The Flowers of Evil

volume 7

Shuzo Oshimi

VERTICAL.

Contents

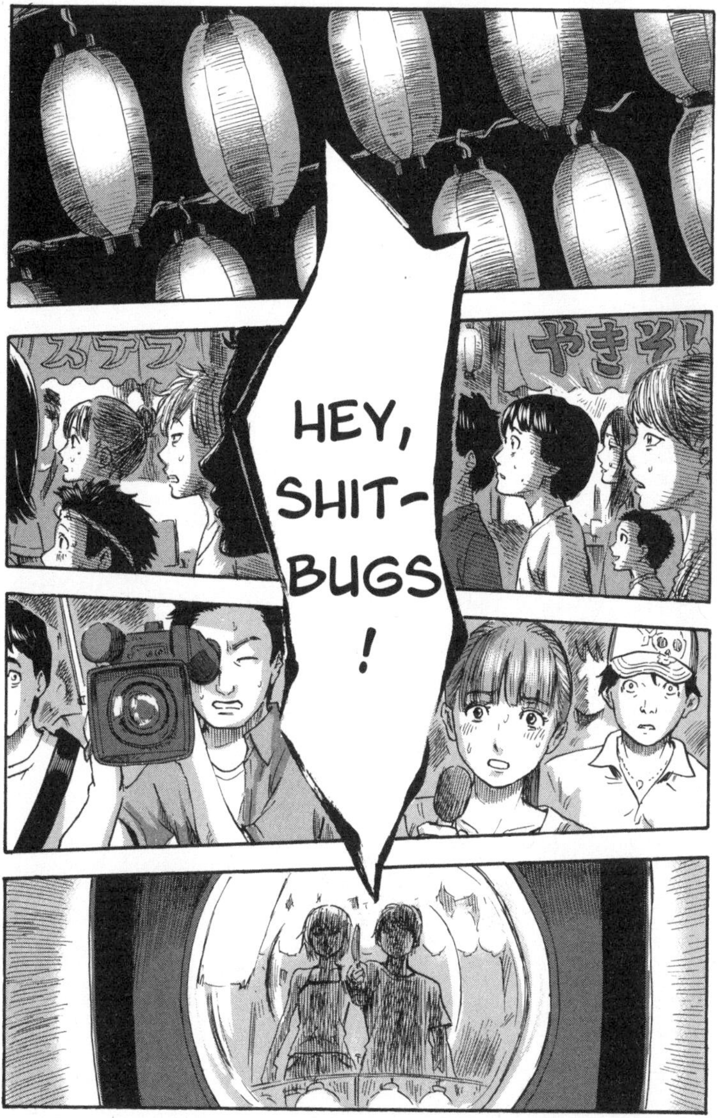
HEY, SHIT-BUGS!

Chapter 33: Happy Are They Who May Take Flight

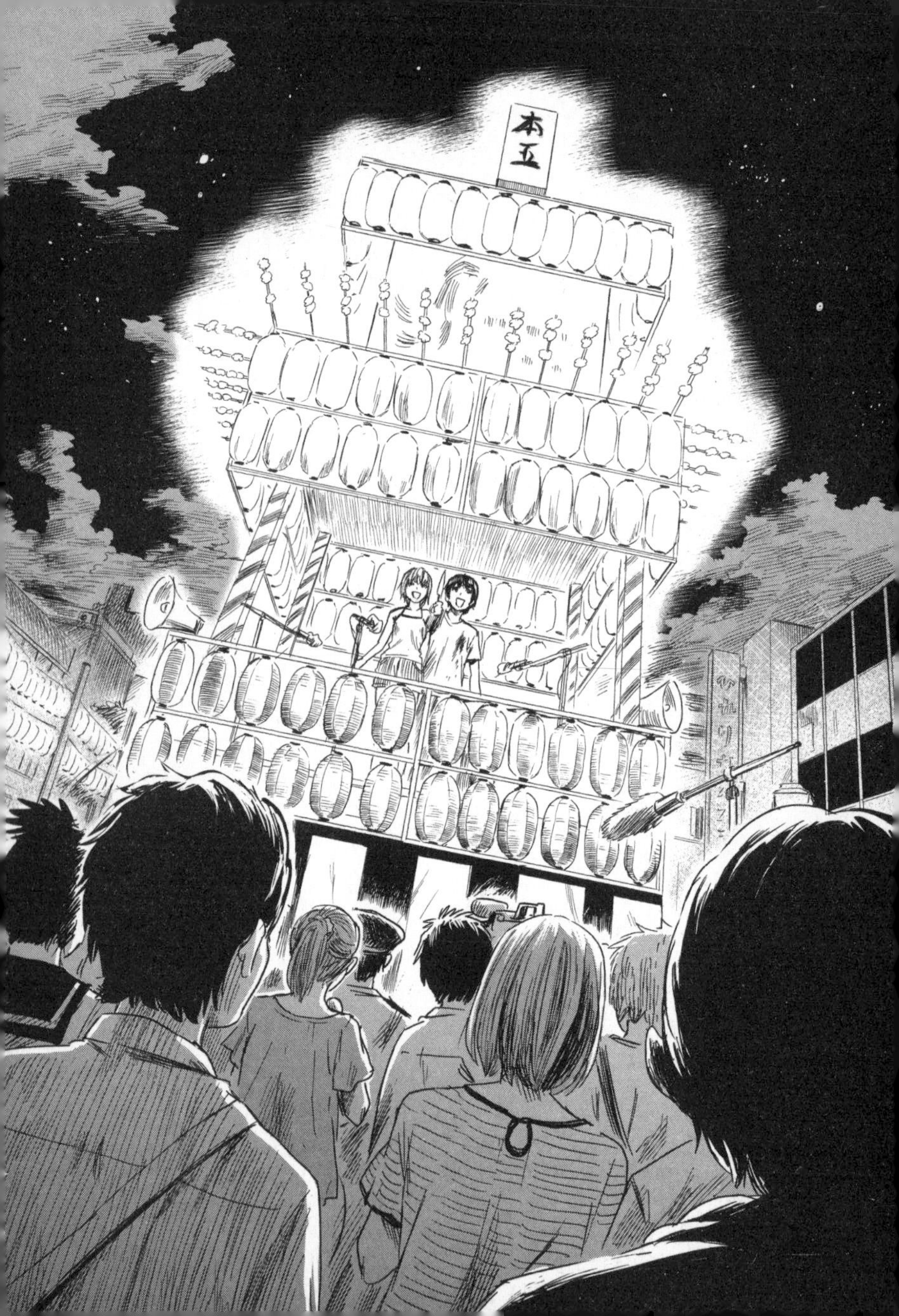
本五

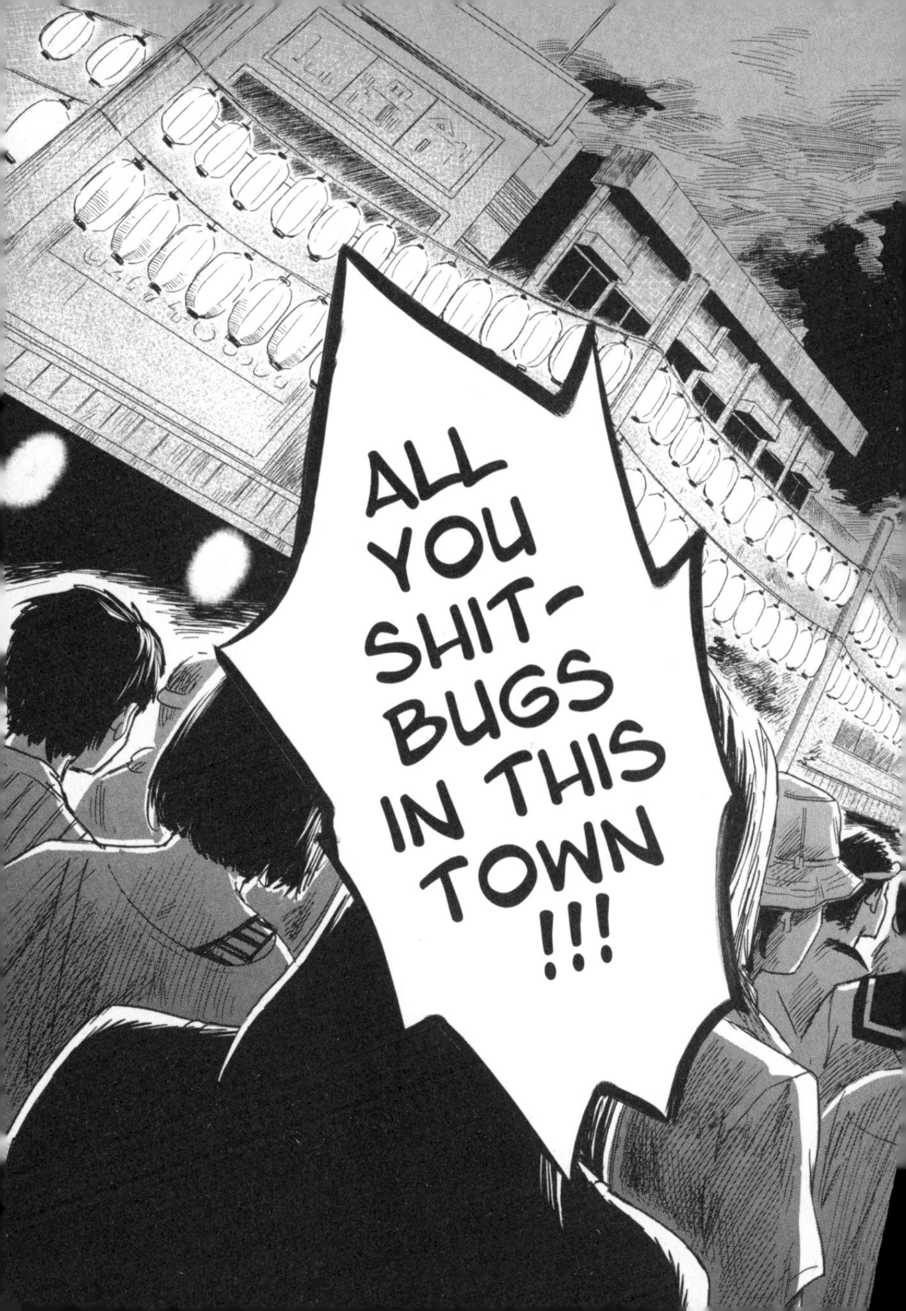
ALL YOU SHIT-BUGS IN THIS TOWN!!!

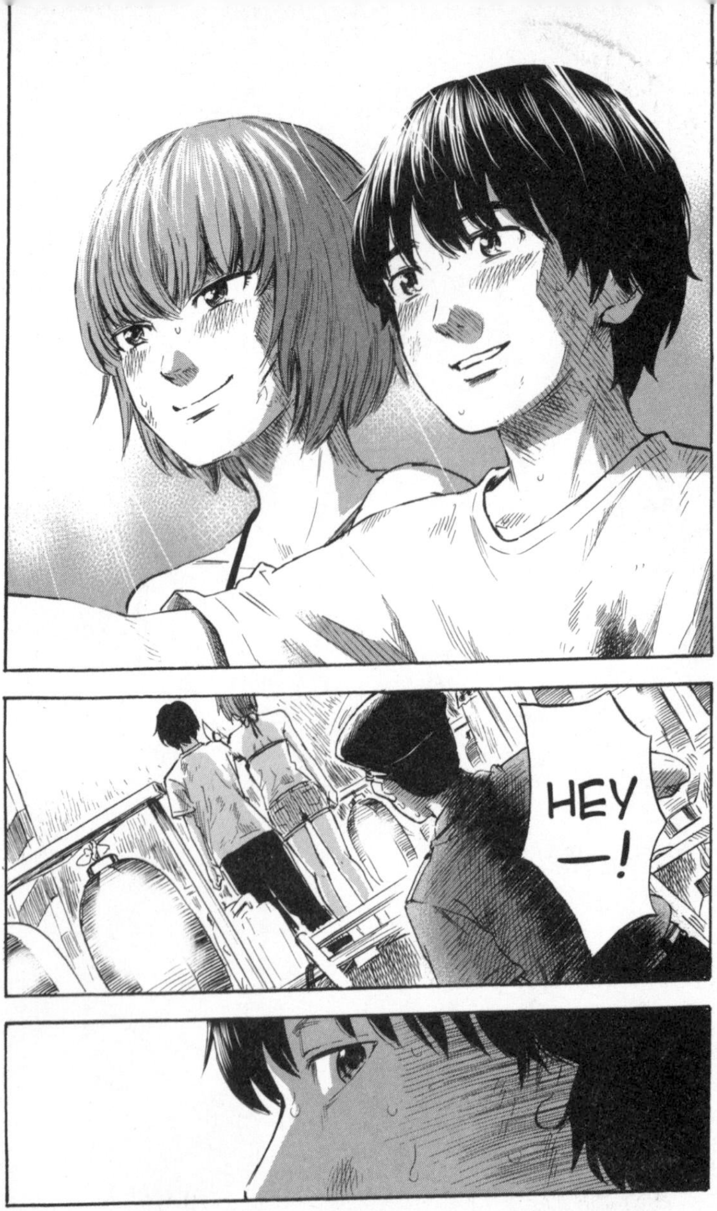
HEY
—!

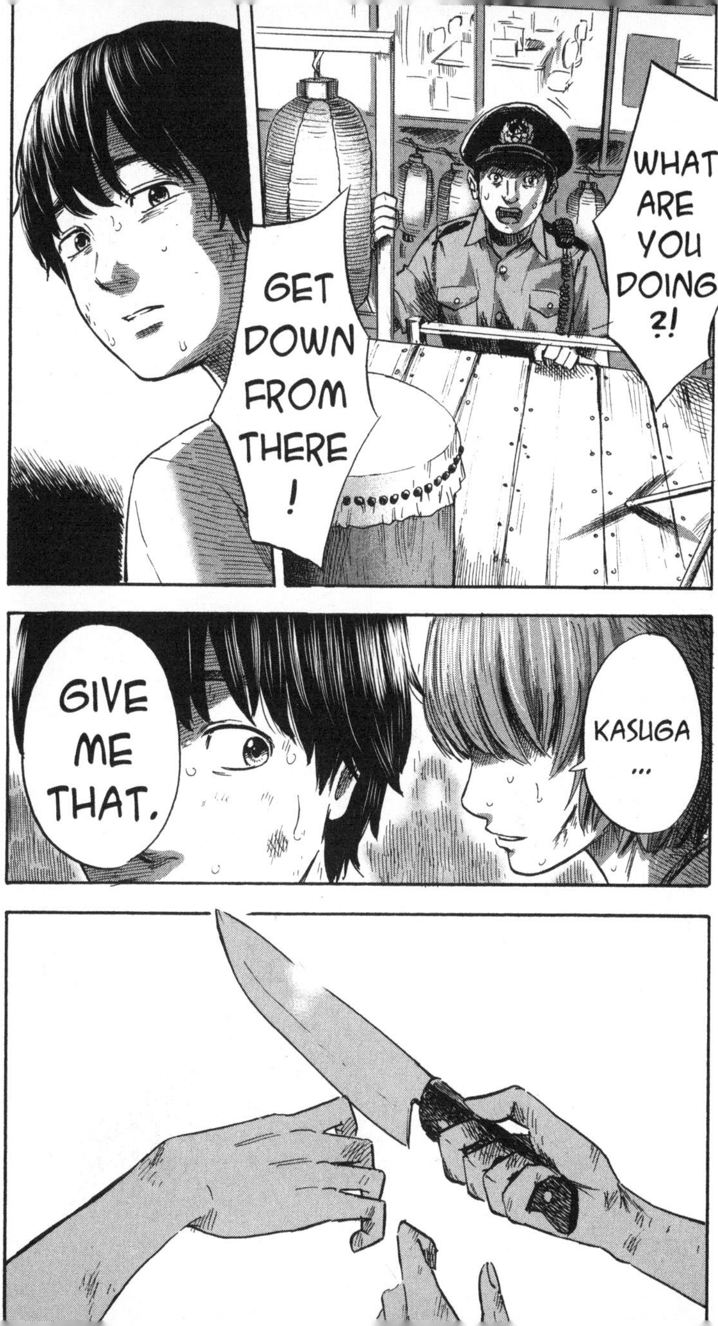
WHAT ARE YOU DOING?!
GET DOWN FROM THERE!
KASUGA...
GIVE ME THAT.

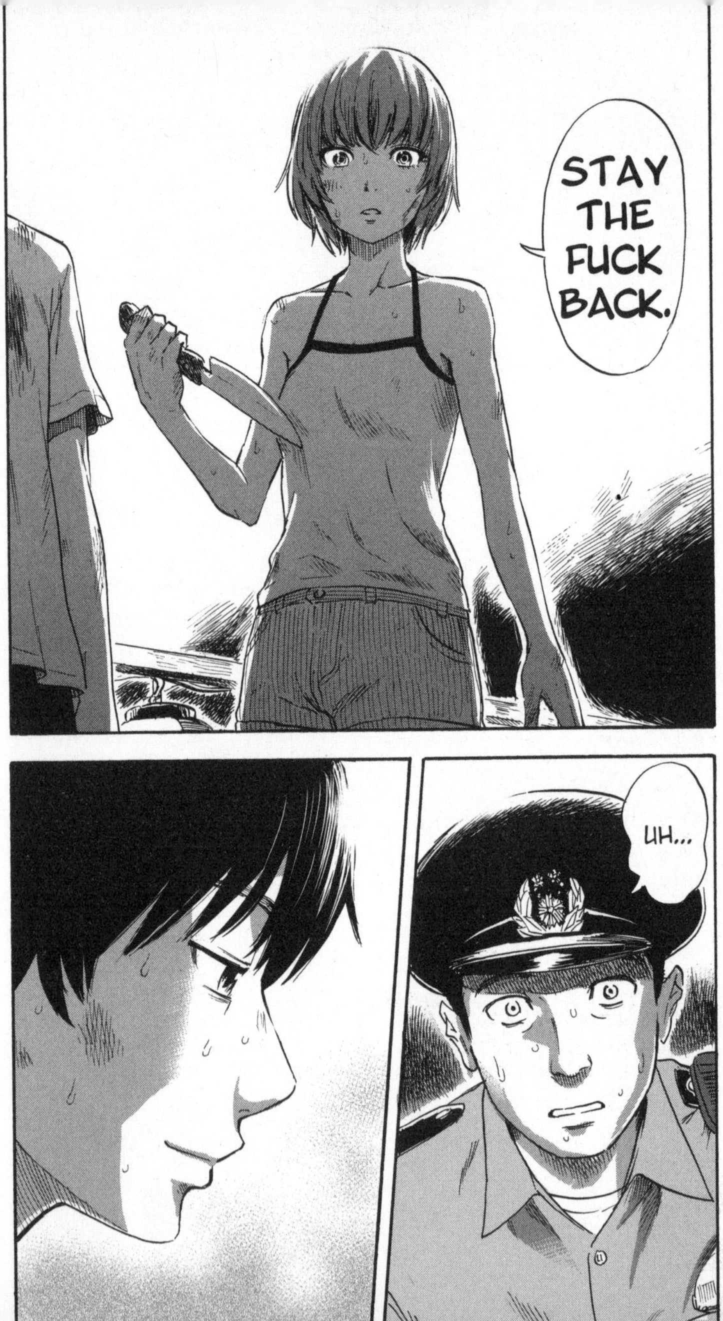
STAY THE FUCK BACK.
UH...

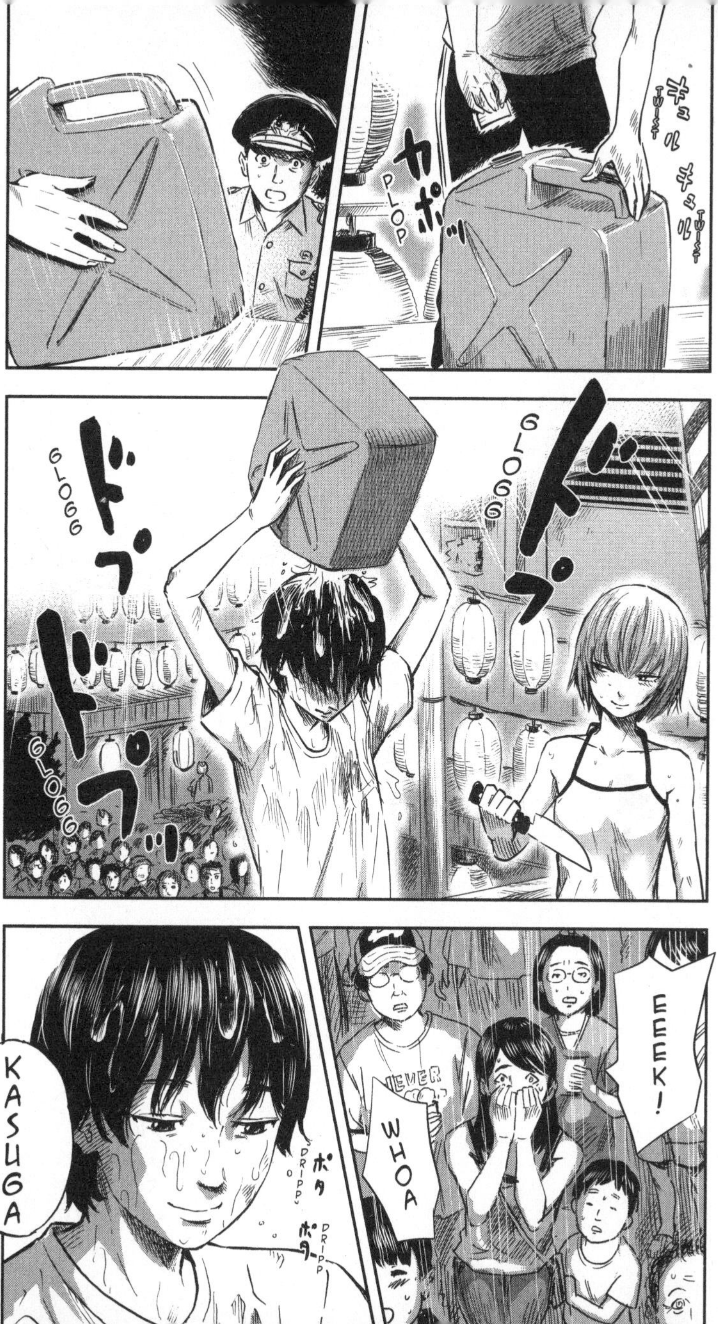
キュル キュル
TWIST TWIST
カポッ
PLOP
ドプ
GLOGG
ドプドプッ
GLOGG
GLOGG
EEEEK!
WHOA
KASUGA
ポタ
DRIPP
ポタ
DRIPP

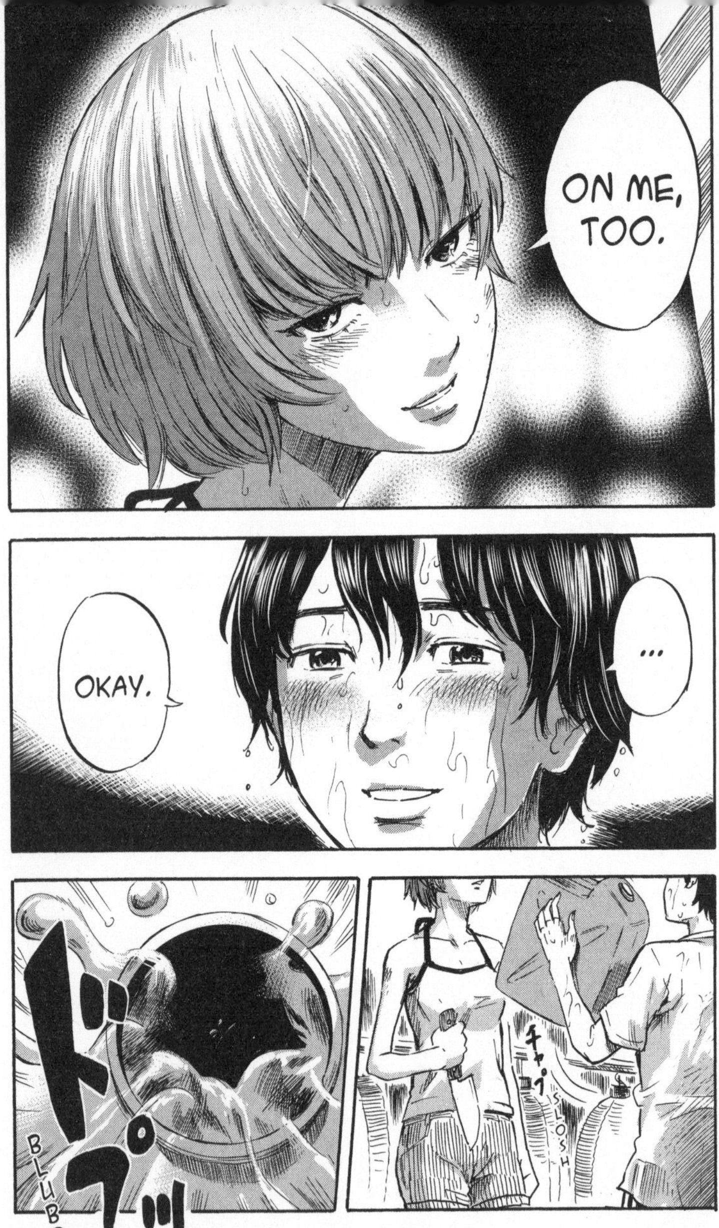
ON ME, TOO.
...
OKAY.
チャプ
SLOSH
ドプッ
BLUBB

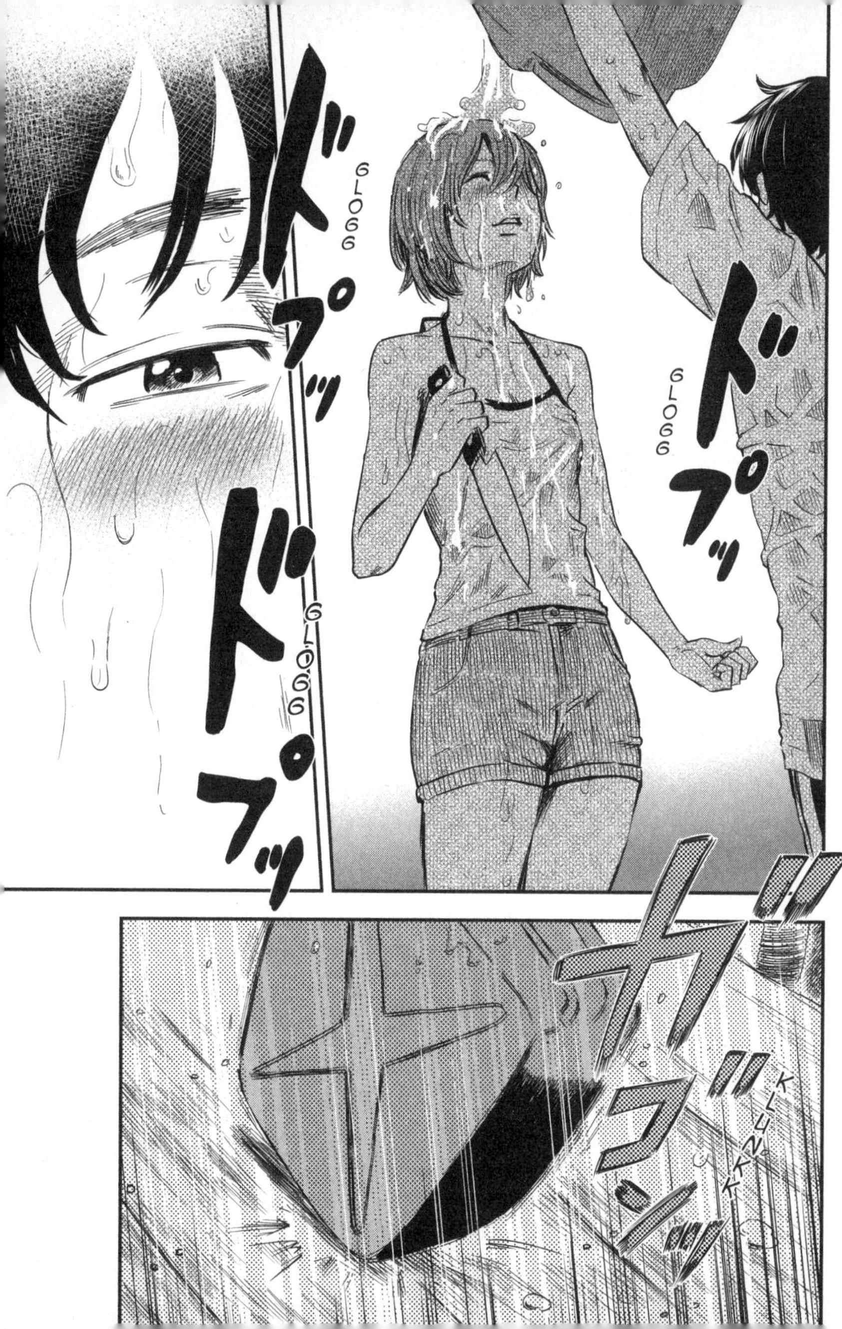
ドプッ
GLOGG
ドプッ
GLOGG
ドプッ
GLOGG
ガコッ
KLUNK

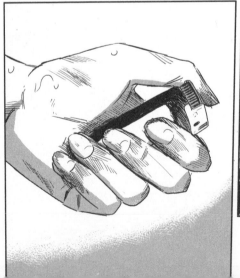

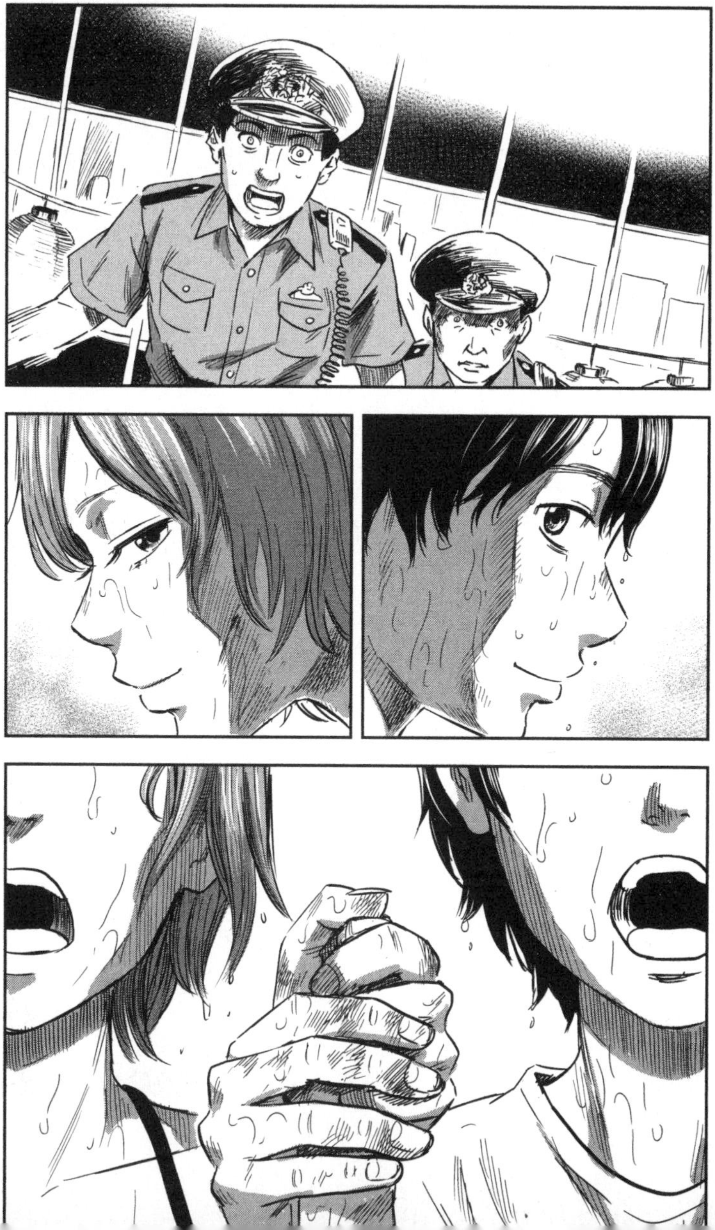

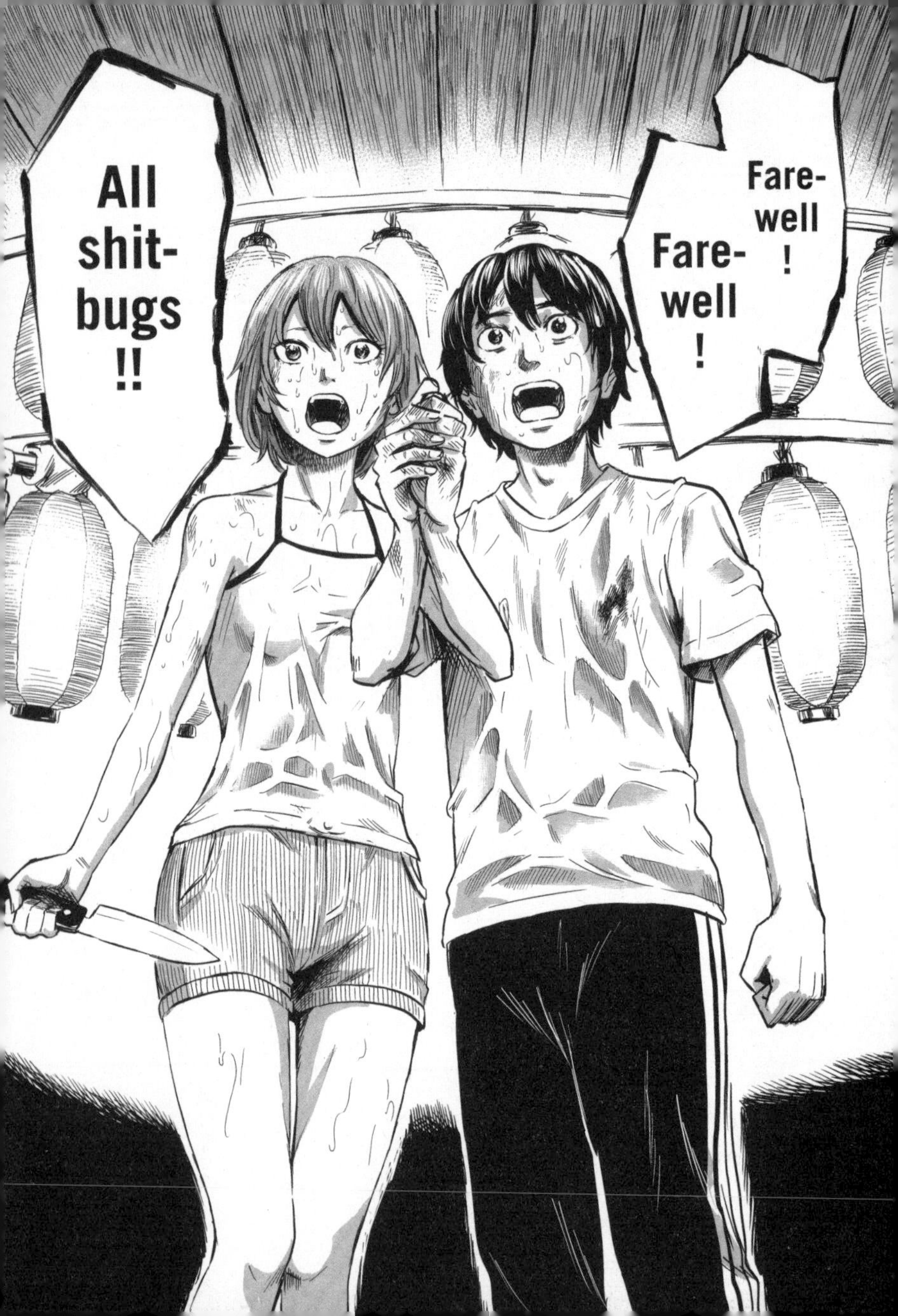
Fare-well!
Fare-well!
All shit-bugs!!

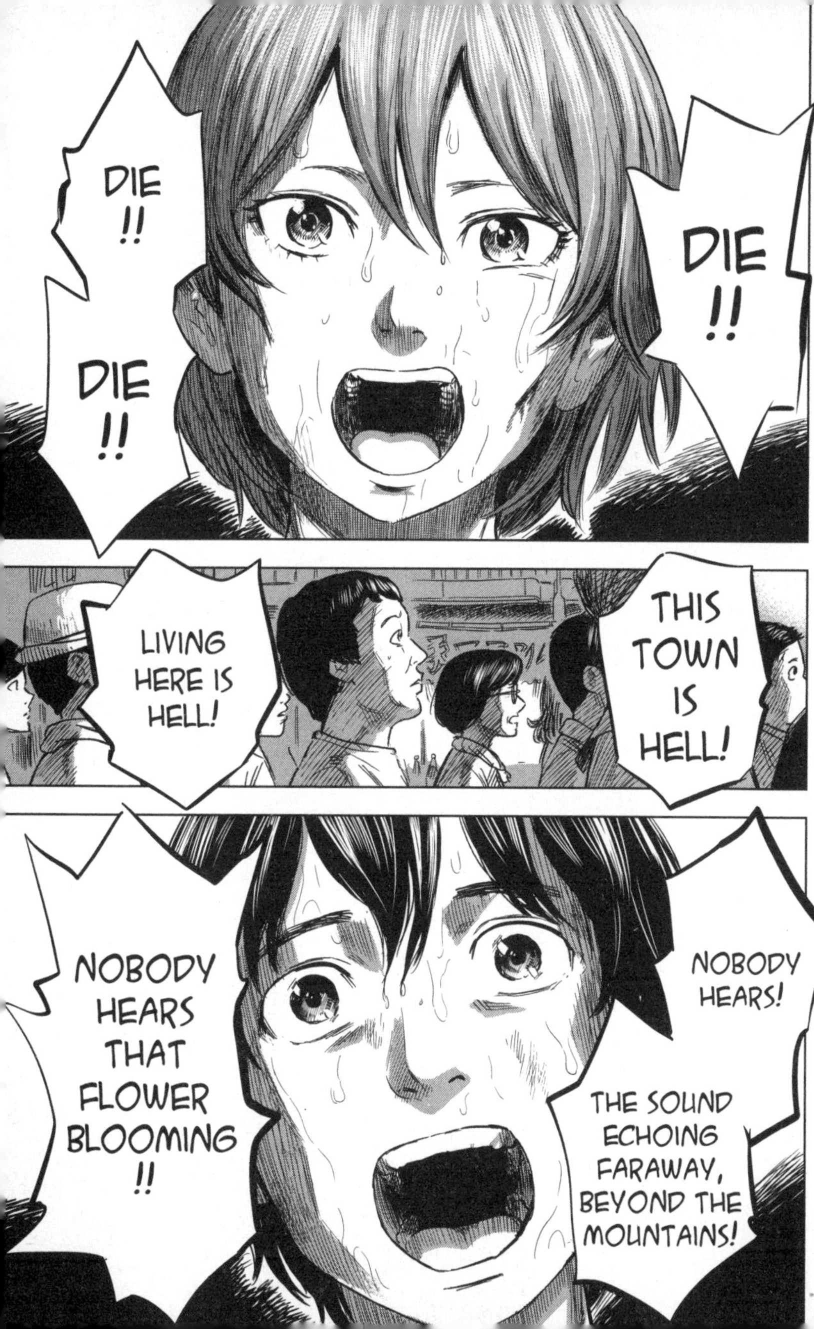
DIE !!
DIE !!
DIE !!
THIS TOWN IS HELL!
LIVING HERE IS HELL!
NOBODY HEARS!
THE SOUND ECHOING FARAWAY, BEYOND THE MOUNTAINS!
NOBODY HEARS THAT FLOWER BLOOMING !!

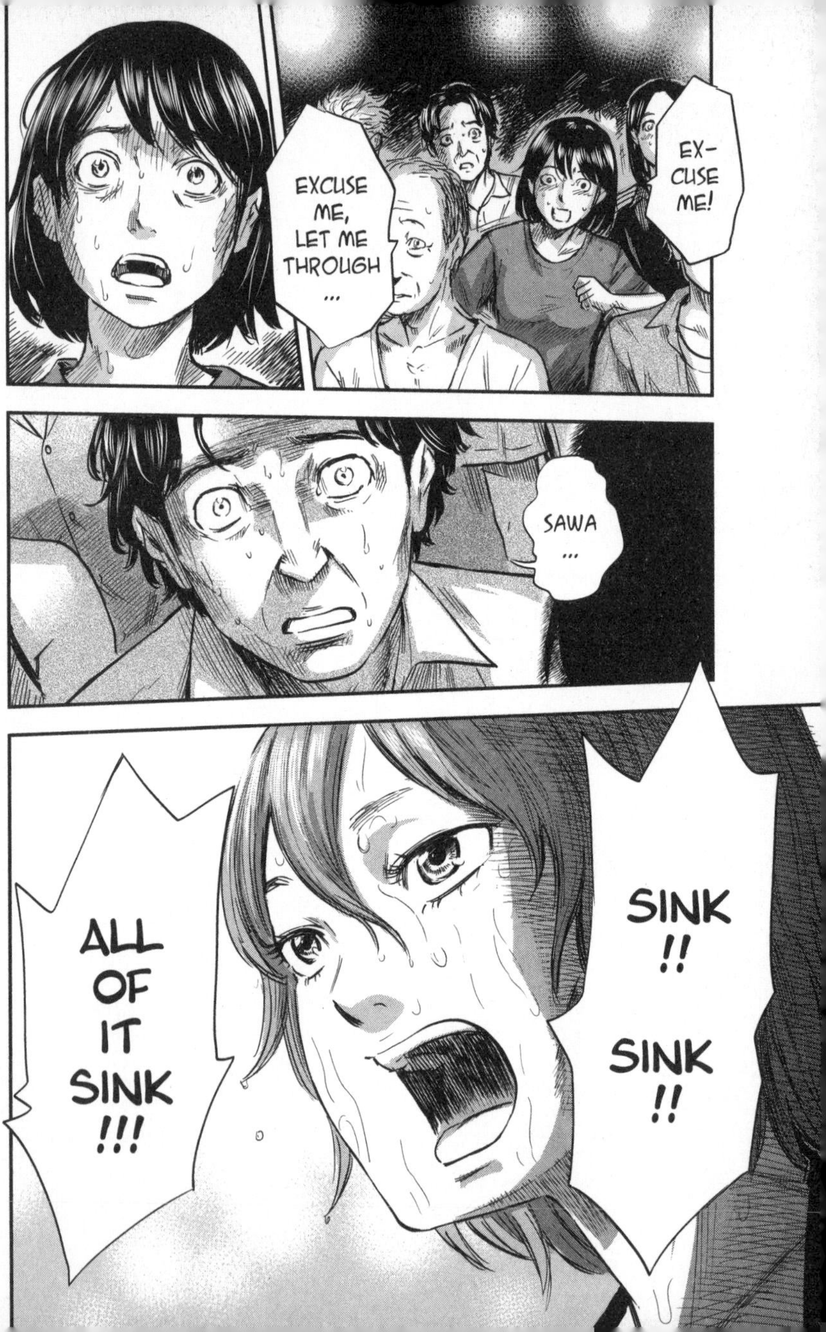
EX-CUSE ME!
EXCUSE ME, LET ME THROUGH ...
SAWA ...
SINK!!
SINK!!
ALL OF IT SINK!!!

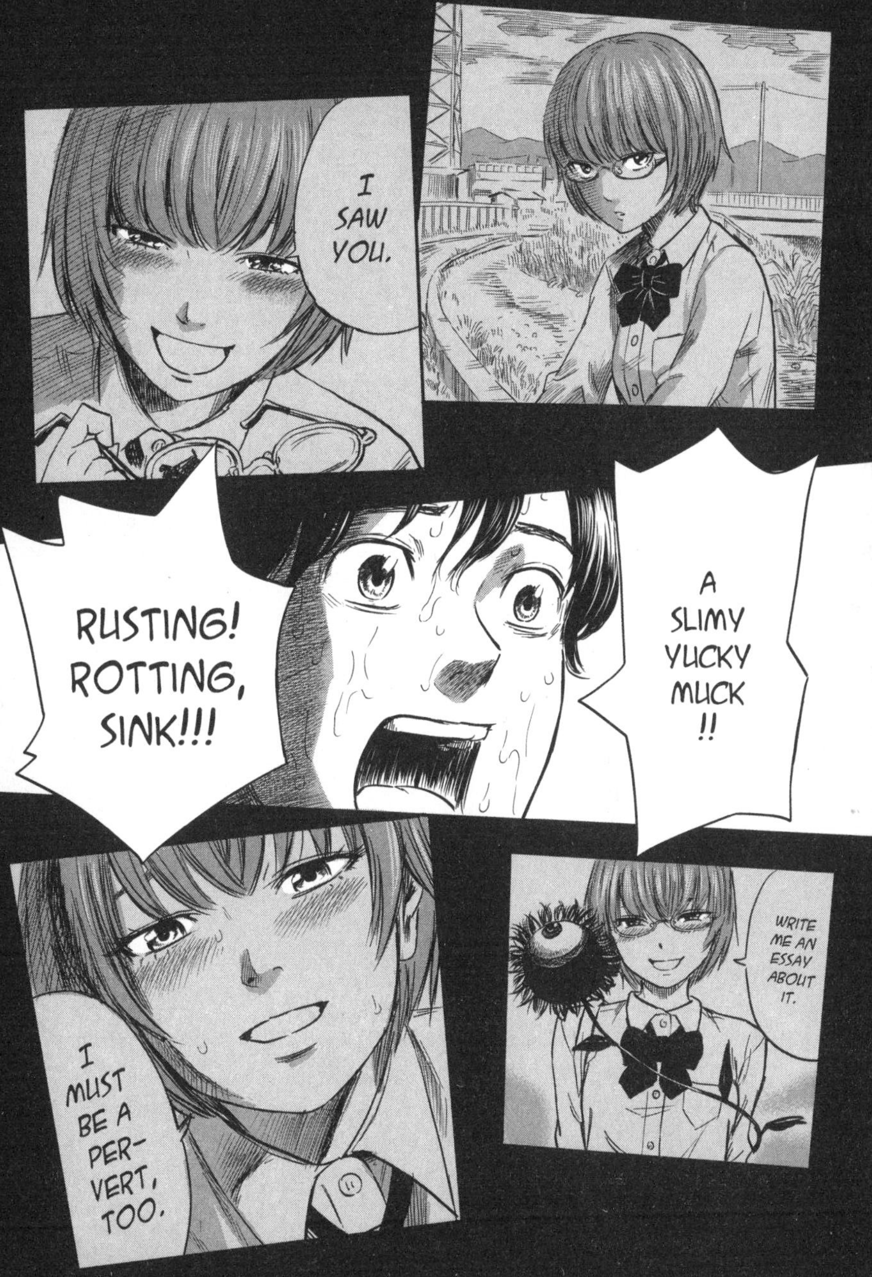
I SAW YOU.
A SLIMY YUCKY MUCK !!
RUSTING! ROTTING, SINK!!!
WRITE ME AN ESSAY ABOUT IT.
I MUST BE A PERVERT, TOO.

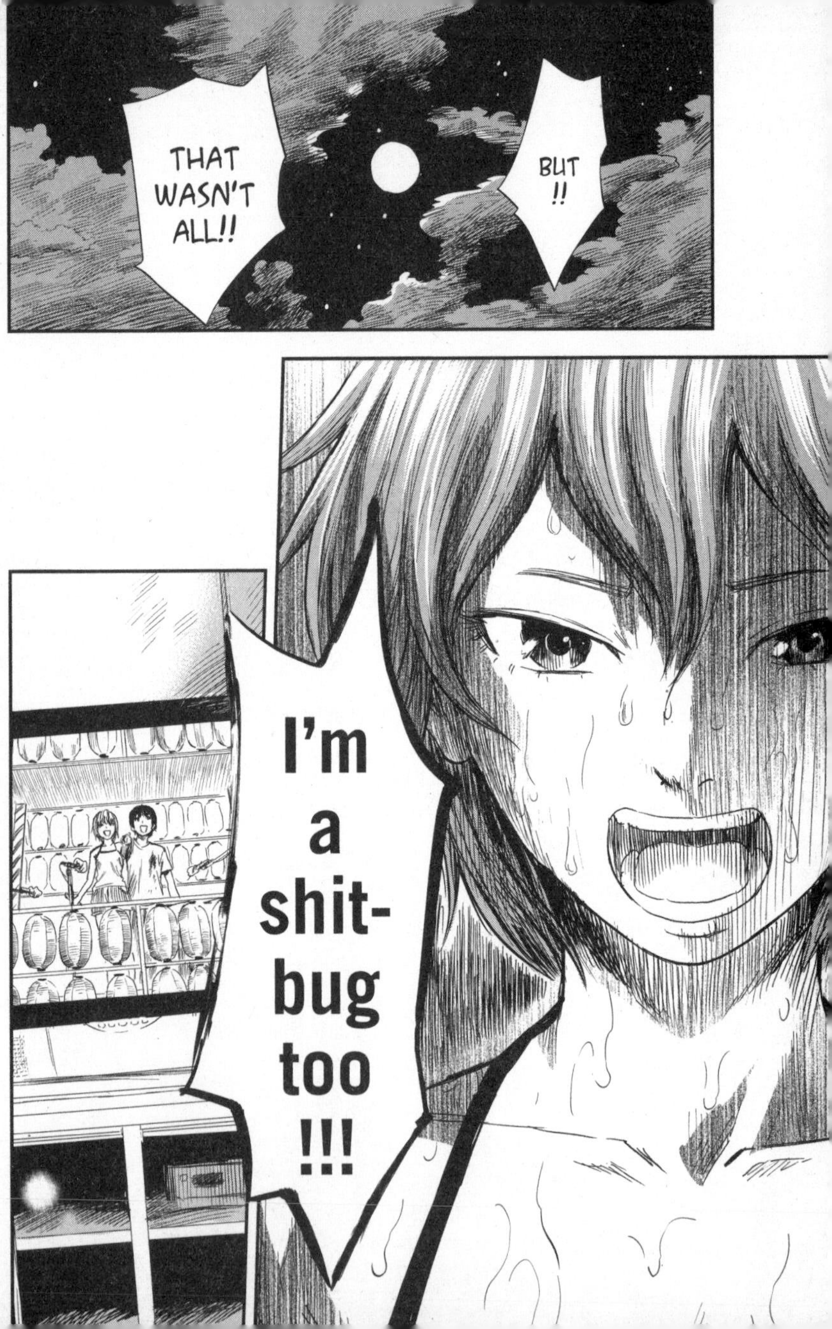
BUT !!
THAT WASN'T ALL!!
I'm a shit-bug too !!!

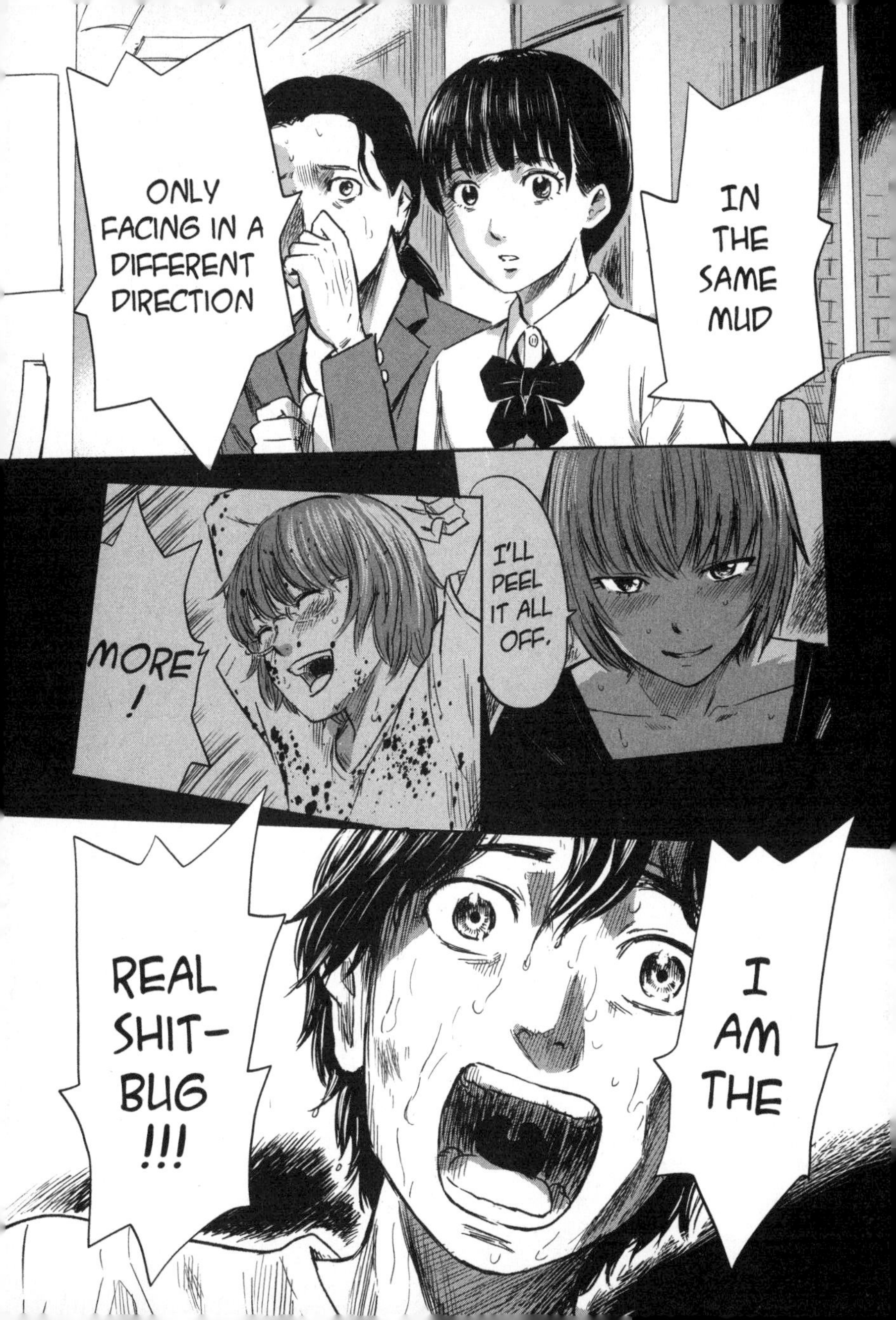
IN THE SAME MUD
ONLY FACING IN A DIFFERENT DIRECTION
I'LL PEEL IT ALL OFF.
MORE!
I AM THE
REAL SHIT-BUG!!!

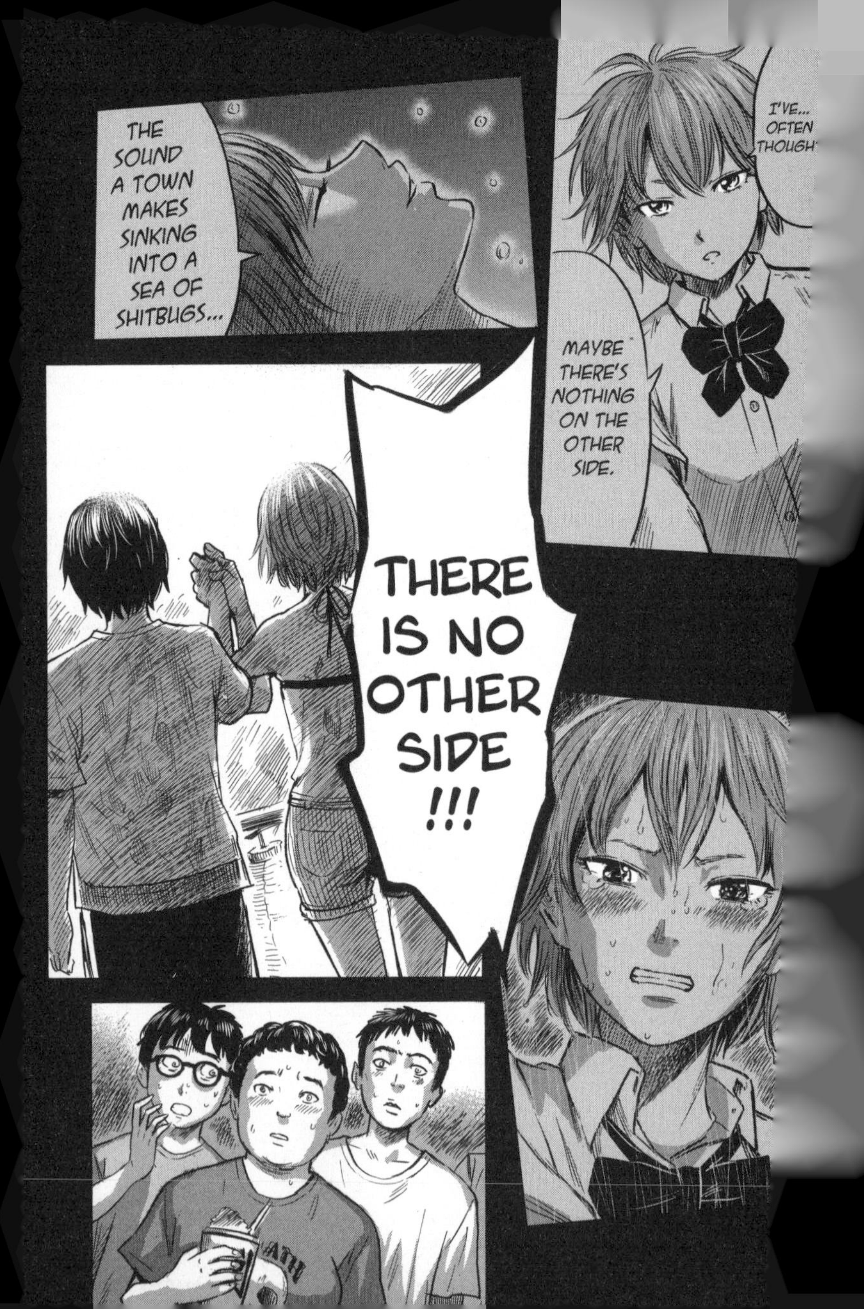
I'VE... OFTEN THOUGH
MAYBE THERE'S NOTHING ON THE OTHER SIDE.
THE SOUND A TOWN MAKES SINKING INTO A SEA OF SHITBUGS...
THERE IS NO OTHER SIDE !!!

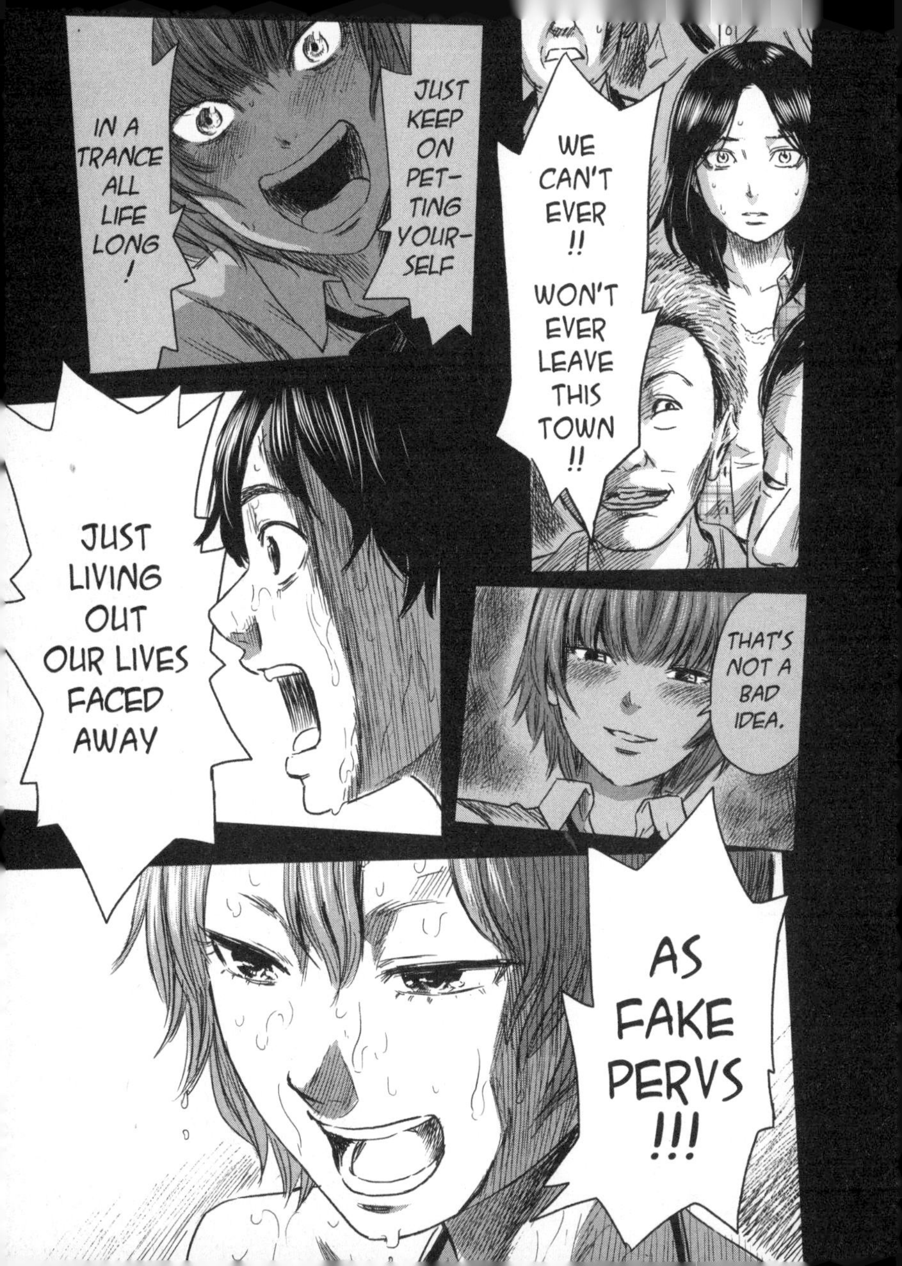
WE CAN'T EVER!!
WON'T EVER LEAVE THIS TOWN!!
JUST KEEP ON PETTING YOURSELF
IN A TRANCE ALL LIFE LONG!
THAT'S NOT A BAD IDEA.
JUST LIVING OUT OUR LIVES FACED AWAY
AS FAKE PERVS!!!

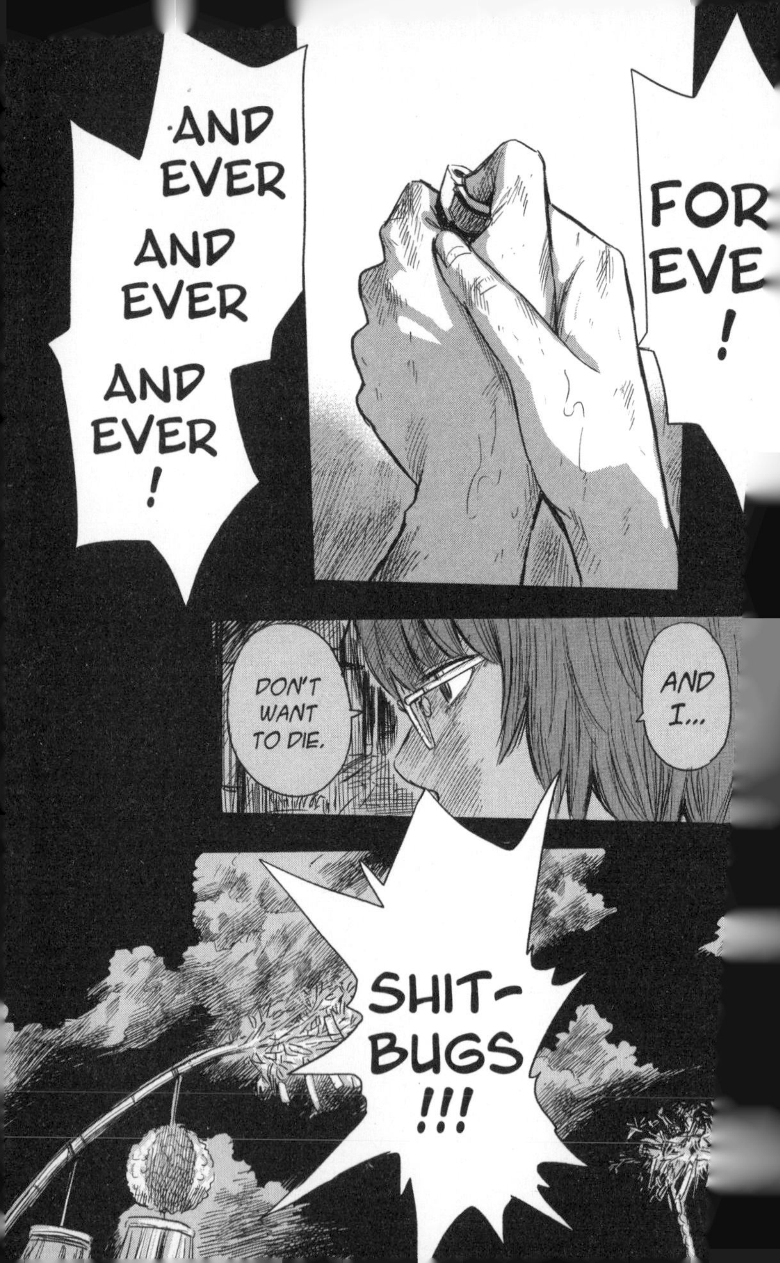
FOR EVE!
AND EVER AND EVER AND EVER!
AND I...
DON'T WANT TO DIE.
SHIT-BUGS!!!

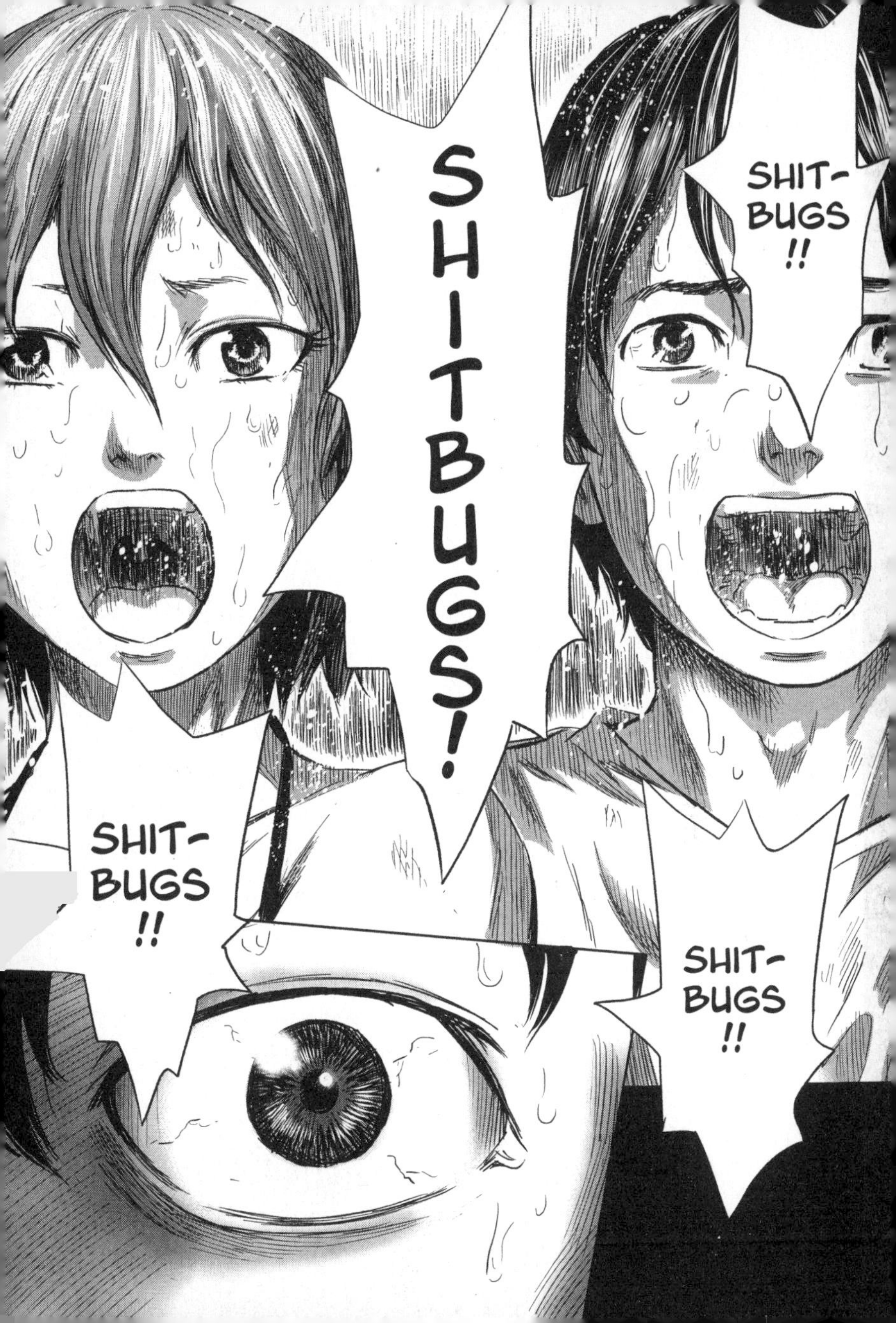
SHIT-BUGS!!
SHITBUGS!
SHIT-BUGS!!
SHIT-BUGS!!

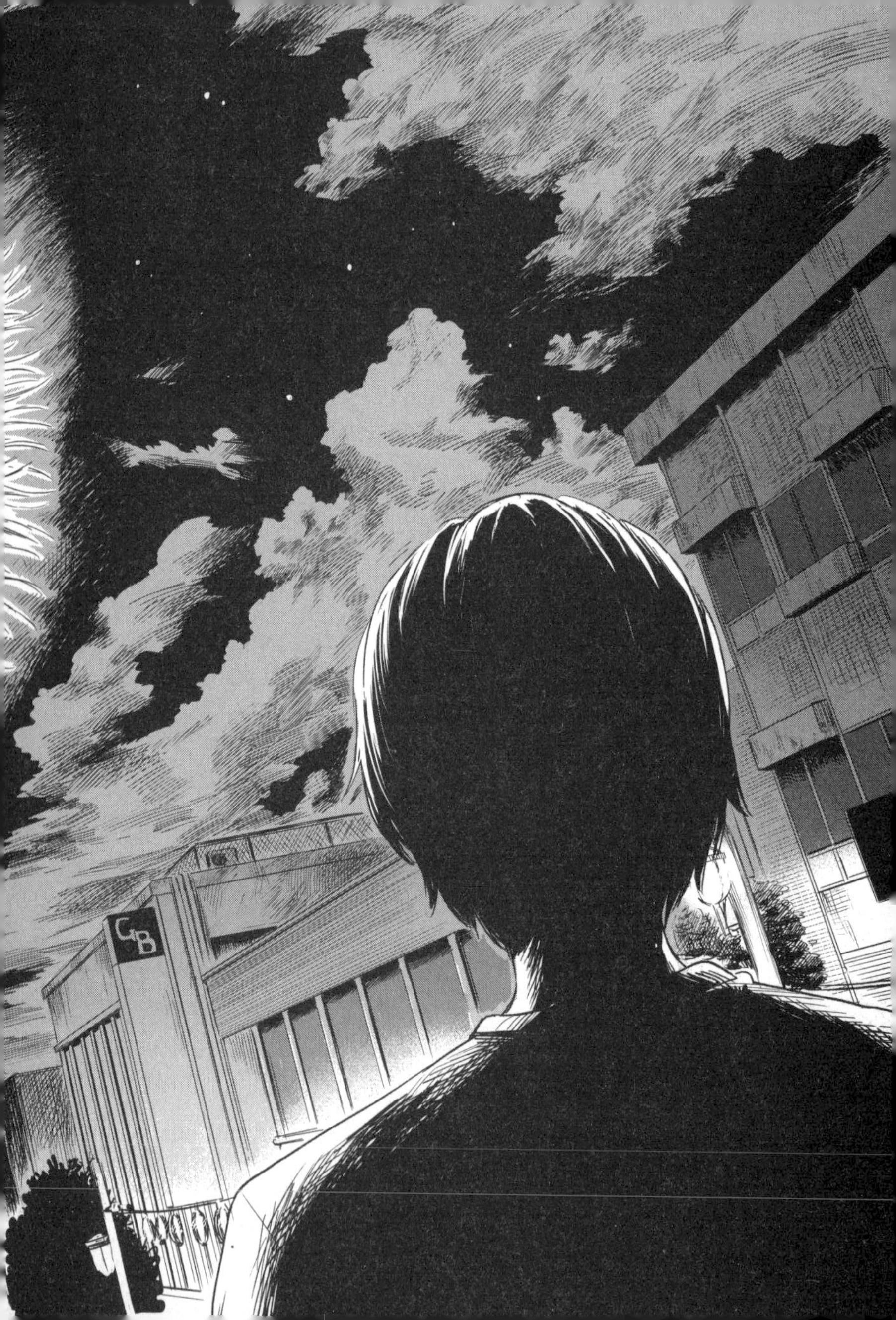
CB

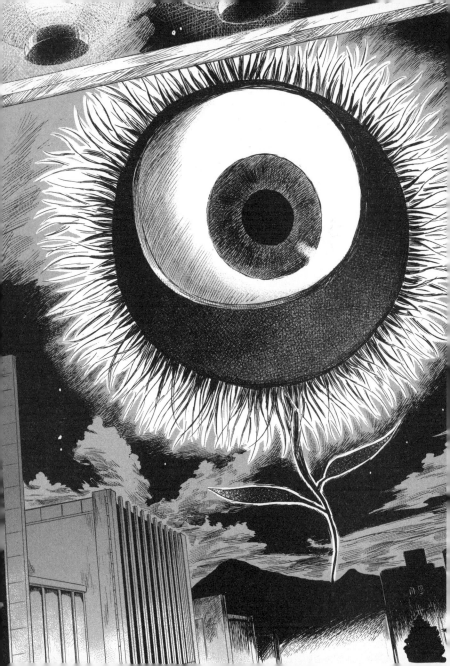

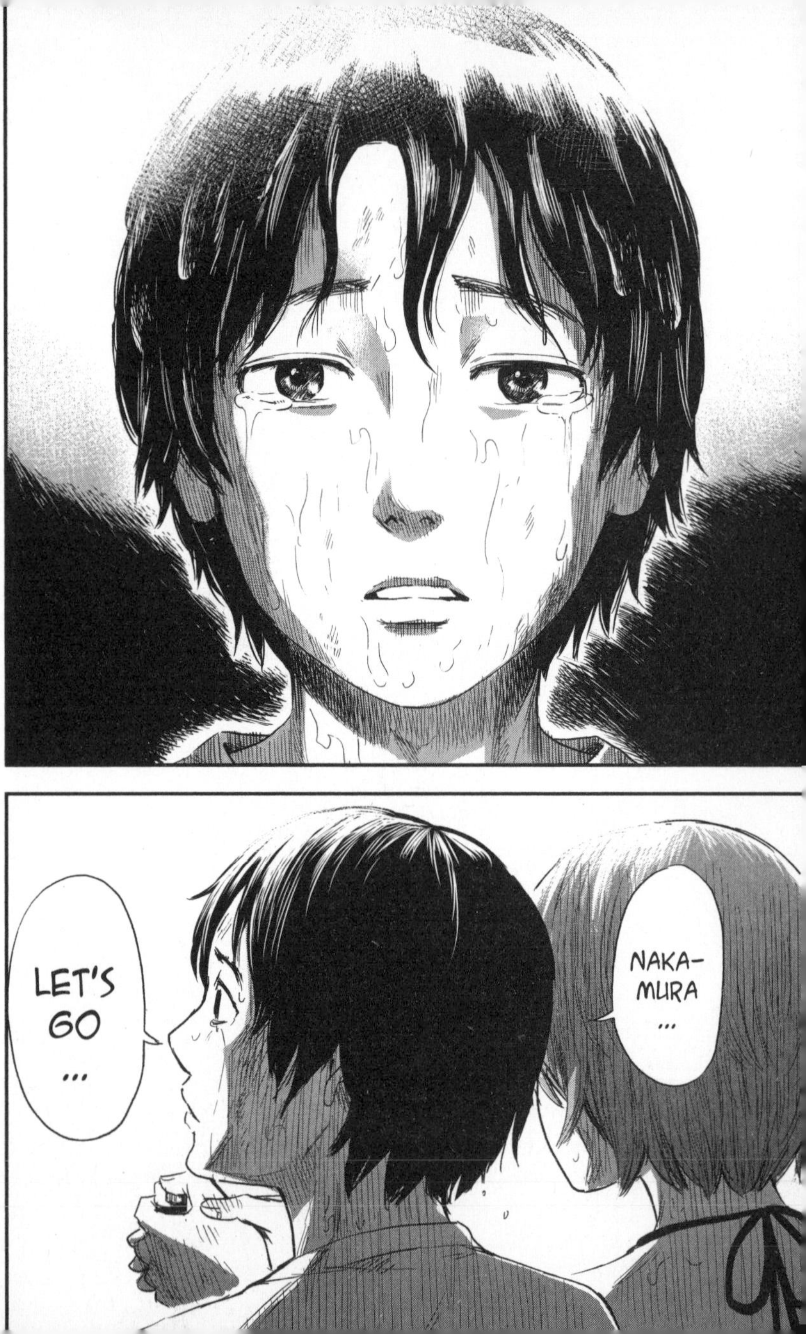
NAKA-MURA ...
LET'S GO ...

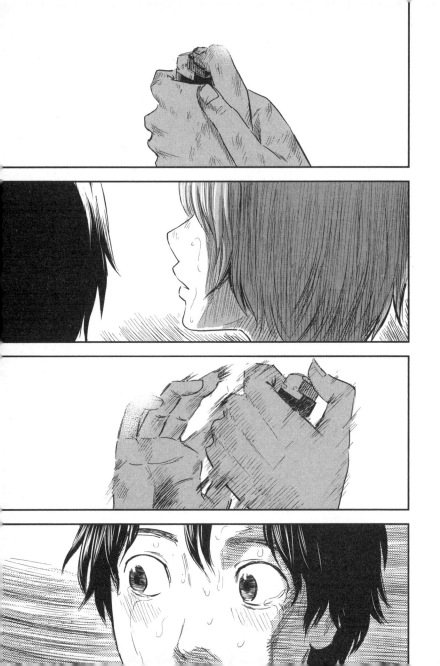

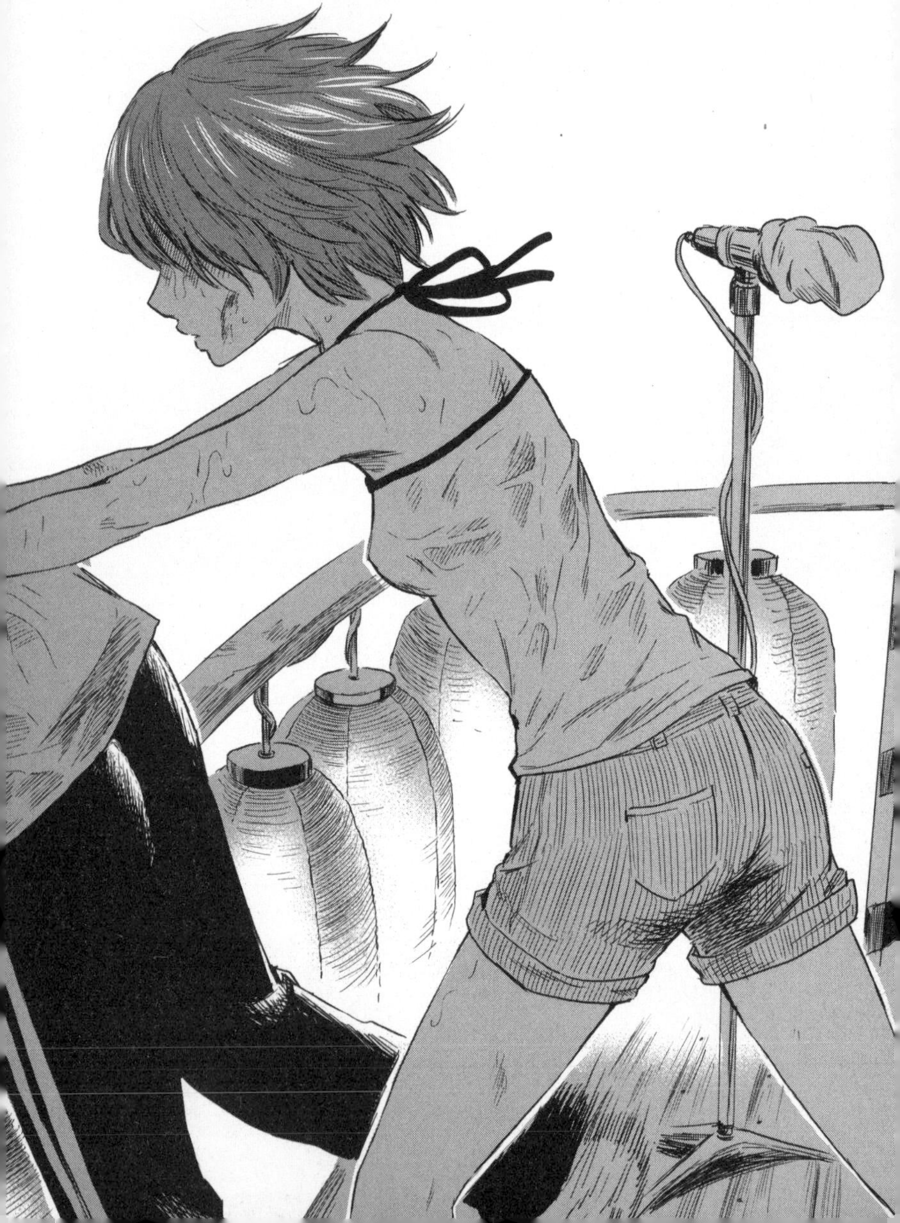

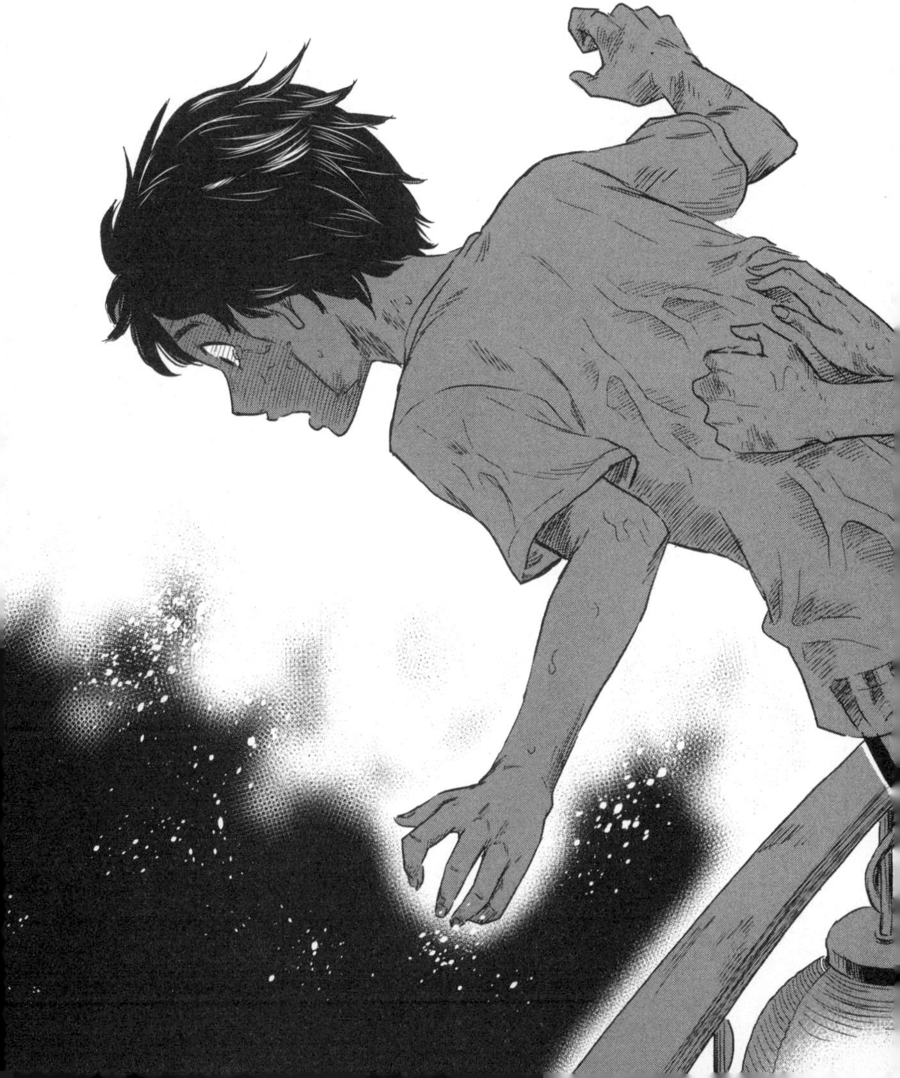

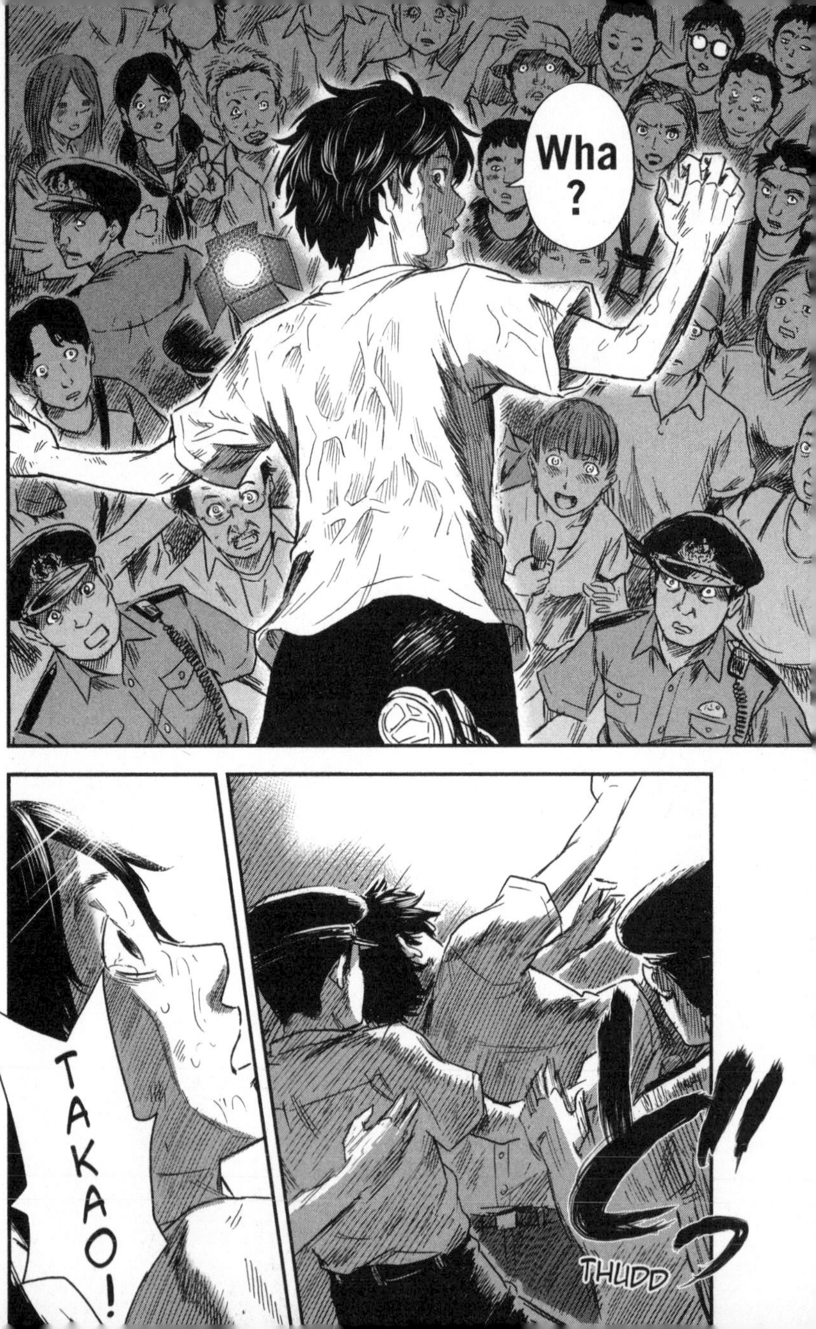
Wha ?
THUDD
TAKAO!

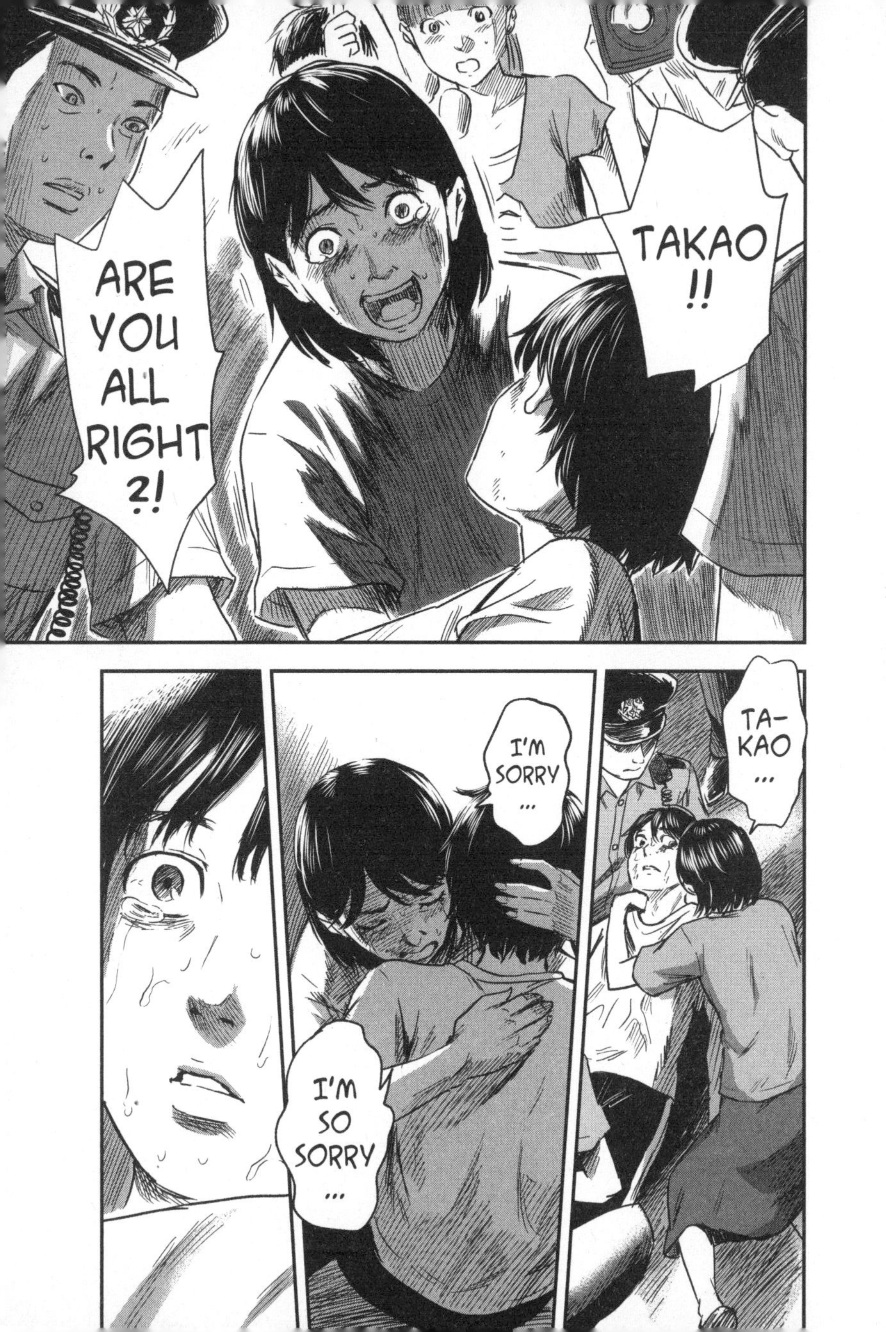
TAKAO !!
ARE YOU ALL RIGHT ?!
TA-KAO ...
I'M SORRY ...
I'M SO SORRY ...

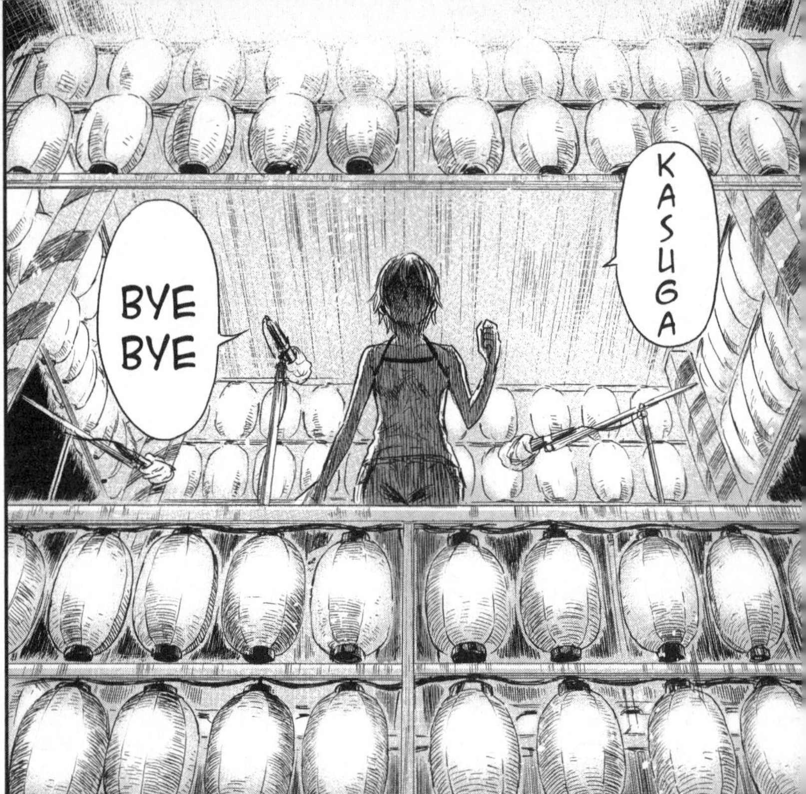
KASUGA
BYE BYE
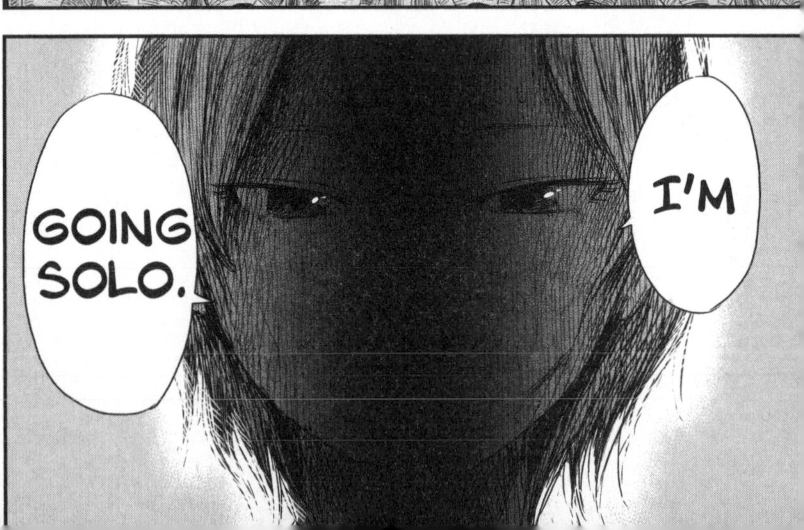
I'M
GOING SOLO.

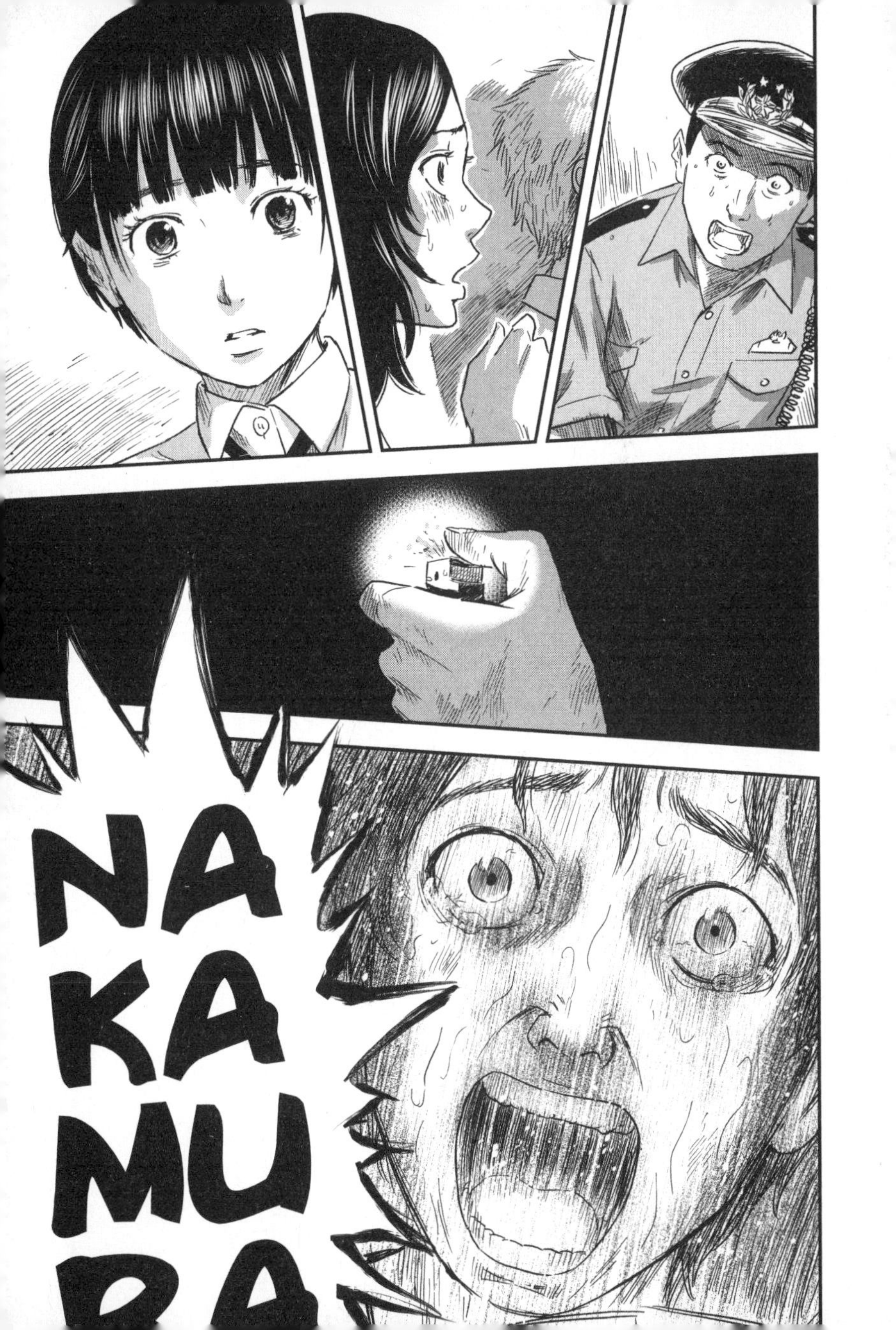
NAKAMURA

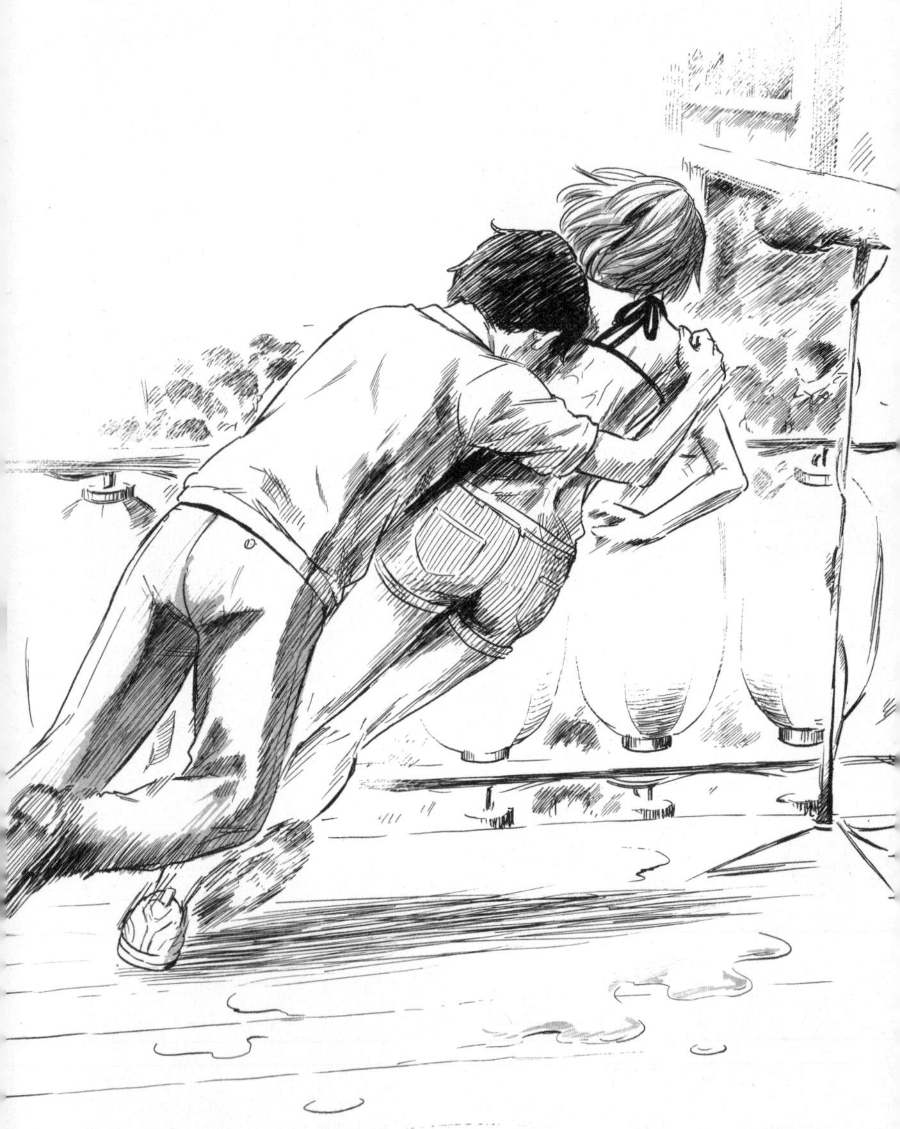

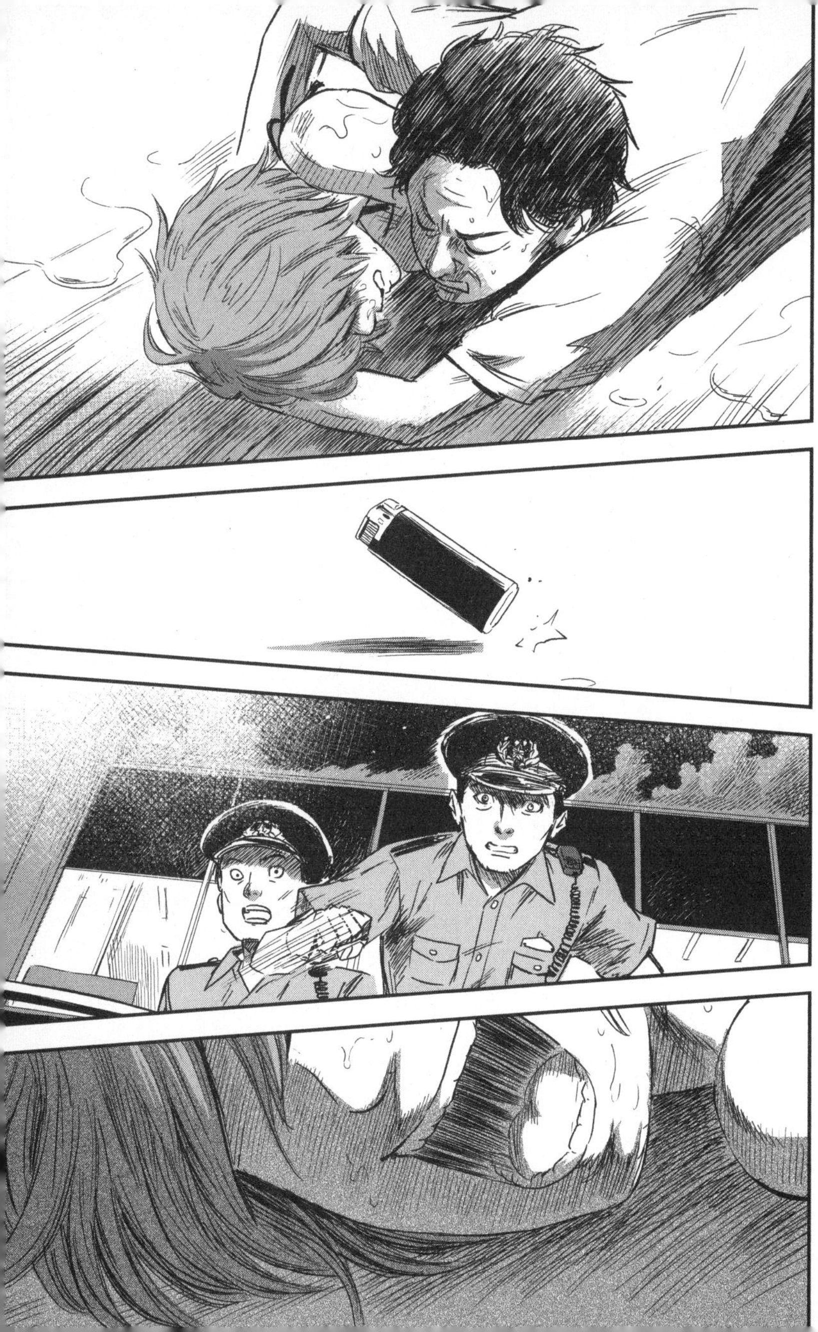

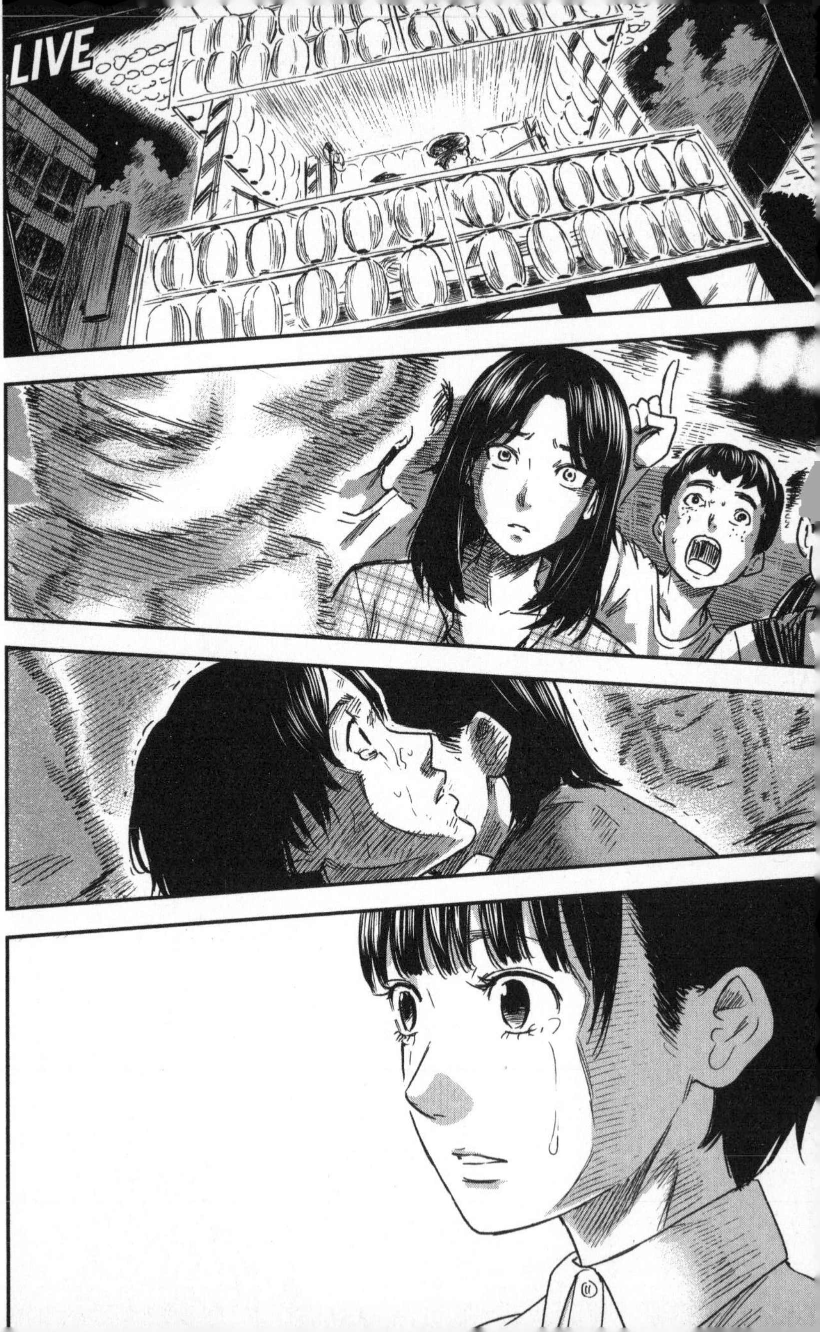
LIVE

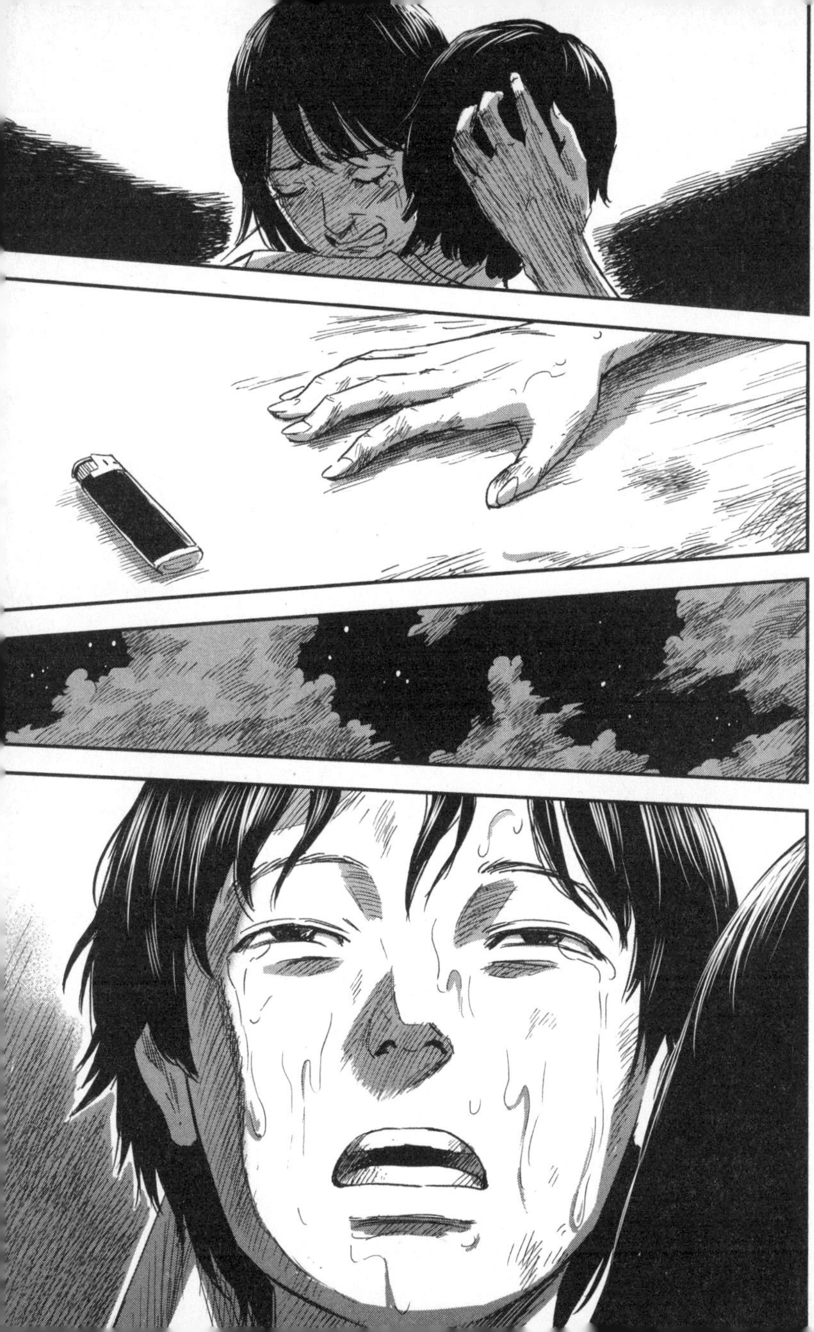

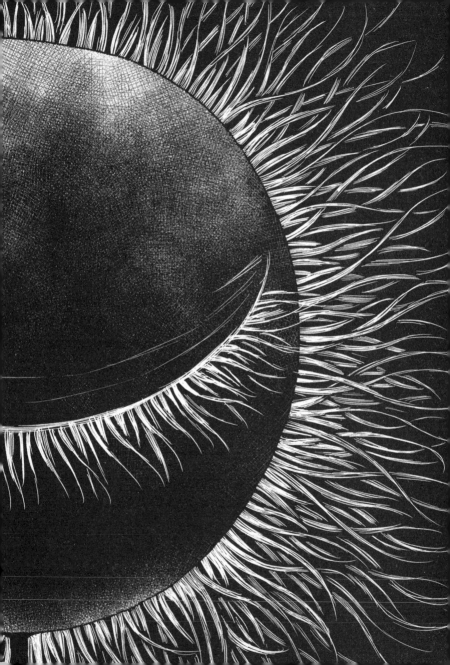

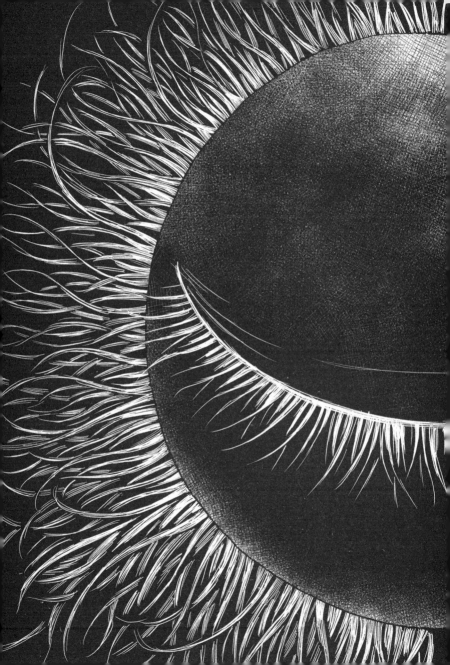

Chapter 34: Precious Thoughts

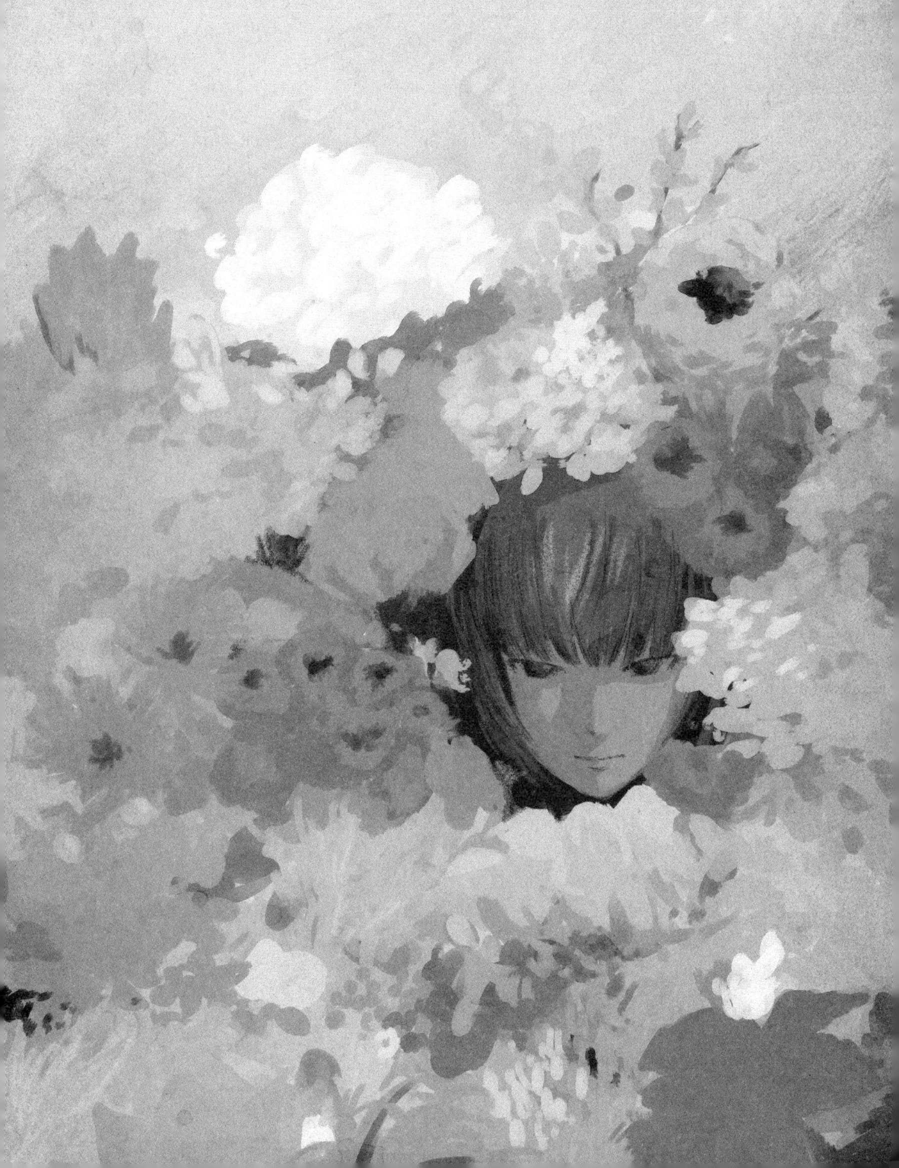

The Flowers
of Evil

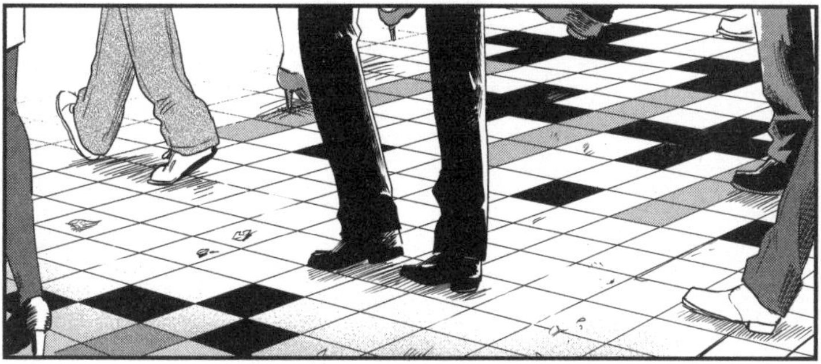
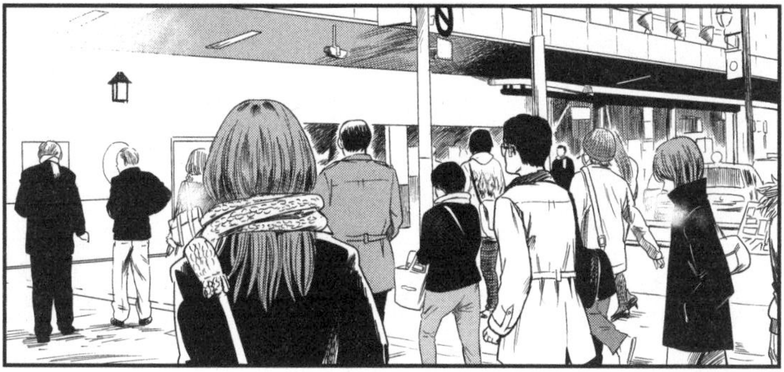
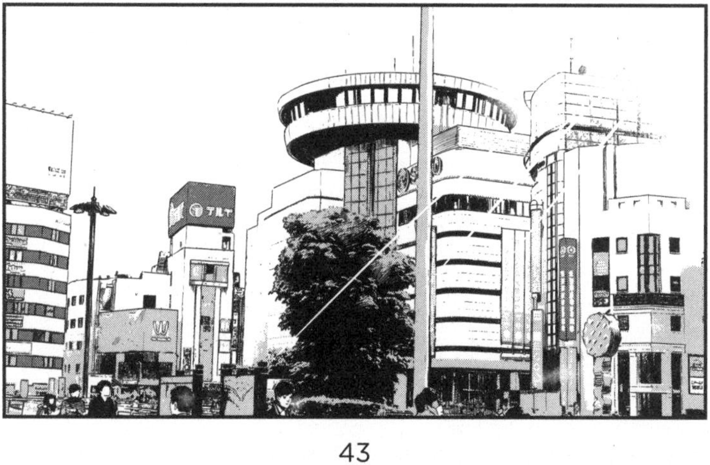

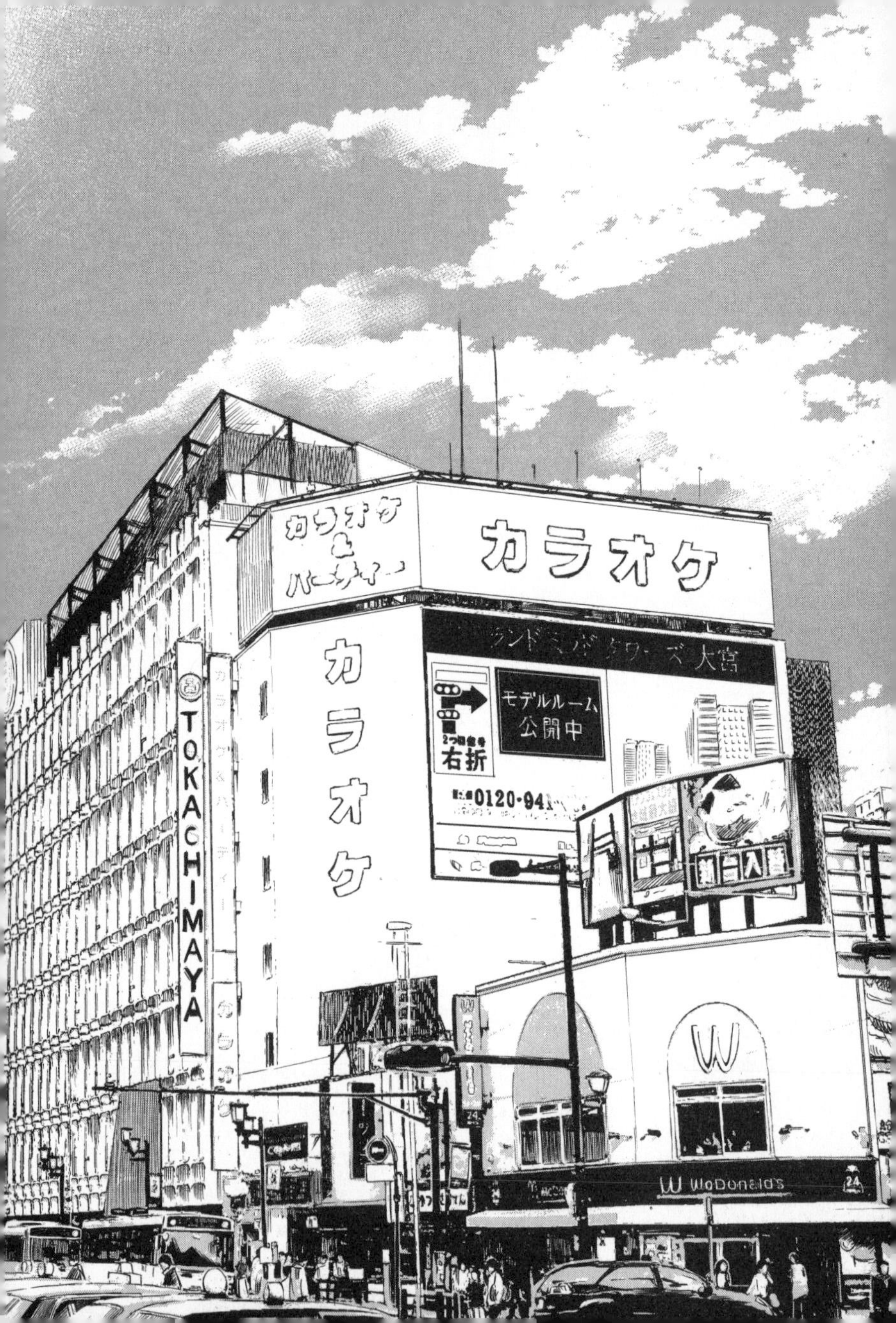

カラオケ
&パーティー
カラオケ
カラオケ
TOKACHIMAYA
タワーズ大宮
モデルルーム
公開中
右折
0120-94
WcDonald's

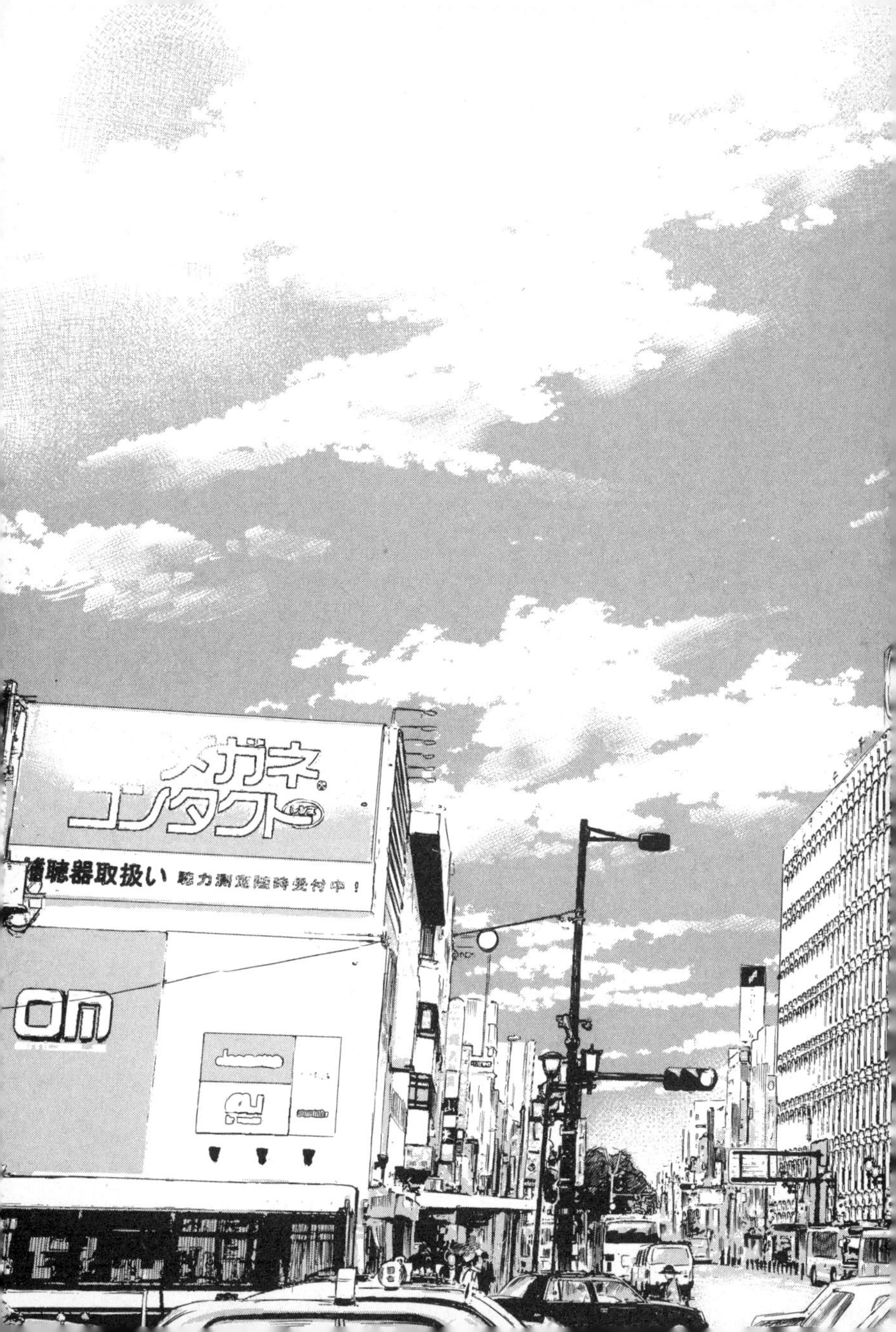
メガネ
コンタクト
補聴器取扱い
聴力測定随時受付中！

SAITAMA PREFECTURAL MIGIWA HIGH SCHOOL

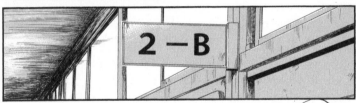

2－B

WHICH MEANS THAT THE AUTHOR'S FEELINGS HERE ...

... SO AS FAR AS THIS ISSUE GOES ...

46

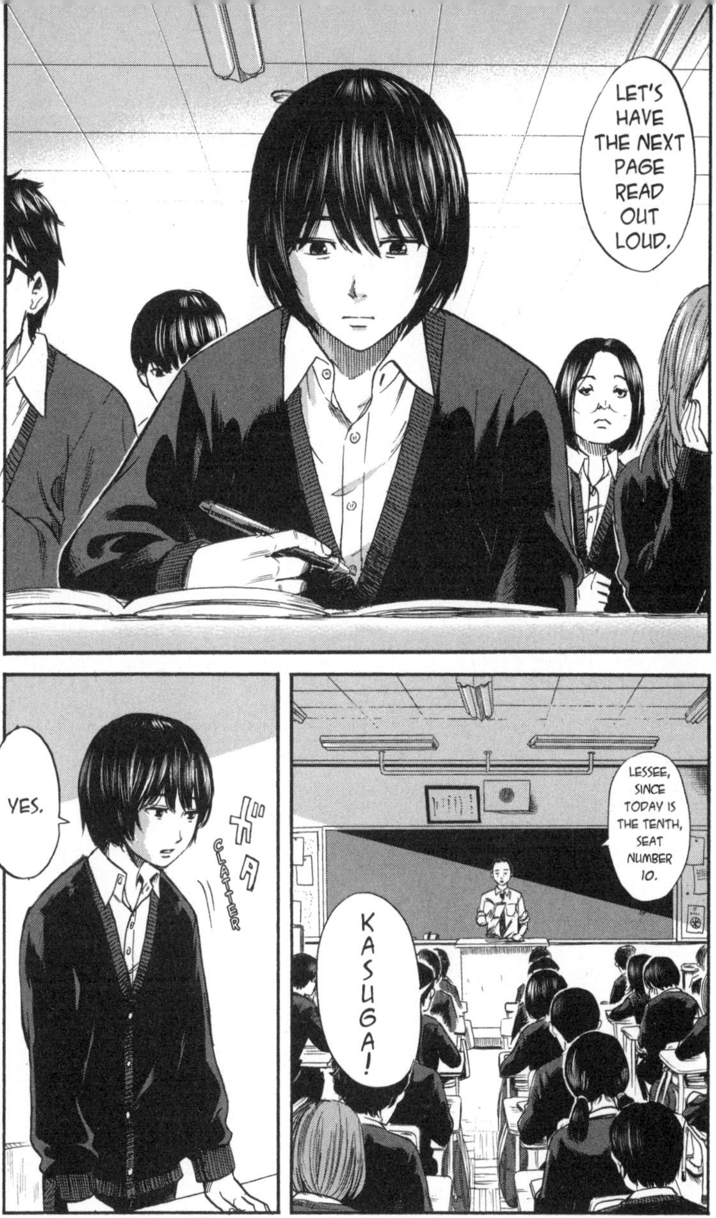
LET'S HAVE THE NEXT PAGE READ OUT LOUD.
LESSEE, SINCE TODAY IS THE TENTH, SEAT NUMBER 10.
KASUGA!
YES.
CLATTER

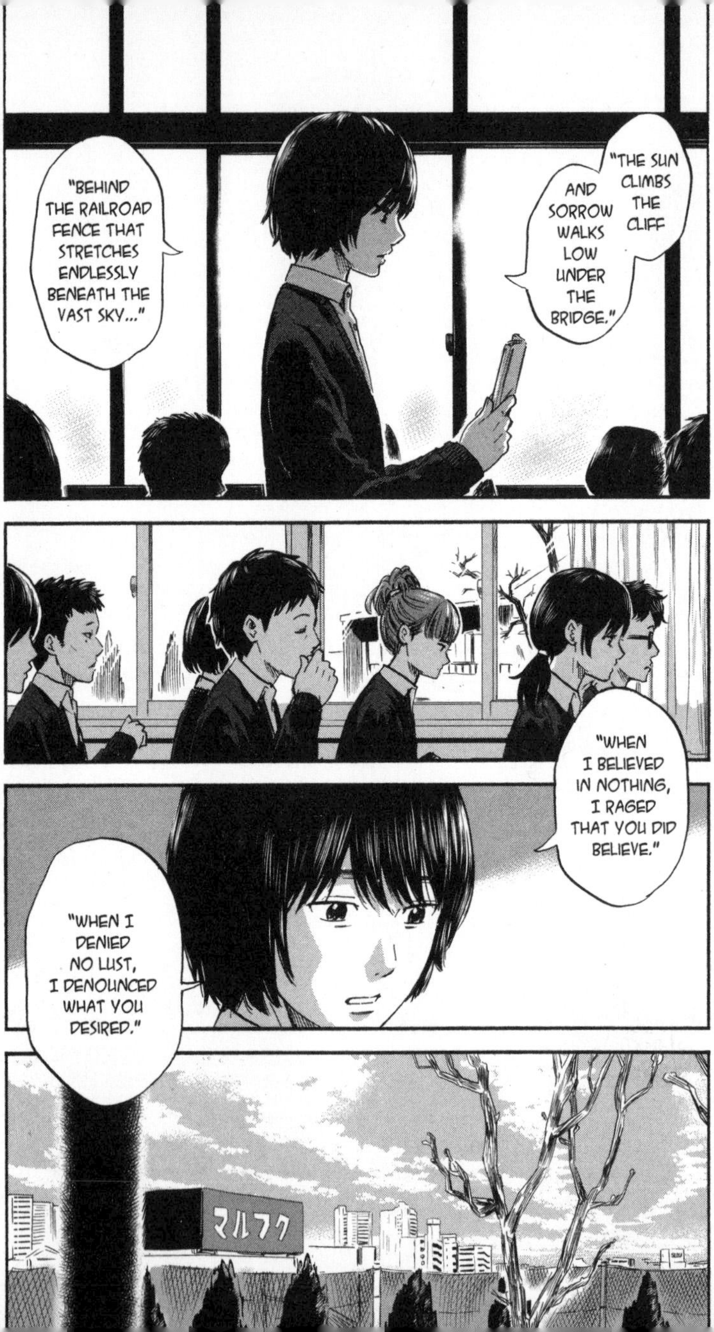
"THE SUN CLIMBS THE CLIFF AND SORROW WALKS LOW UNDER THE BRIDGE."
"BEHIND THE RAILROAD FENCE THAT STRETCHES ENDLESSLY BENEATH THE VAST SKY..."
"WHEN I BELIEVED IN NOTHING, I RAGED THAT YOU DID BELIEVE."
"WHEN I DENIED NO LUST, I DENOUNCED WHAT YOU DESIRED."
マルフク

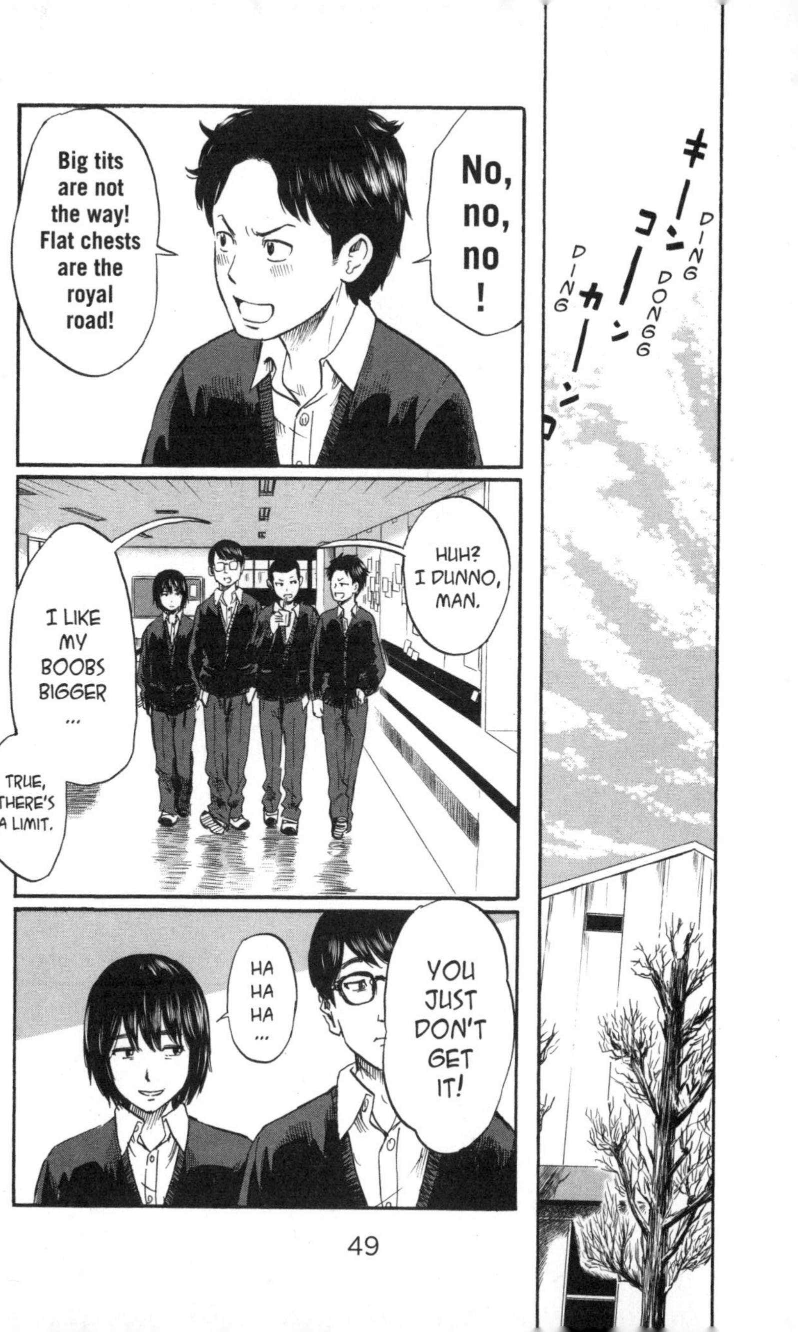
キーン
DING
コーン
DONG
カーン
DING
コ
No, no, no!
Big tits are not the way! Flat chests are the royal road!
HUH? I DUNNO, MAN.
I LIKE MY BOOBS BIGGER ...
TRUE, THERE'S A LIMIT.
YOU JUST DON'T GET IT!
HA HA HA ...

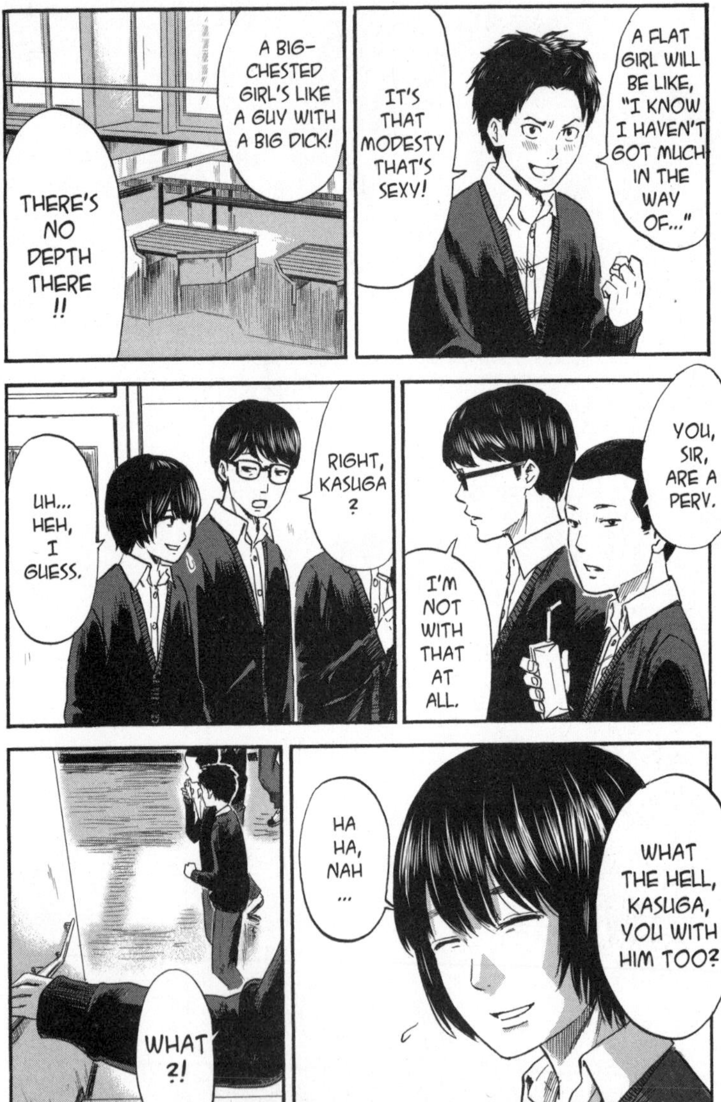
A FLAT GIRL WILL BE LIKE, "I KNOW I HAVEN'T GOT MUCH IN THE WAY OF..."
IT'S THAT MODESTY THAT'S SEXY!
A BIG-CHESTED GIRL'S LIKE A GUY WITH A BIG DICK!
THERE'S NO DEPTH THERE!!
YOU, SIR, ARE A PERV.
I'M NOT WITH THAT AT ALL.
RIGHT, KASUGA?
UH... HEH, I GUESS.
WHAT THE HELL, KASUGA, YOU WITH HIM TOO?
HA HA, NAH...
WHAT?!

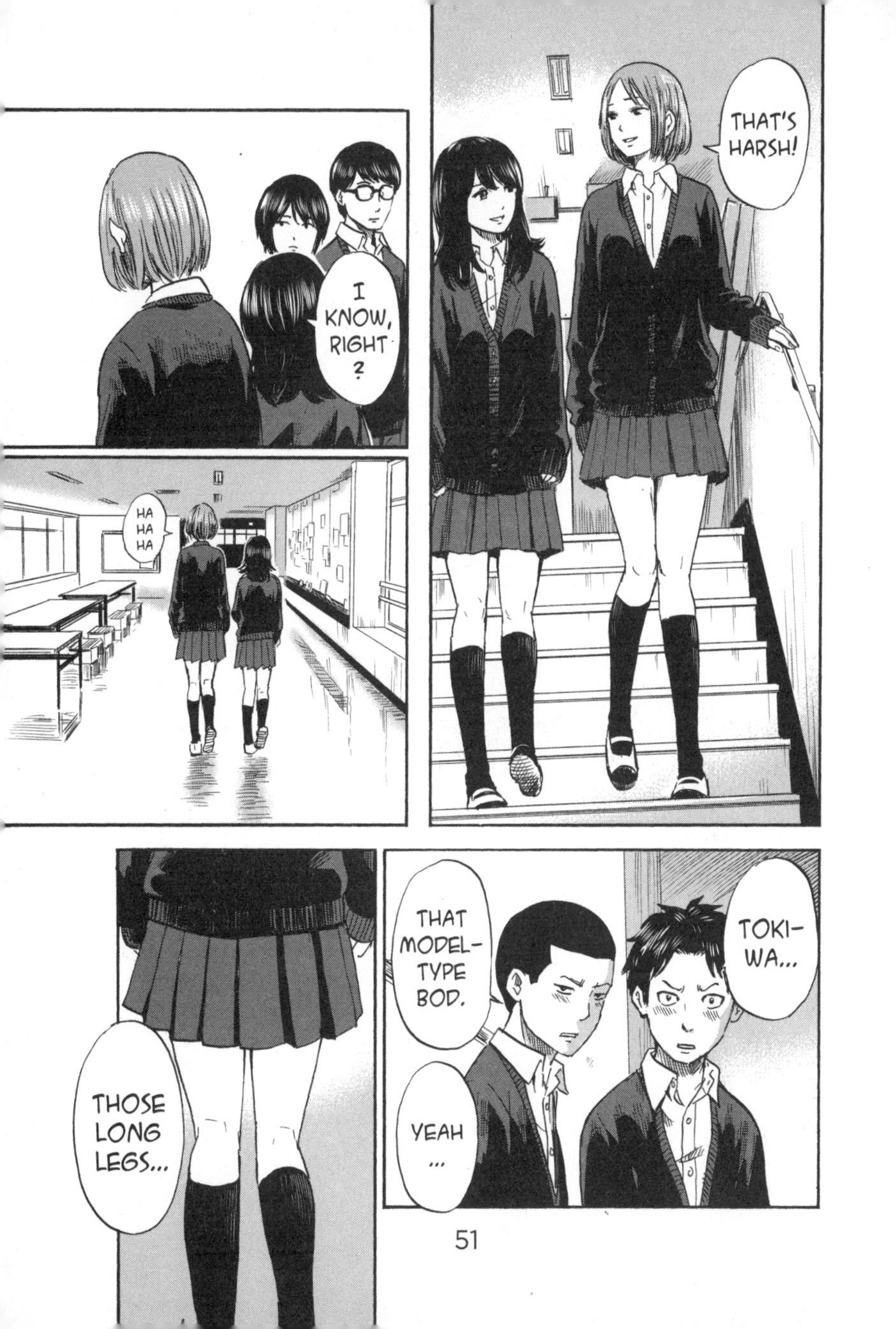
THAT'S HARSH!
I KNOW, RIGHT?
HA HA HA
TOKI-WA...
THAT MODEL-TYPE BOD.
YEAH...
THOSE LONG LEGS...

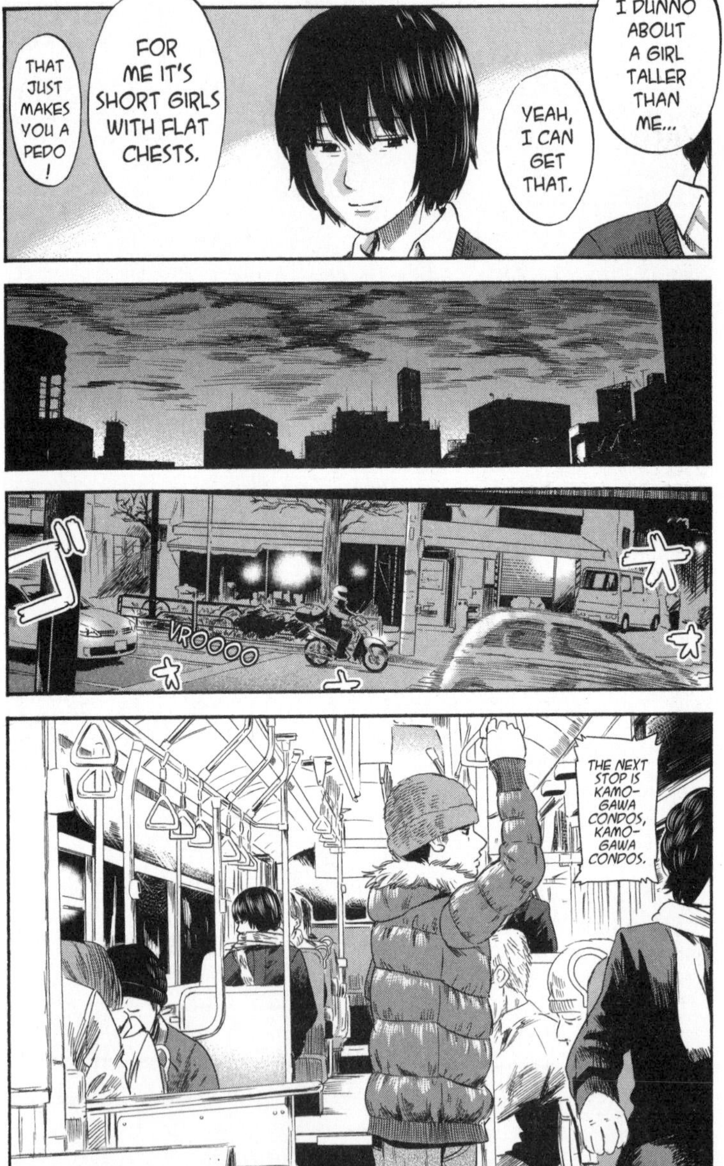
BUT I DUNNO ABOUT A GIRL TALLER THAN ME...
YEAH, I CAN GET THAT.
FOR ME IT'S SHORT GIRLS WITH FLAT CHESTS.
THAT JUST MAKES YOU A PEDO!
ゴオオオ
VROOOO
THE NEXT STOP IS KAMO-GAWA CONDOS, KAMO-GAWA CONDOS.

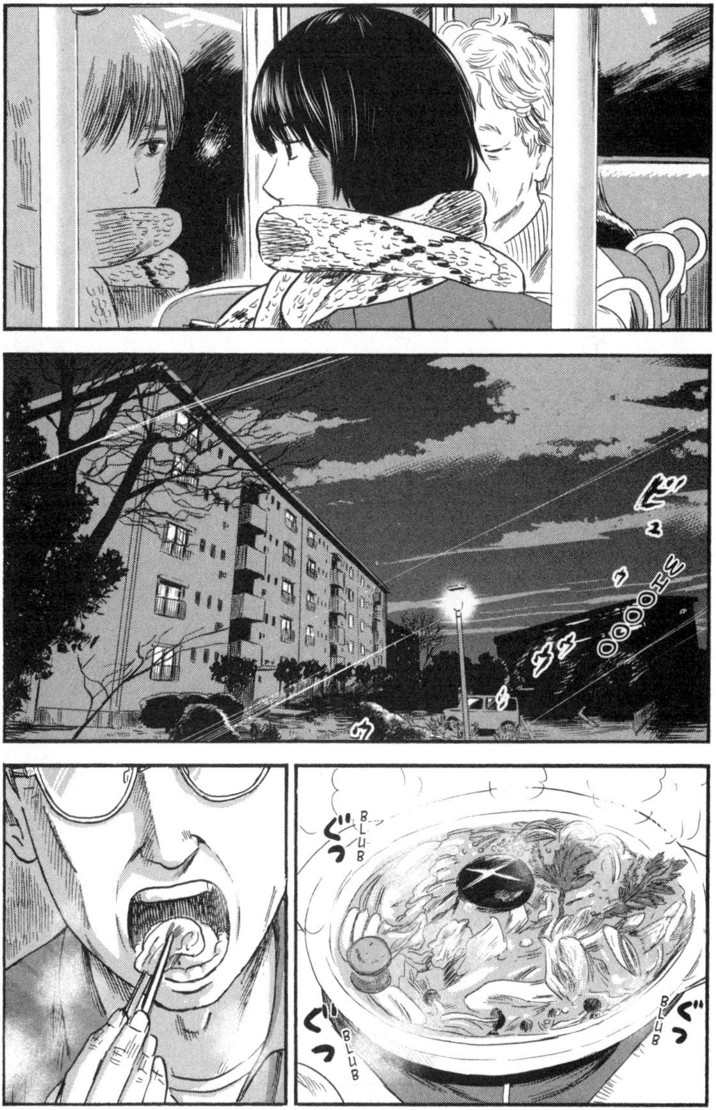
WHOOOOO
BLUB
BLUB
BLUB

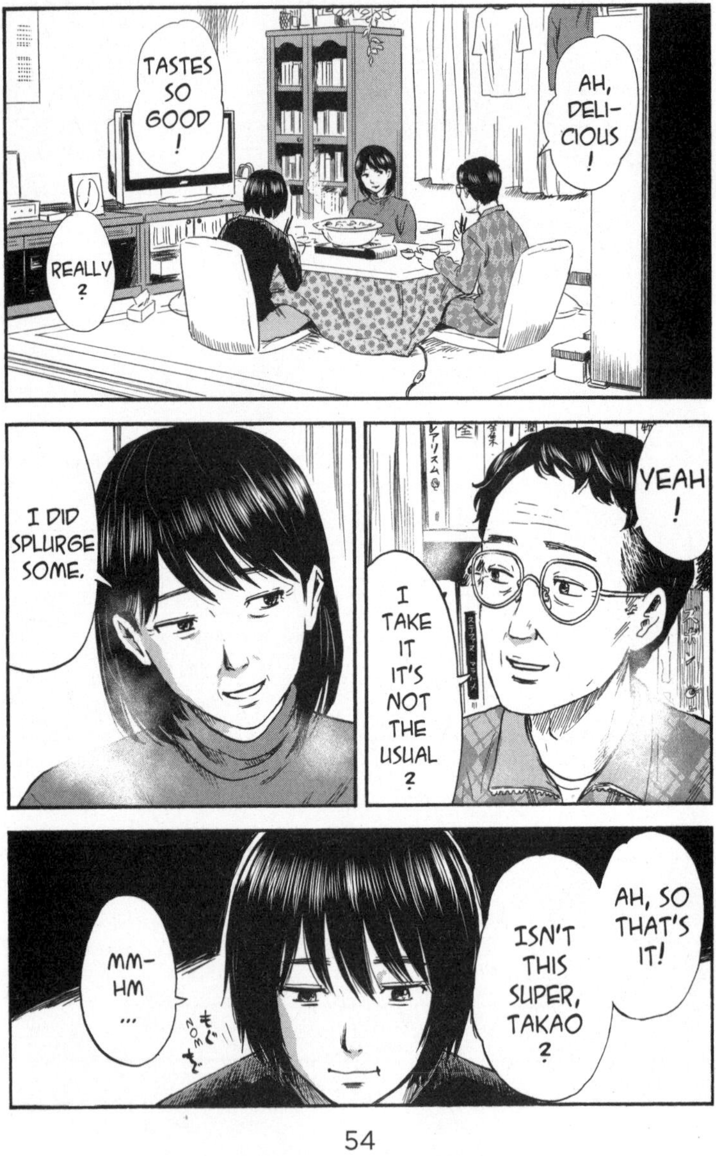
AH, DELICIOUS!
TASTES SO GOOD!
REALLY?
YEAH!
I TAKE IT IT'S NOT THE USUAL?
I DID SPLURGE SOME.
AH, SO THAT'S IT!
ISN'T THIS SUPER, TAKAO?
MM-HM ...
NOM

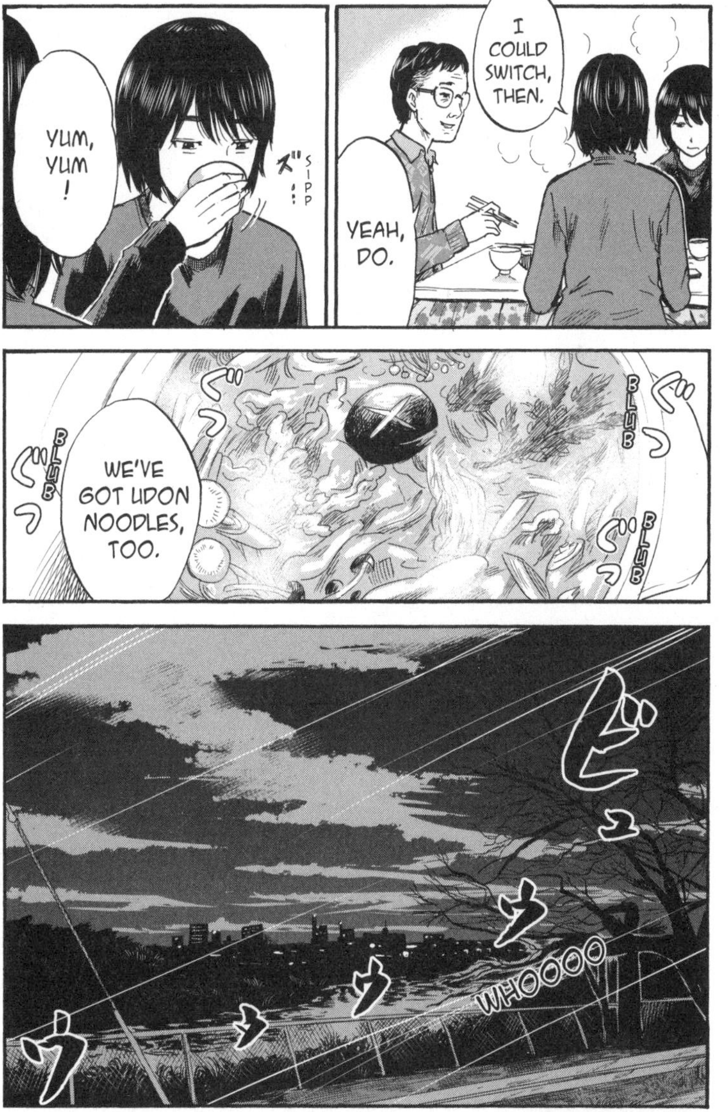
I COULD SWITCH, THEN.
YEAH, DO.
YUM, YUM!
SIPP
BLUB
BLUB
WE'VE GOT UDON NOODLES, TOO.
BLUB
WHOOOO

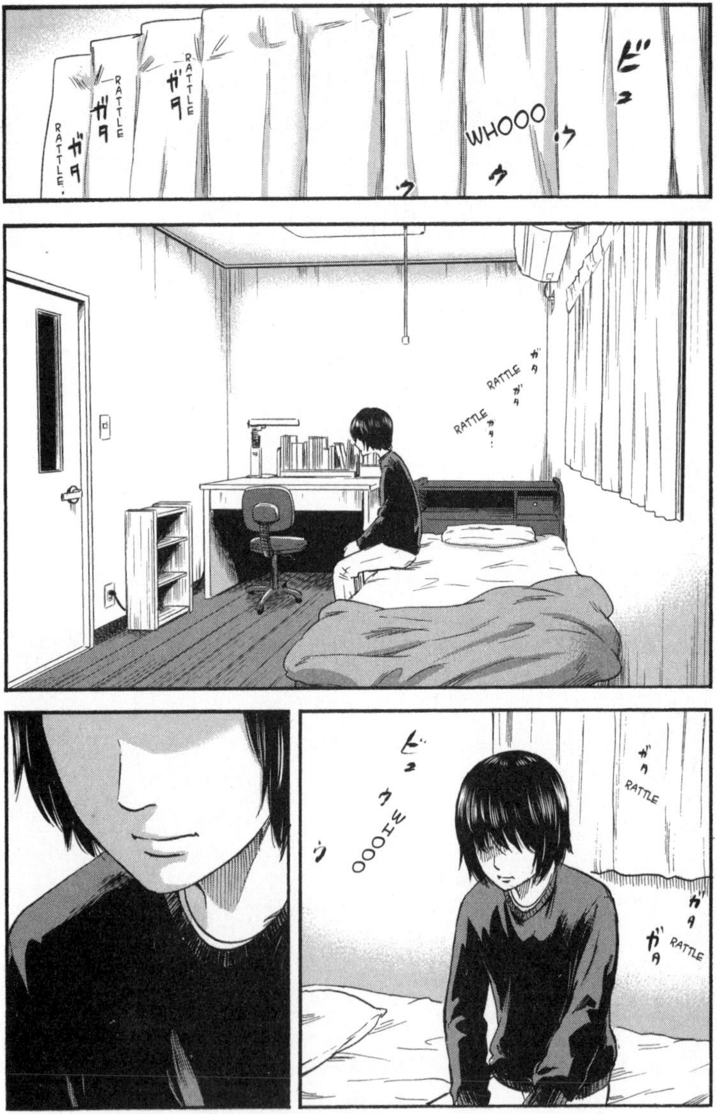
ビュ
ゥ
WHOOO
ゥ
ゥ
ガタ
RATTLE
ガタ
RATTLE
ガタ
RATTLE...
ガタ
RATTLE
ガタ
RATTLE
ガタ...
ガタ
RATTLE
ガタ
ガタ
RATTLE
ビュ
ゥ
WHOOO
ゥ

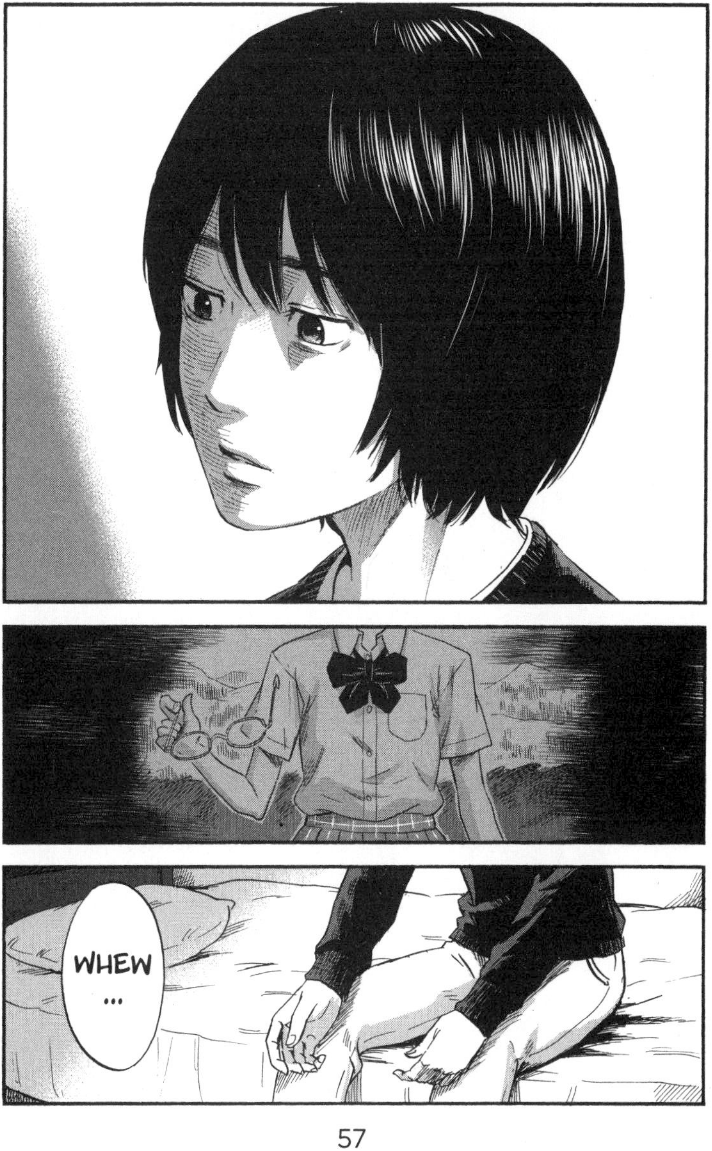
WHEW ...

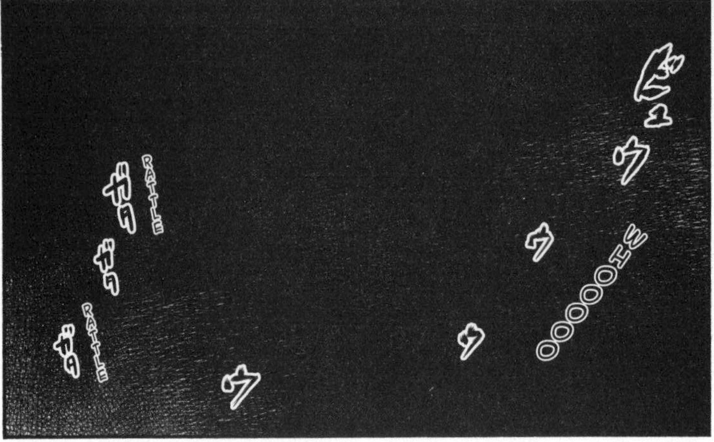
WHOOOOOOO
RATTLE
RATTLE

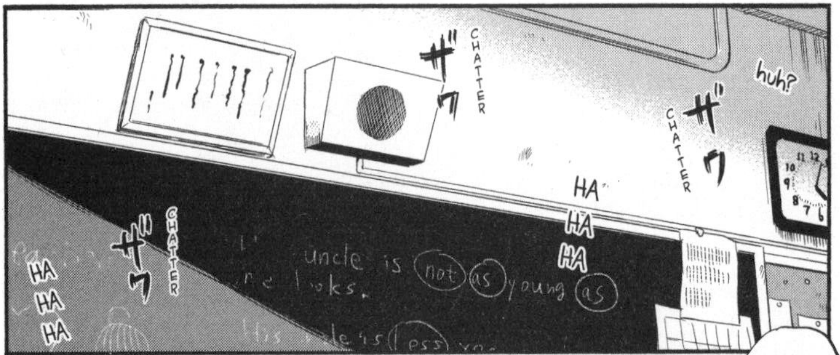
huh?
CHATTER
HA HA HA
CHATTER
CHATTER
HA HA HA

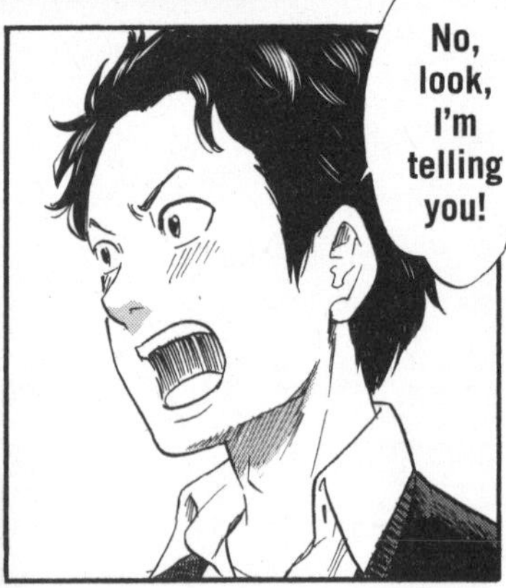
No, look, I'm telling you!

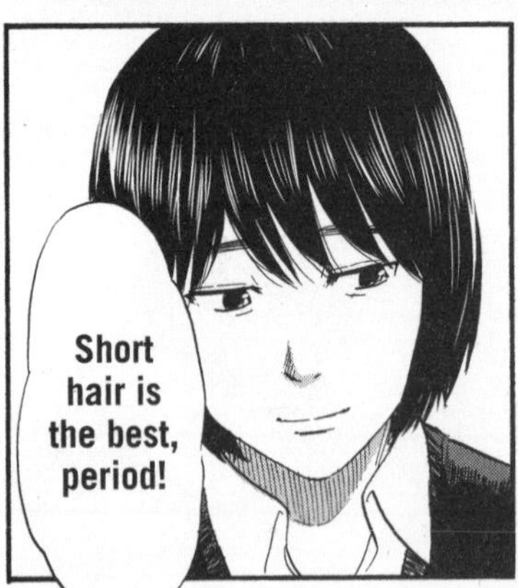
Short hair is the best, period!

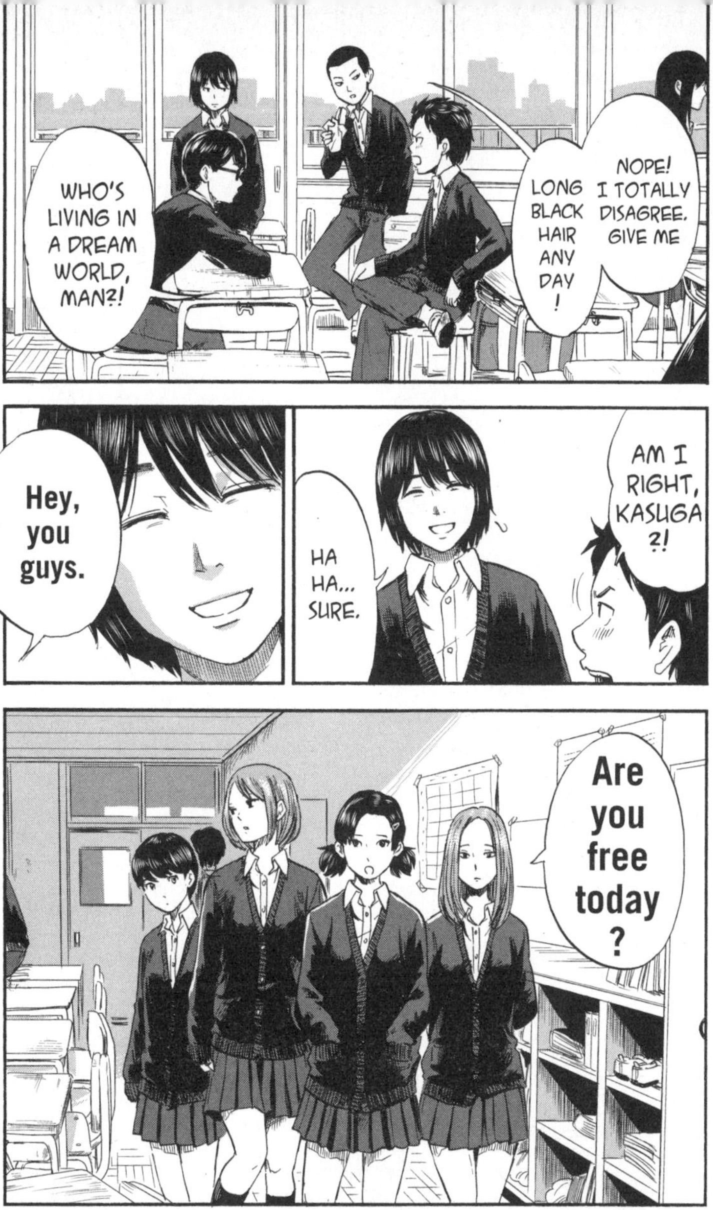
NOPE! I TOTALLY DISAGREE. GIVE ME
LONG BLACK HAIR ANY DAY!
WHO'S LIVING IN A DREAM WORLD, MAN?!
AM I RIGHT, KASUGA?!
HA HA... SURE.
Hey, you guys.
Are you free today?

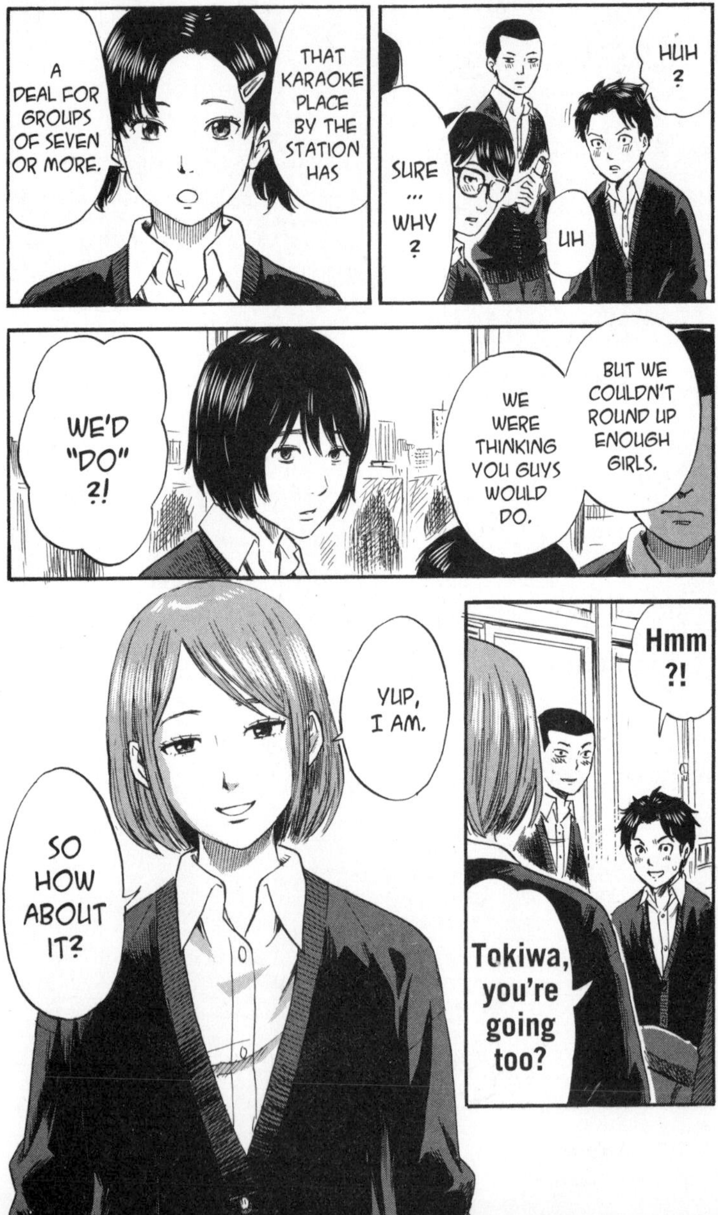
HUH?
UH
SURE ... WHY?
THAT KARAOKE PLACE BY THE STATION HAS
A DEAL FOR GROUPS OF SEVEN OR MORE.
BUT WE COULDN'T ROUND UP ENOUGH GIRLS.
WE WERE THINKING YOU GUYS WOULD DO.
WE'D "DO"?!
Hmm?!
Tokiwa, you're going too?
YUP, I AM.
SO HOW ABOUT IT?

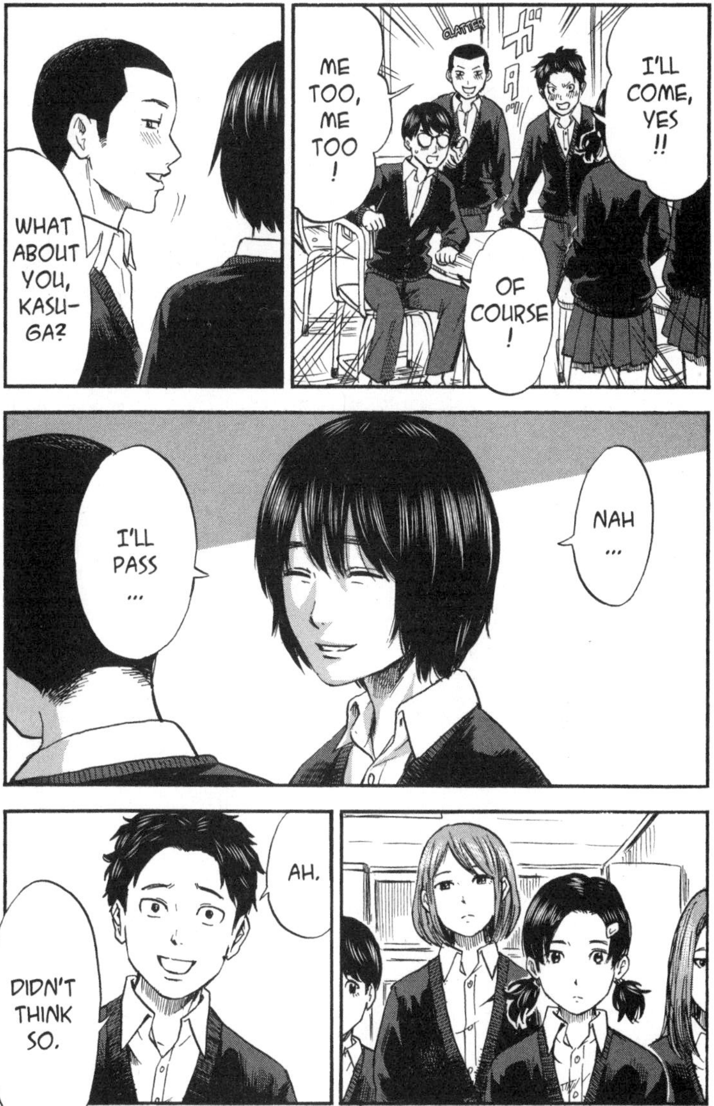
I'LL COME, YES!!
CLATTER
ME TOO, ME TOO!
OF COURSE!
WHAT ABOUT YOU, KASU-GA?
NAH...
I'LL PASS...
AH.
DIDN'T THINK SO.

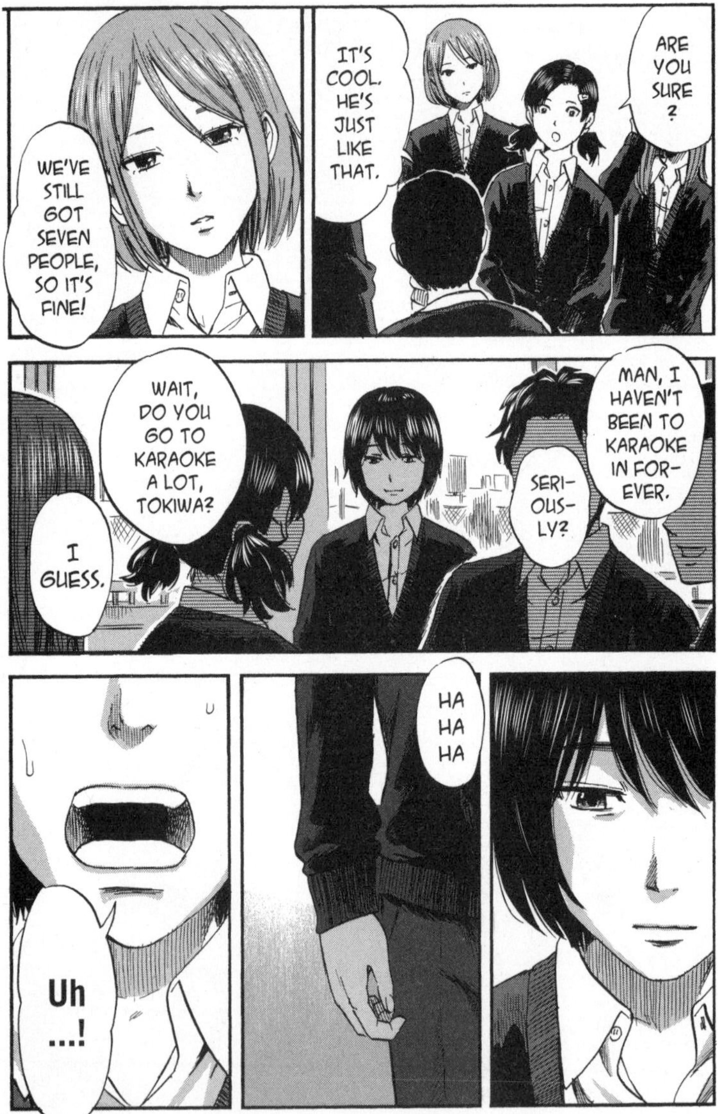
ARE YOU SURE?
IT'S COOL. HE'S JUST LIKE THAT.
WE'VE STILL GOT SEVEN PEOPLE, SO IT'S FINE!
MAN, I HAVEN'T BEEN TO KARAOKE IN FOR-EVER.
SERI-OUS-LY?
WAIT, DO YOU GO TO KARAOKE A LOT, TOKIWA?
I GUESS.
HA HA HA
Uh ...!

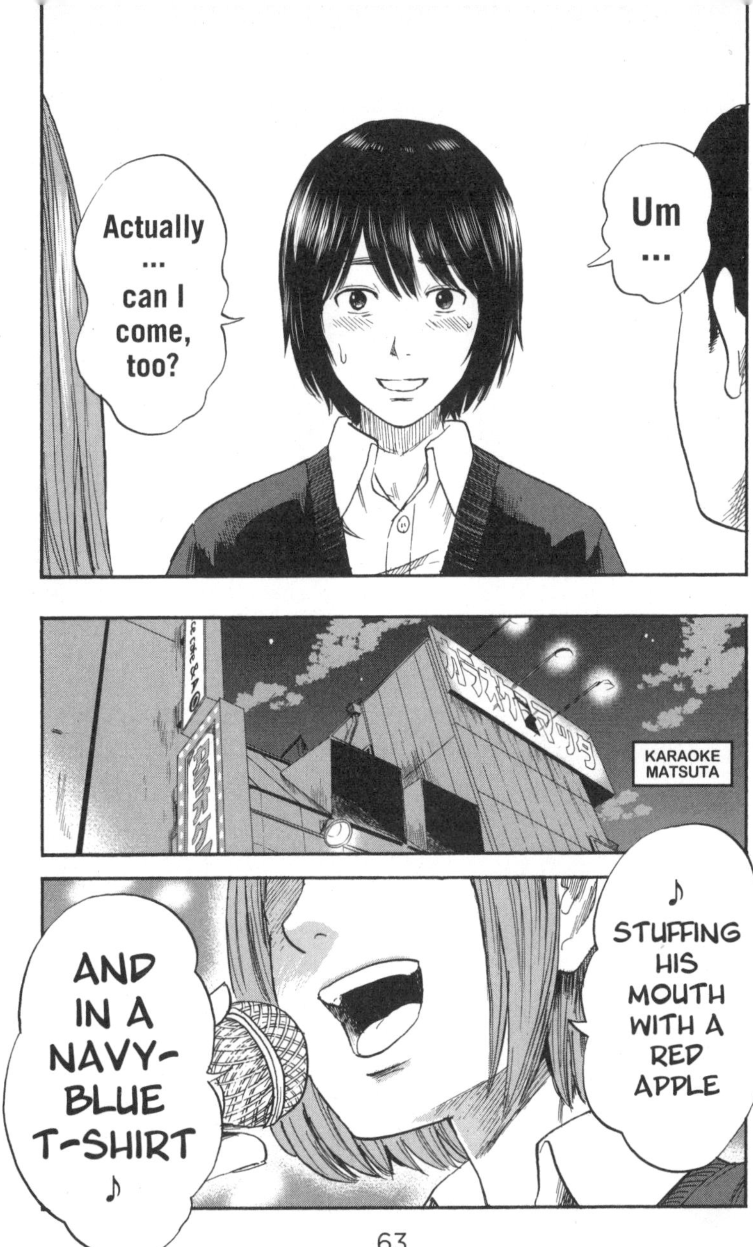
Um ...
Actually ... can I come, too?
KARAOKE MATSUTA
♪ STUFFING HIS MOUTH WITH A RED APPLE
AND IN A NAVY-BLUE T-SHIRT ♪

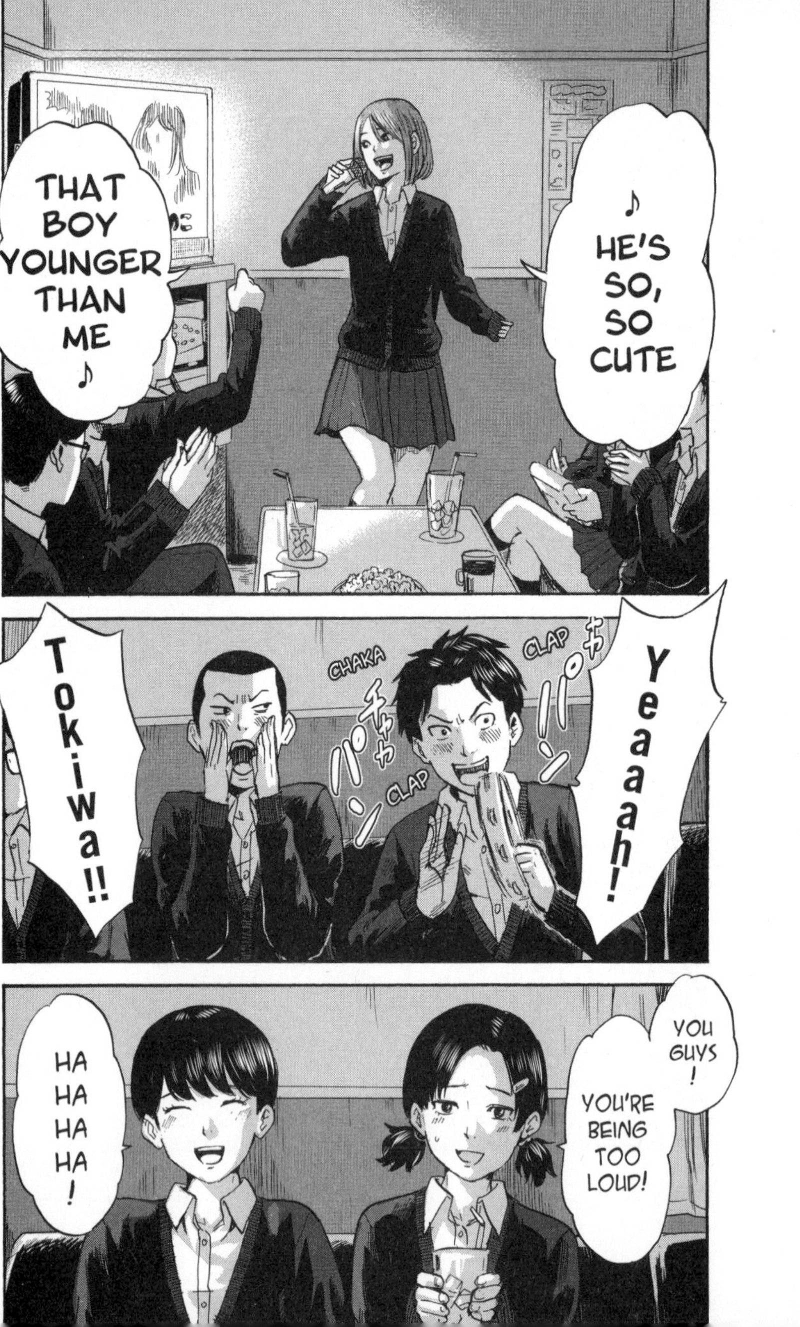
THAT BOY YOUNGER THAN ME ♪
♪ HE'S SO, SO CUTE
Yeaaaah!
CLAP
CHAKA
CLAP
Tokiwa!!
YOU GUYS!
YOU'RE BEING TOO LOUD!
HA HA HA HA!

OKAY! MY TURN NEXT!

Yay, Sasaki!

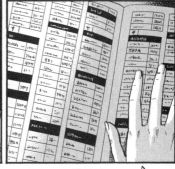

HMM... UH...

HA HA HA HA

Ultra Soul!

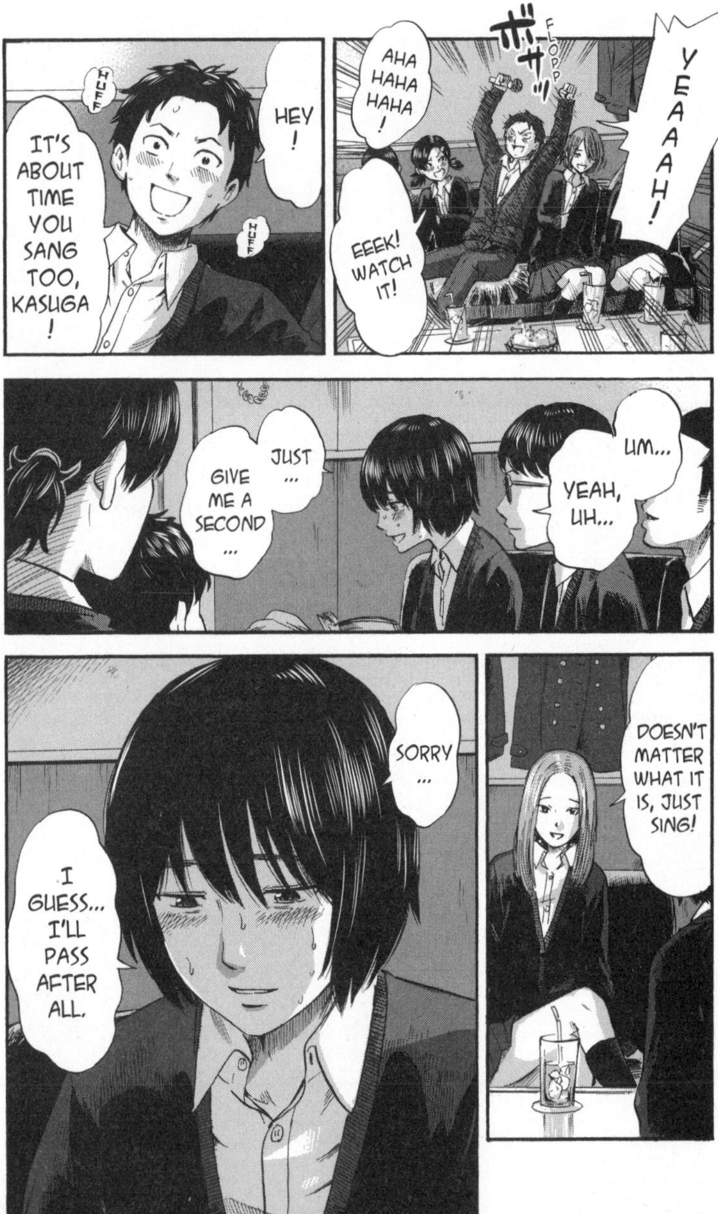
YEAAAAH!
FLOPP
AHA HAHA HAHA!
EEEK! WATCH IT!
HEY!
HUFF
IT'S ABOUT TIME YOU SANG TOO, KASUGA!
HUFF
UM...
YEAH, UH...
JUST...
GIVE ME A SECOND...
DOESN'T MATTER WHAT IT IS, JUST SING!
SORRY...
I GUESS... I'LL PASS AFTER ALL.

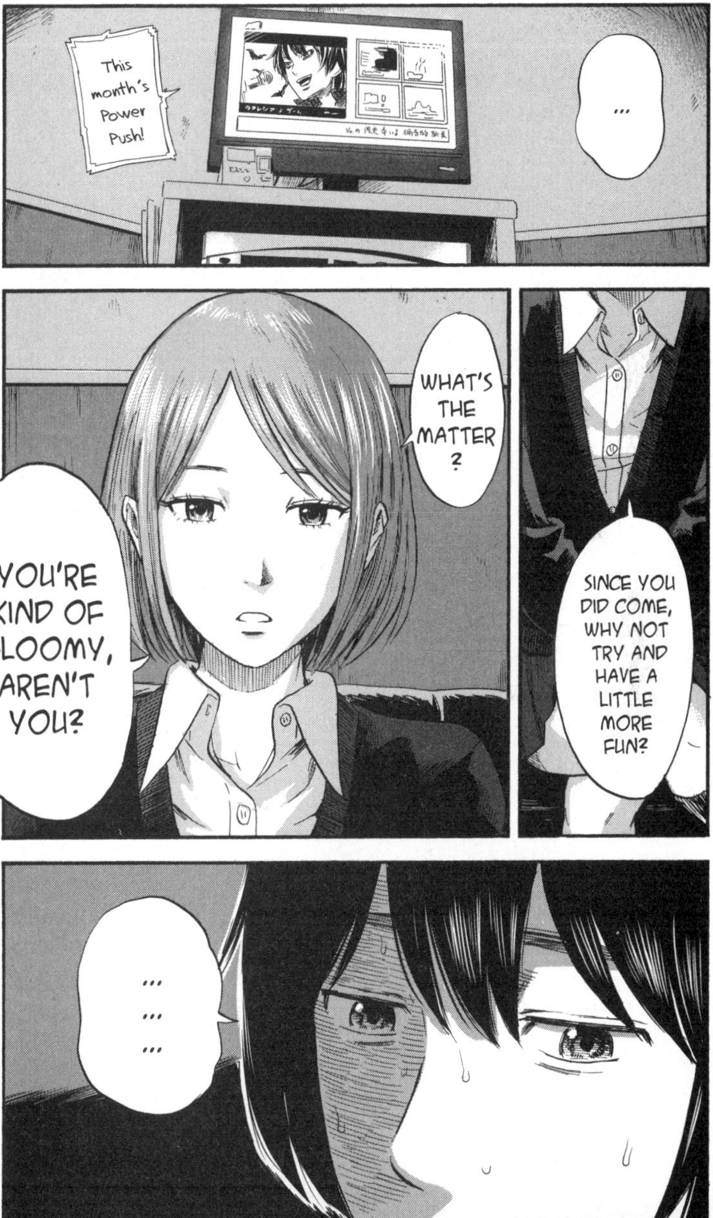
...
This month's Power Push!
SINCE YOU DID COME, WHY NOT TRY AND HAVE A LITTLE MORE FUN?
WHAT'S THE MATTER?
YOU'RE KIND OF GLOOMY, AREN'T YOU?
... ...

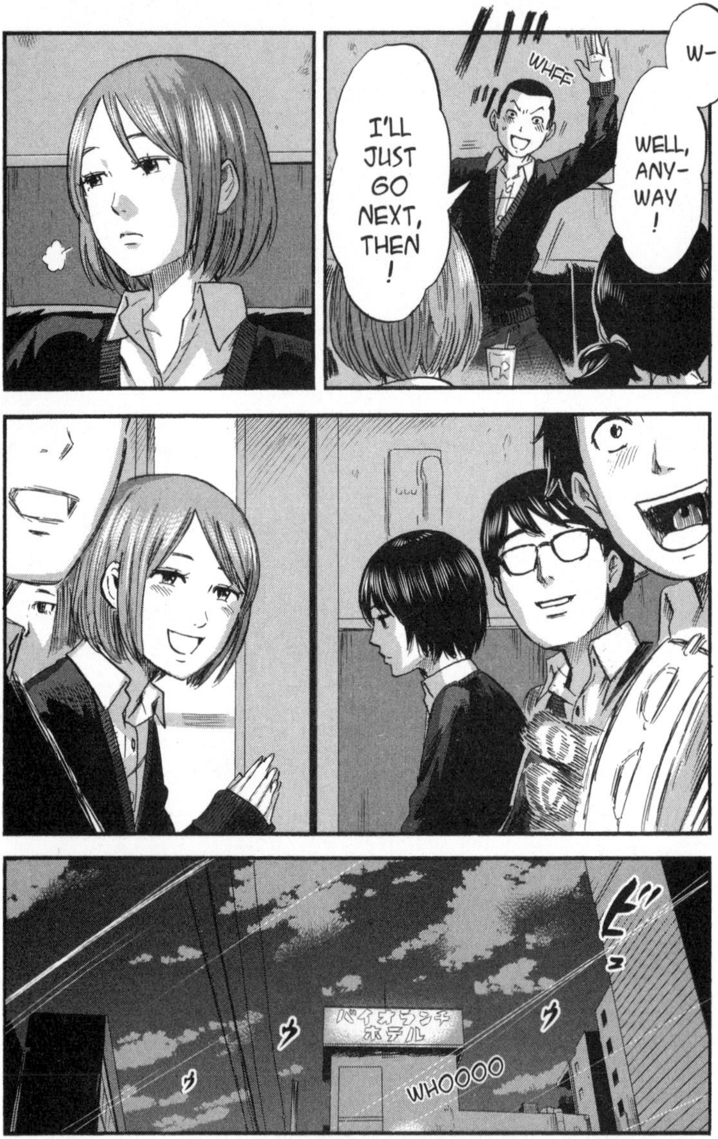
W-
WELL, ANY-WAY!
WHFF
I'LL JUST GO NEXT, THEN!
バイオランチ ホテル
WHOOOO

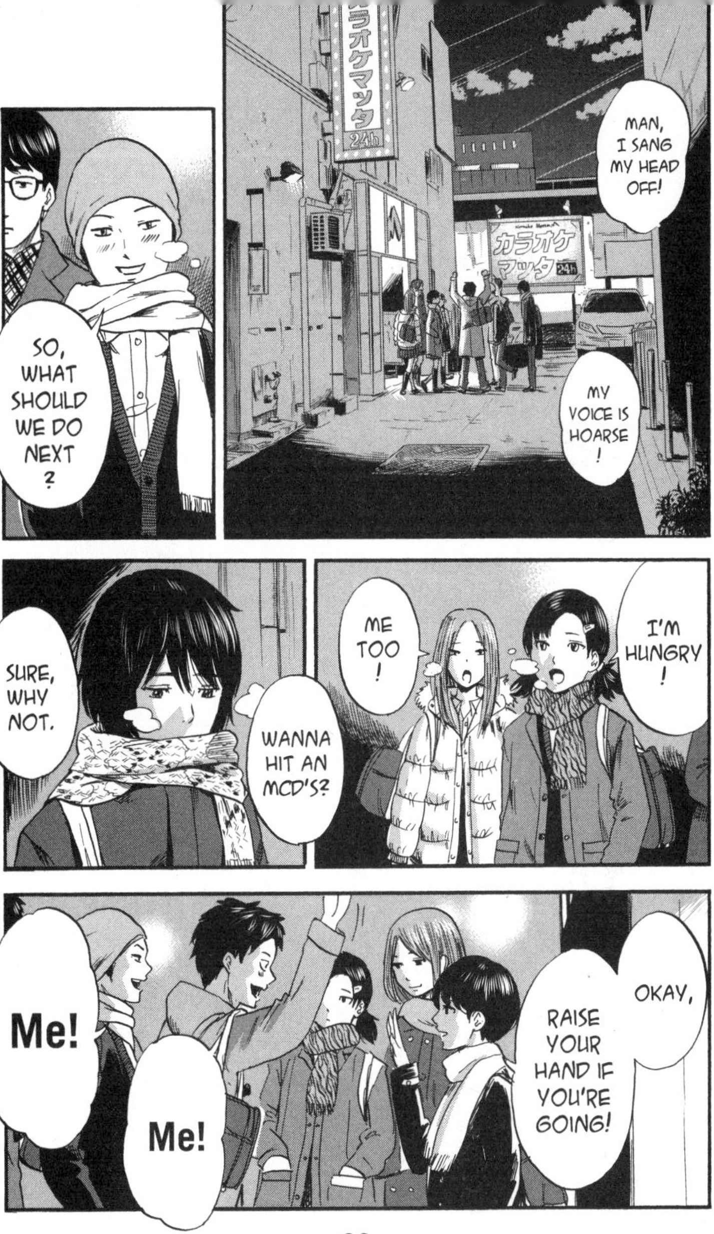
カラオケマッタ 24h
MAN, I SANG MY HEAD OFF!
MY VOICE IS HOARSE!
SO, WHAT SHOULD WE DO NEXT?
I'M HUNGRY!
ME TOO!
WANNA HIT AN MCD'S?
SURE, WHY NOT.
OKAY, RAISE YOUR HAND IF YOU'RE GOING!
Me!
Me!

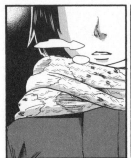

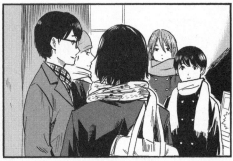

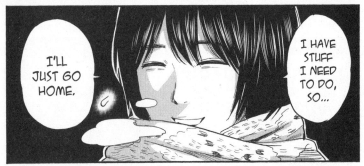

I HAVE STUFF I NEED TO DO, SO...
I'LL JUST GO HOME.
OH... OKAY.
THANKS FOR COMIN'.
BYE!

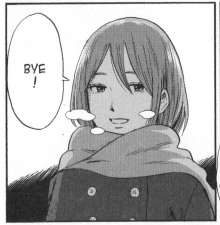

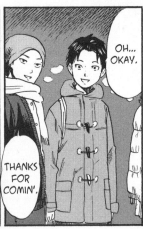

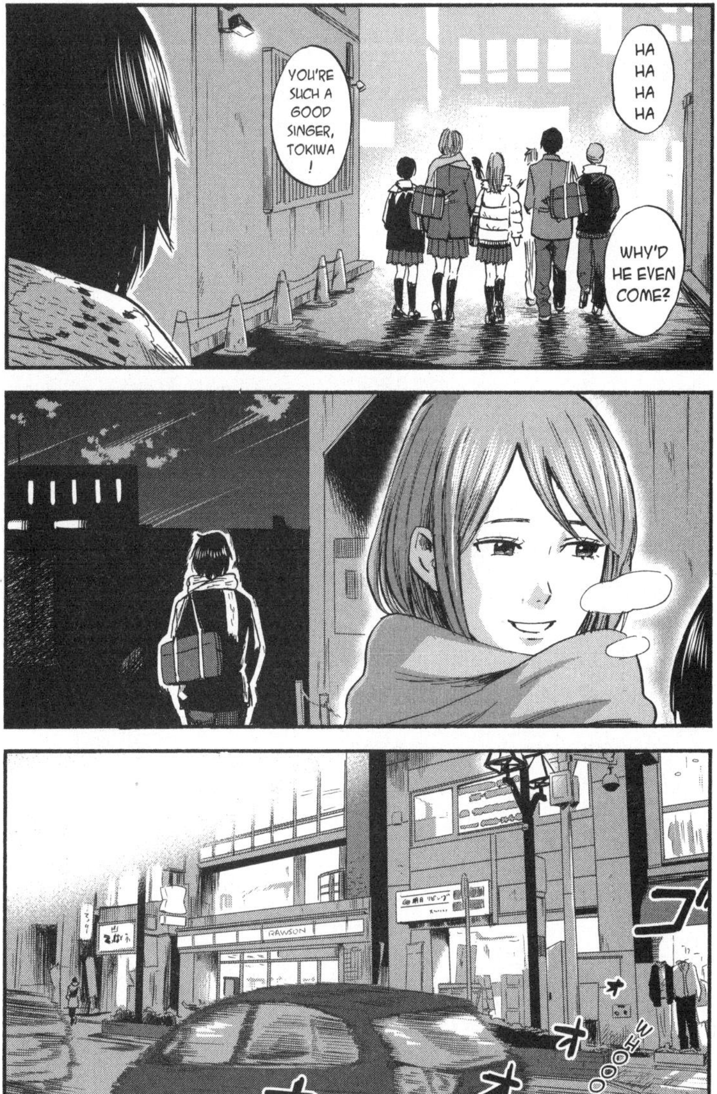
HA HA HA HA
YOU'RE SUCH A GOOD SINGER, TOKIWA!
WHY'D HE EVEN COME?
RAWSON
WHOOOO

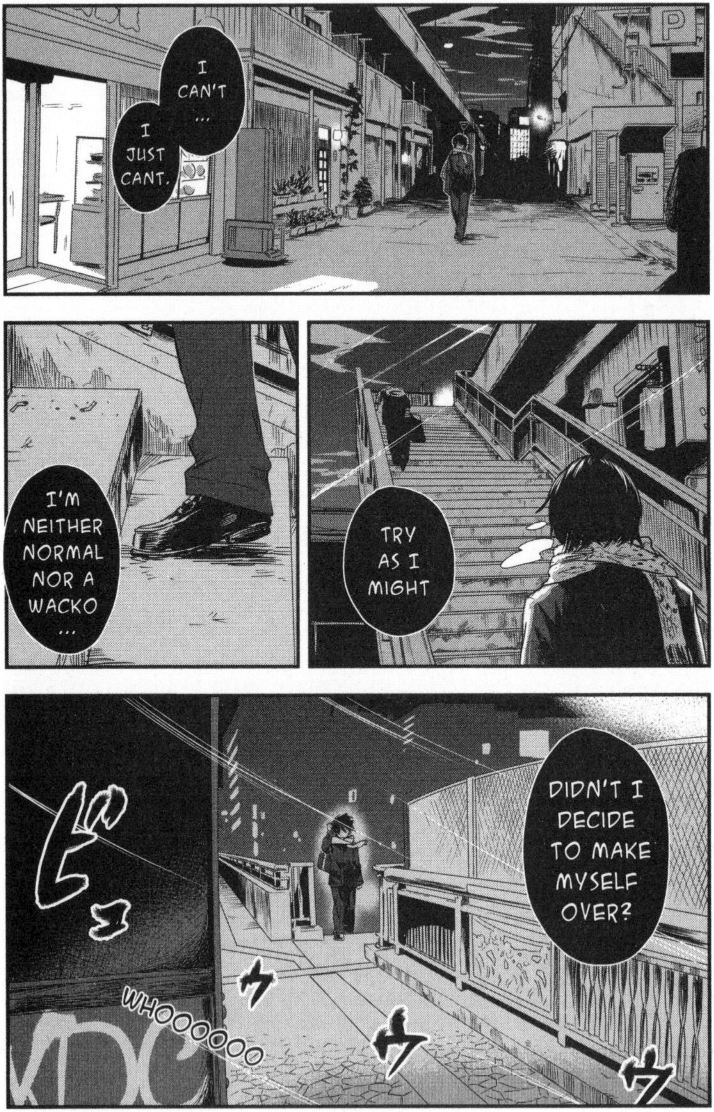
I CAN'T ...
I JUST CANT.
TRY AS I MIGHT
I'M NEITHER NORMAL NOR A WACKO ...
DIDN'T I DECIDE TO MAKE MYSELF OVER?
ビュ
ウウウ
WHOOOOOOO

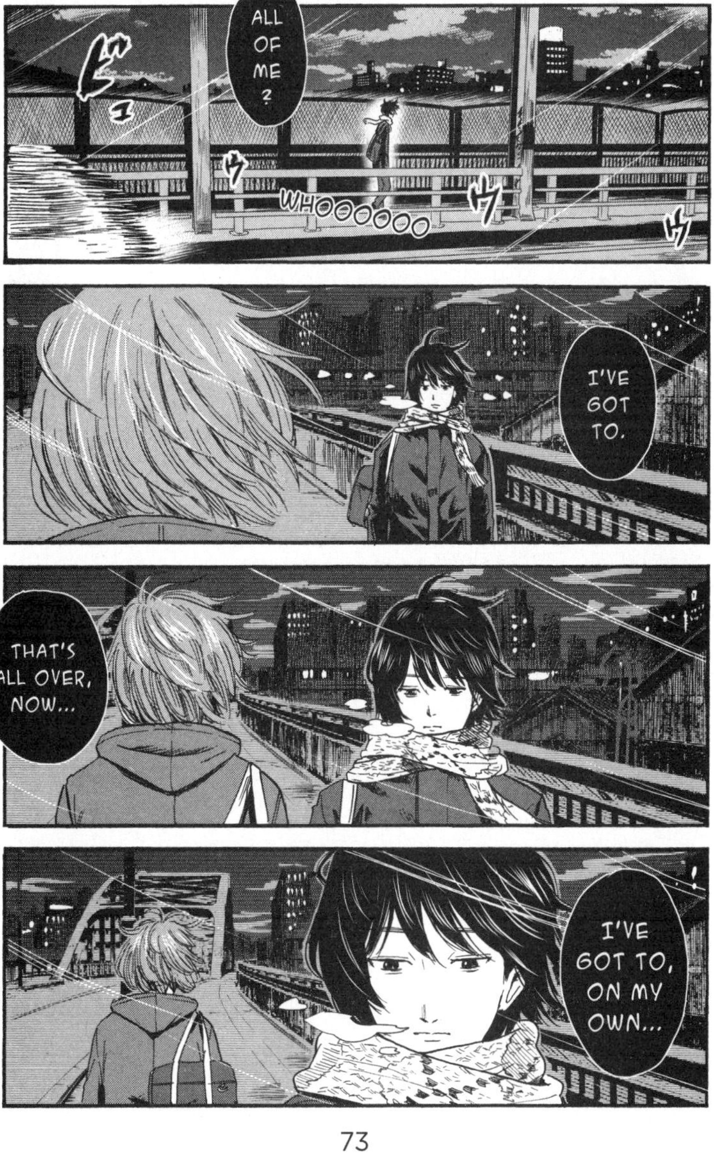
ALL OF ME?
WHOOOOOO
I'VE GOT TO.
THAT'S ALL OVER, NOW...
I'VE GOT TO, ON MY OWN...

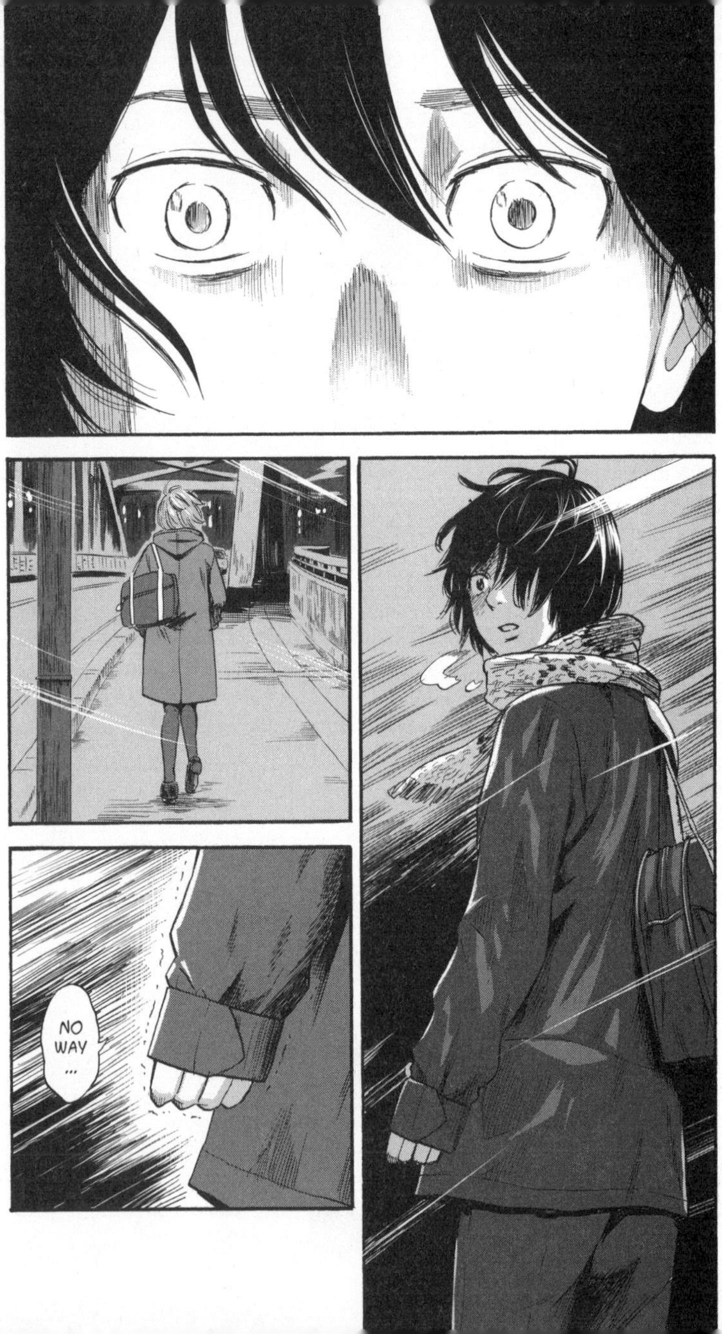
NO WAY ...

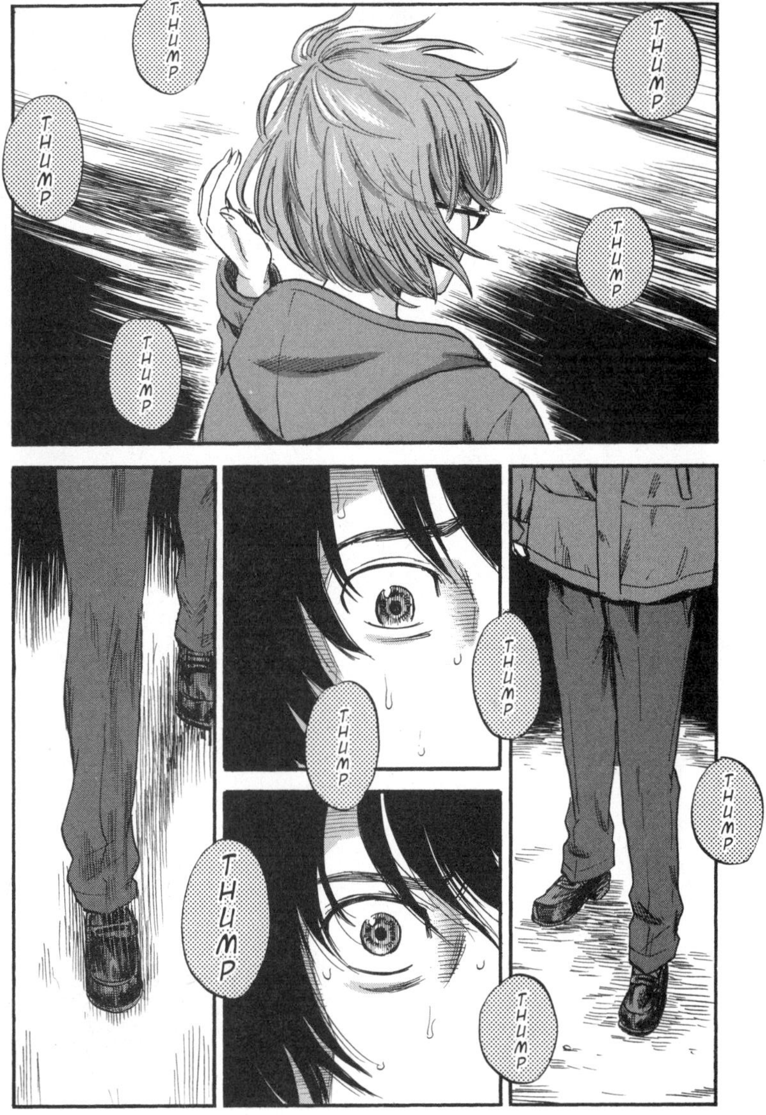
THUMP
THUMP
THUMP
THUMP
THUMP
THUMP
THUMP
THUMP
THUMP
THUMP
THUMP
THUMP

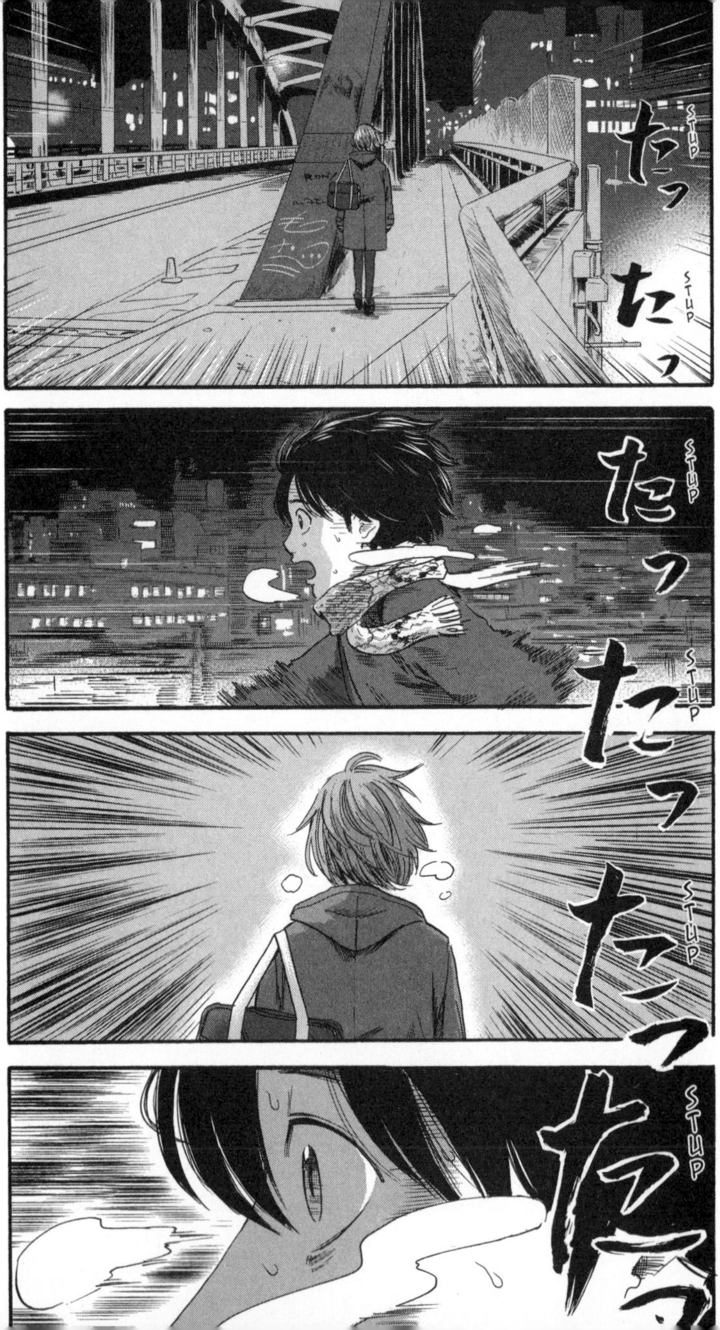
たっ
STUP
たっ
STUP
たっ
STUP
たっ
STUP
たっ
STUP
たっ
STUP

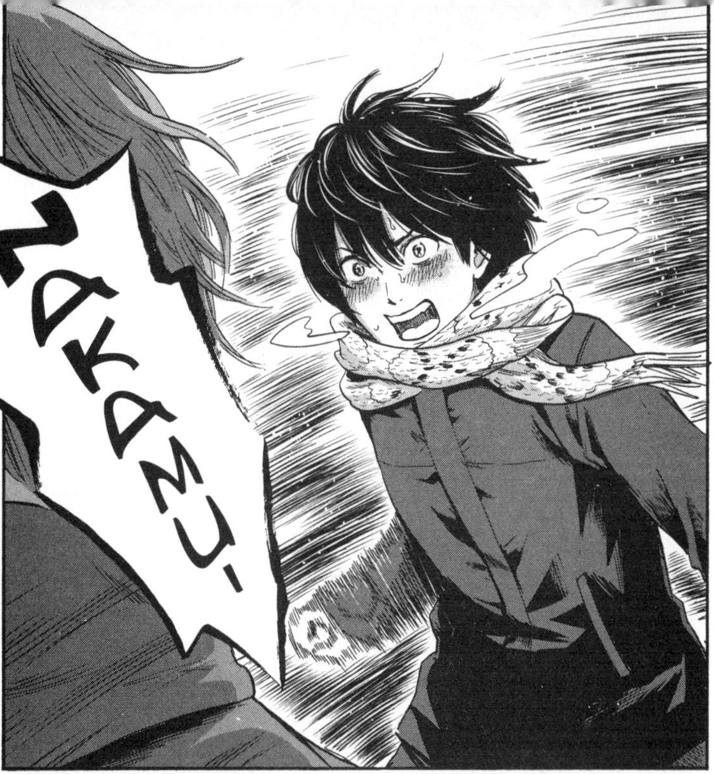
ZAKAMU-

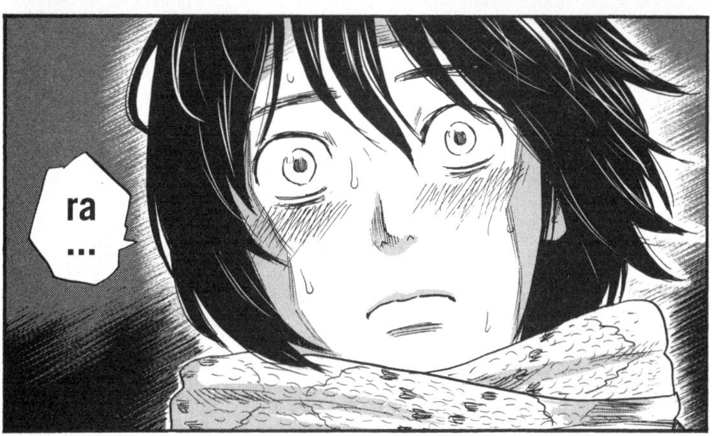
ra ...

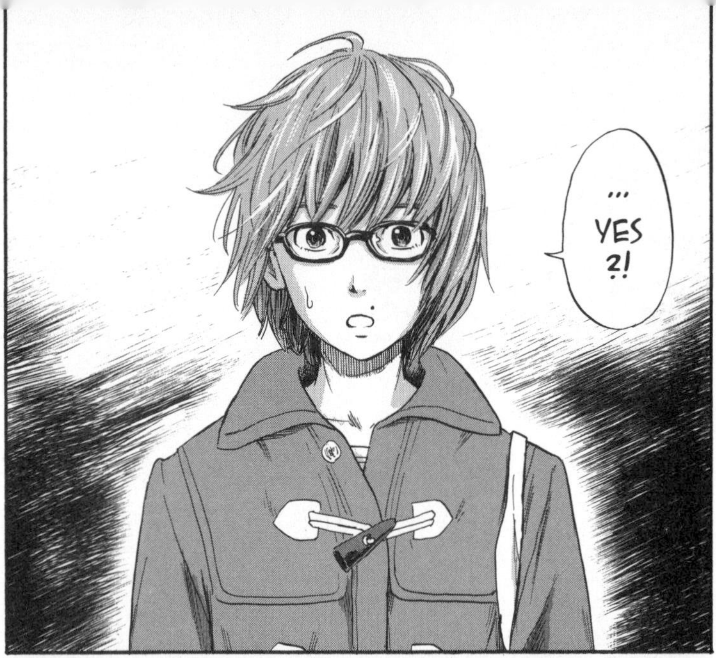
... YES ?!

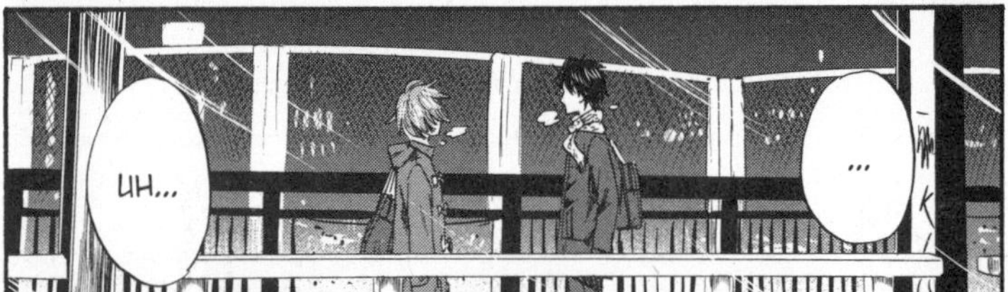
...
UH...

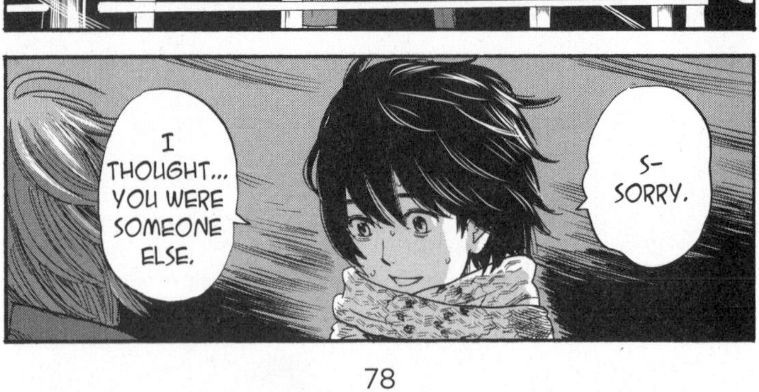
S-SORRY.
I THOUGHT... YOU WERE SOMEONE ELSE.

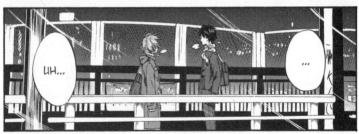

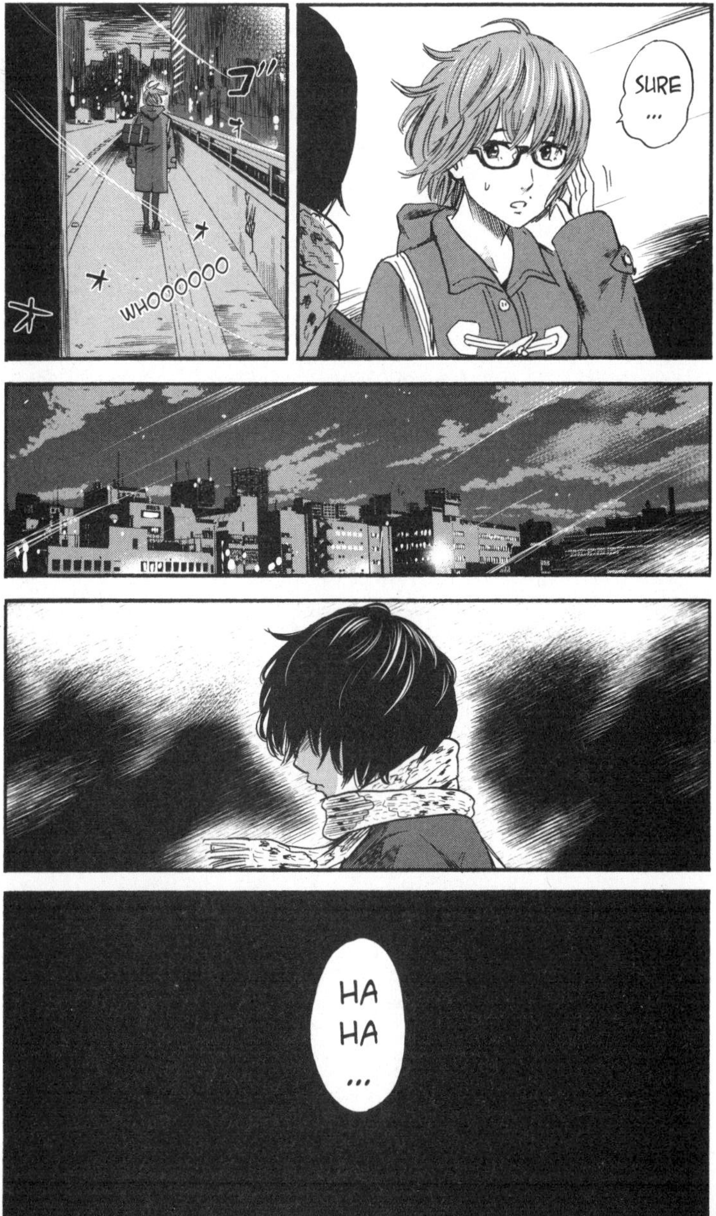
SURE ...
WHOOOOOO
HA HA ...

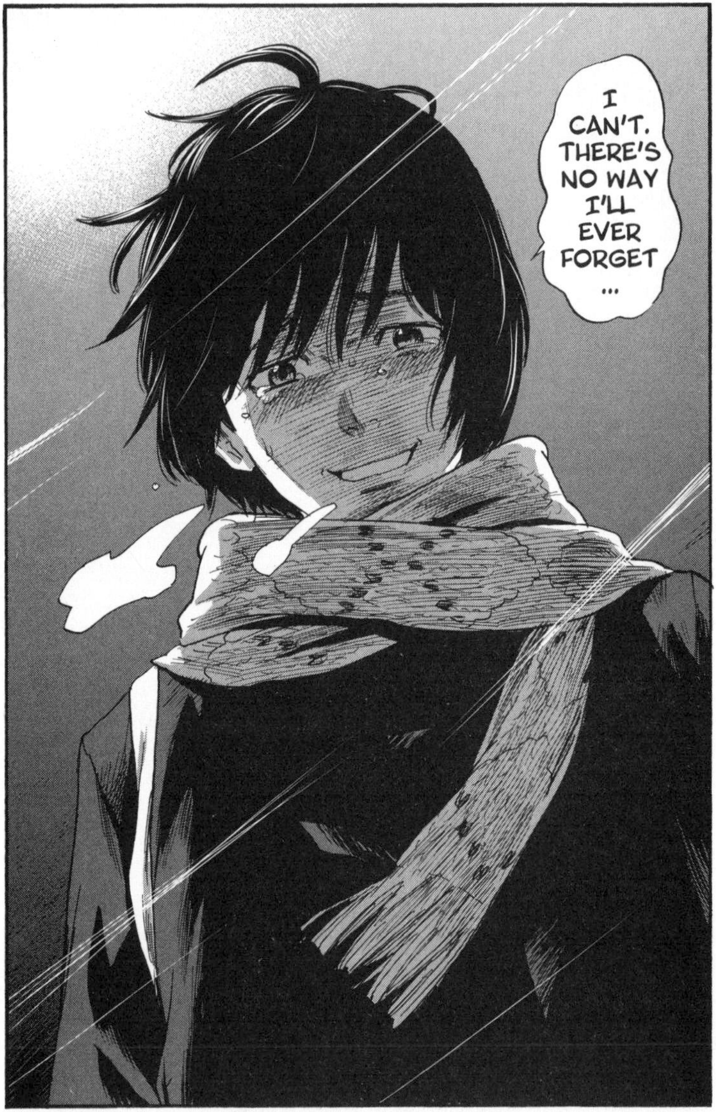
I CAN'T. THERE'S NO WAY I'LL EVER FORGET ...

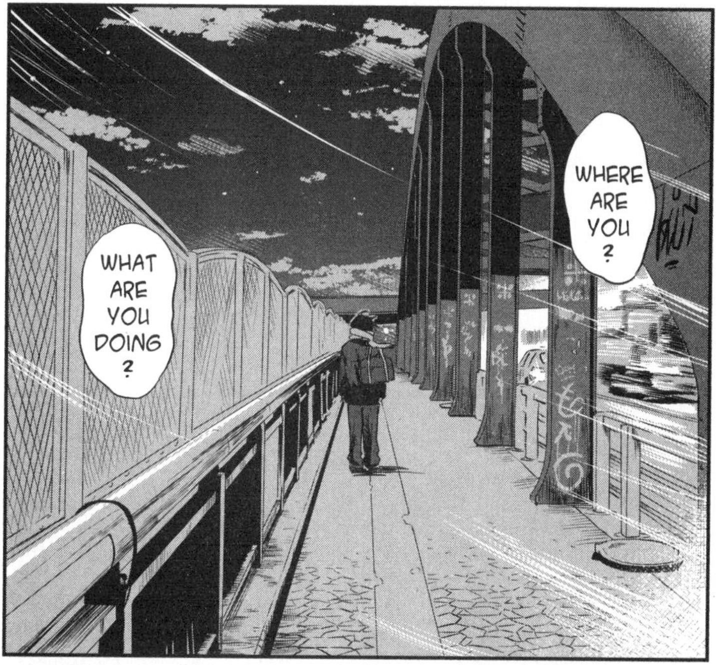
WHERE ARE YOU?
WHAT ARE YOU DOING?
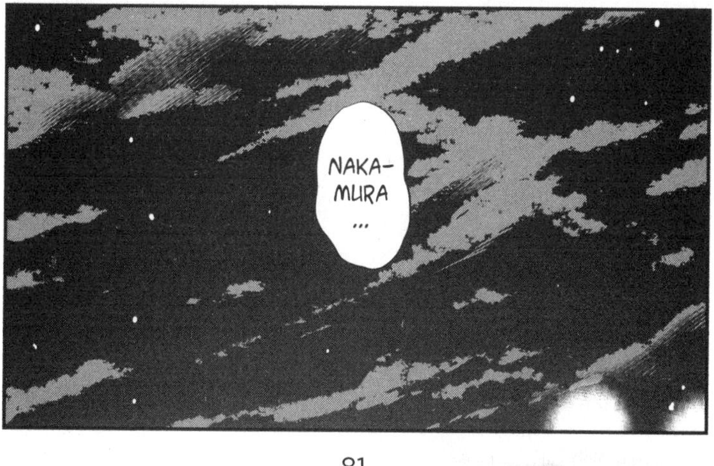
NAKA-MURA...

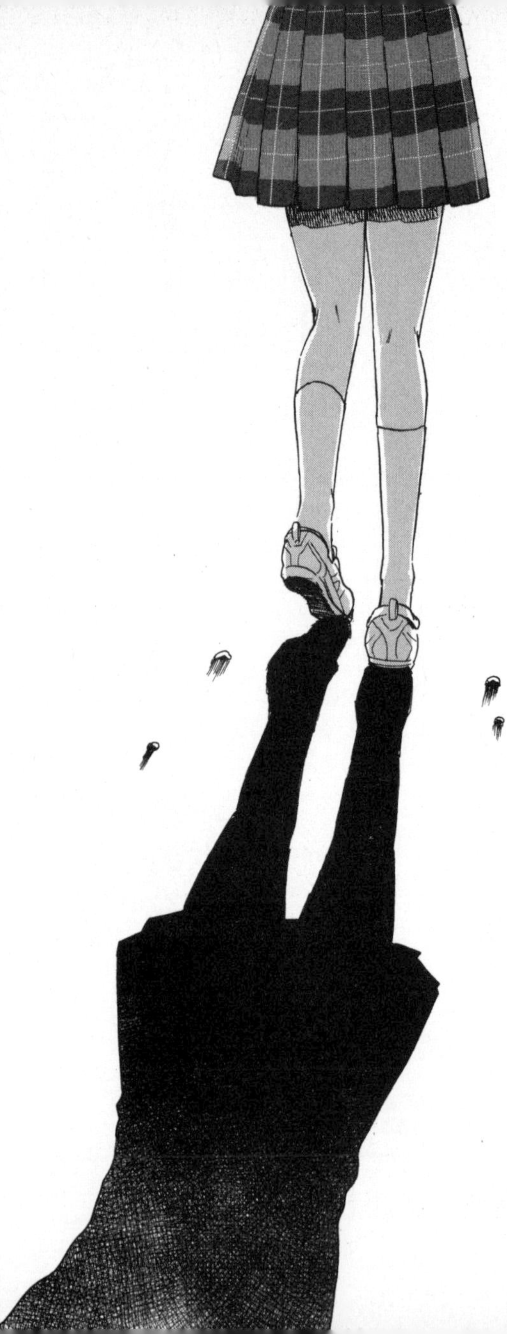

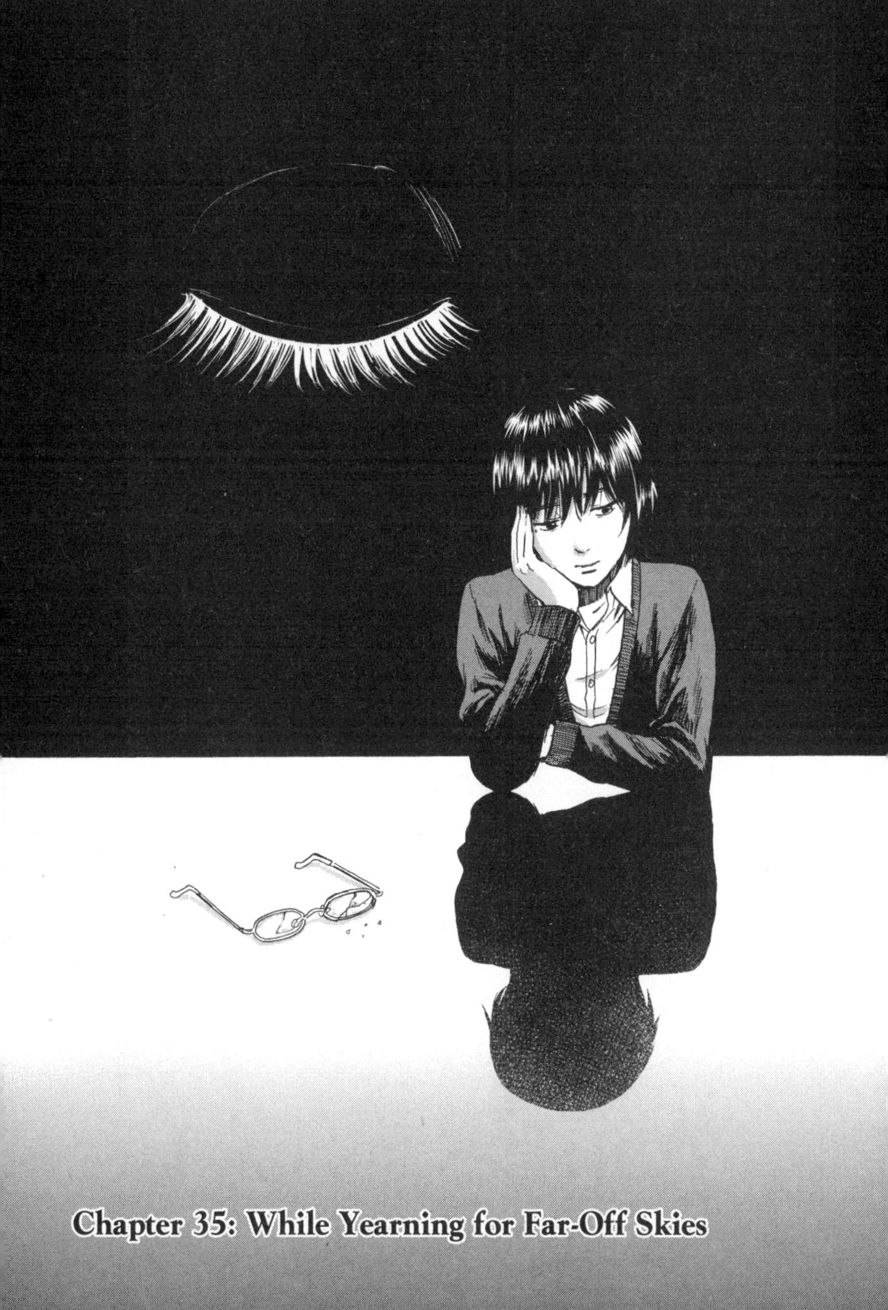

Chapter 35: While Yearning for Far-Off Skies

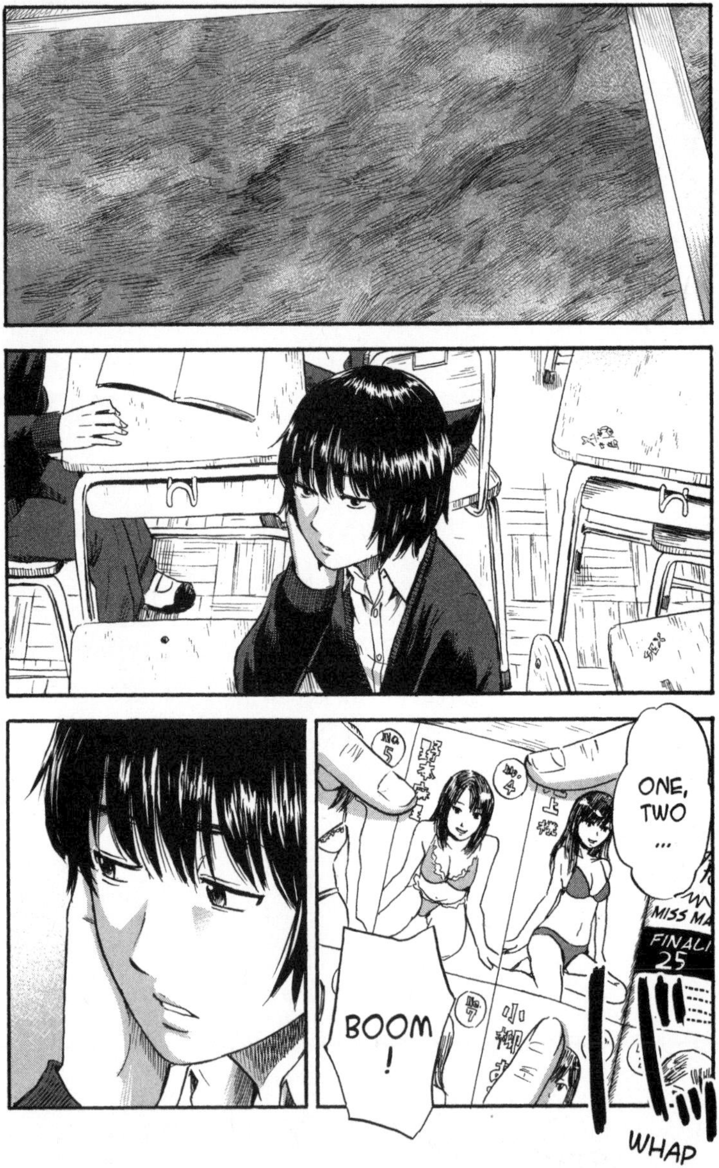
ONE, TWO ...
BOOM !
WHAP

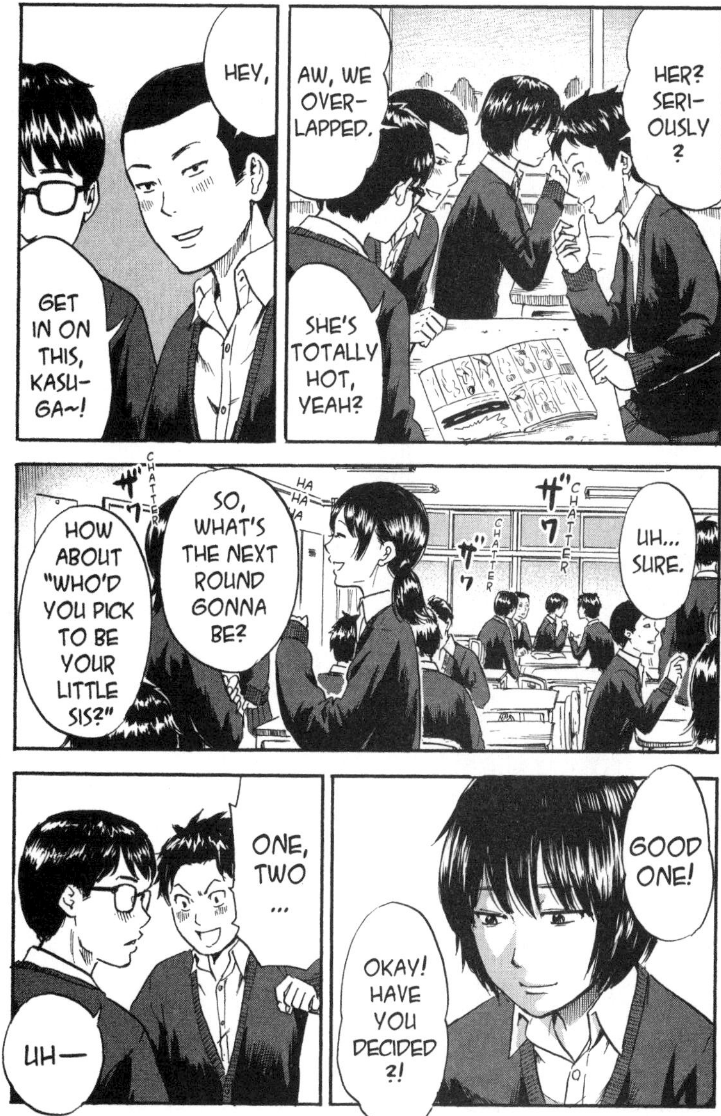
HER? SERI-OUSLY?
AW, WE OVER-LAPPED.
SHE'S TOTALLY HOT, YEAH?
HEY,
GET IN ON THIS, KASU-GA~!
CHATTER
ザワ
CHATTER
UH... SURE.
CHATTER
ザワ
HA HA HA
SO, WHAT'S THE NEXT ROUND GONNA BE?
ザワ
CHATTER
HOW ABOUT "WHO'D YOU PICK TO BE YOUR LITTLE SIS?"
GOOD ONE!
OKAY! HAVE YOU DECIDED?!
ONE, TWO ...
UH—

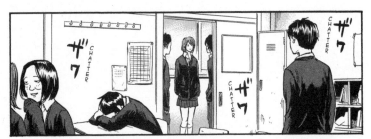

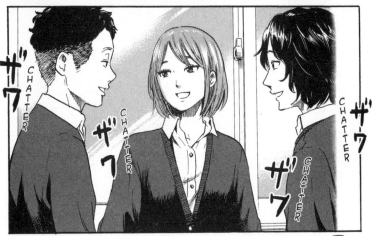

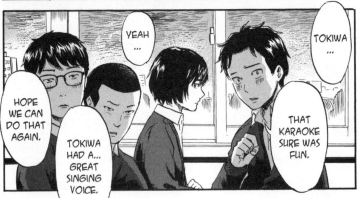

ザワ
CHATTER
ザワ
CHATTER
ザワ
CHATTER
ザワ
CHATTER
ザワ
CHATTER
ザワ
CHATTER
ザワ
CHATTER
TOKIWA ...
YEAH ...
THAT KARAOKE SURE WAS FUN.
TOKIWA HAD A... GREAT SINGING VOICE.
HOPE WE CAN DO THAT AGAIN.

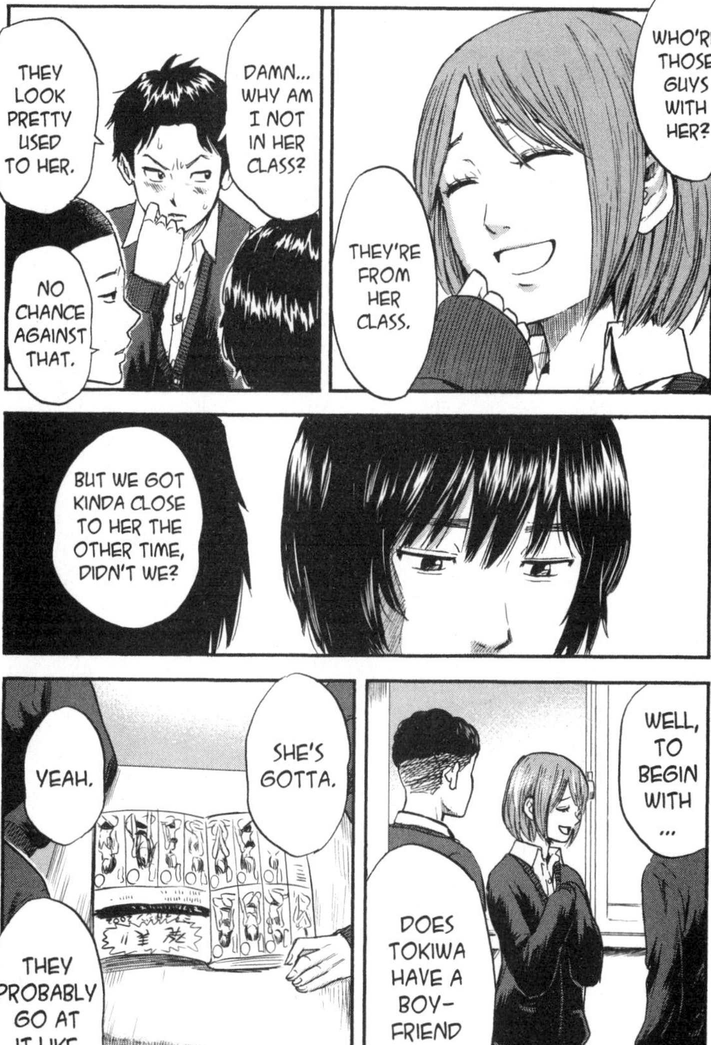
WHO'RE THOSE GUYS WITH HER?
THEY'RE FROM HER CLASS.
DAMN... WHY AM I NOT IN HER CLASS?
THEY LOOK PRETTY USED TO HER.
NO CHANCE AGAINST THAT.
BUT WE GOT KINDA CLOSE TO HER THE OTHER TIME, DIDN'T WE?
WELL, TO BEGIN WITH ...
DOES TOKIWA HAVE A BOY-FRIEND?
SHE'S GOTTA.
YEAH.
THEY PROBABLY GO AT IT LIKE CRAZY.

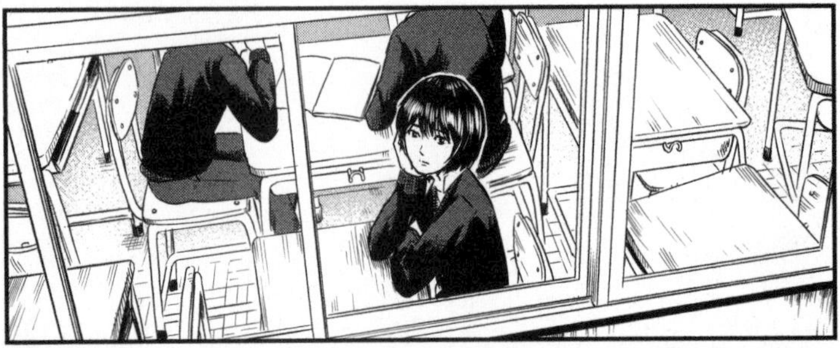

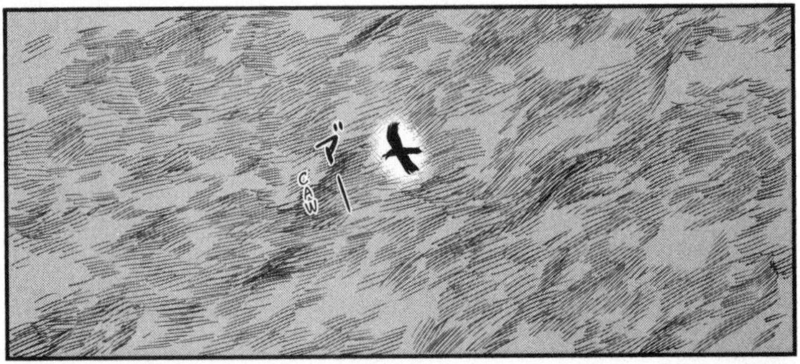
ア゙ー
CAW

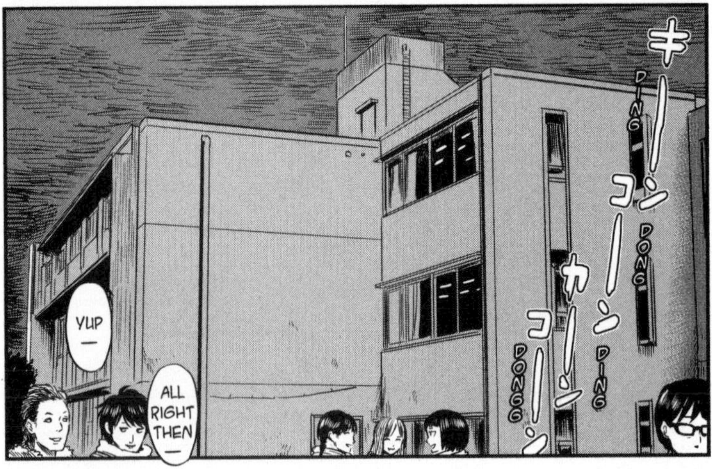
キーンコーンカーンコーン
DING
DONG
DING
DONGG
ALL RIGHT THEN —
YUP —

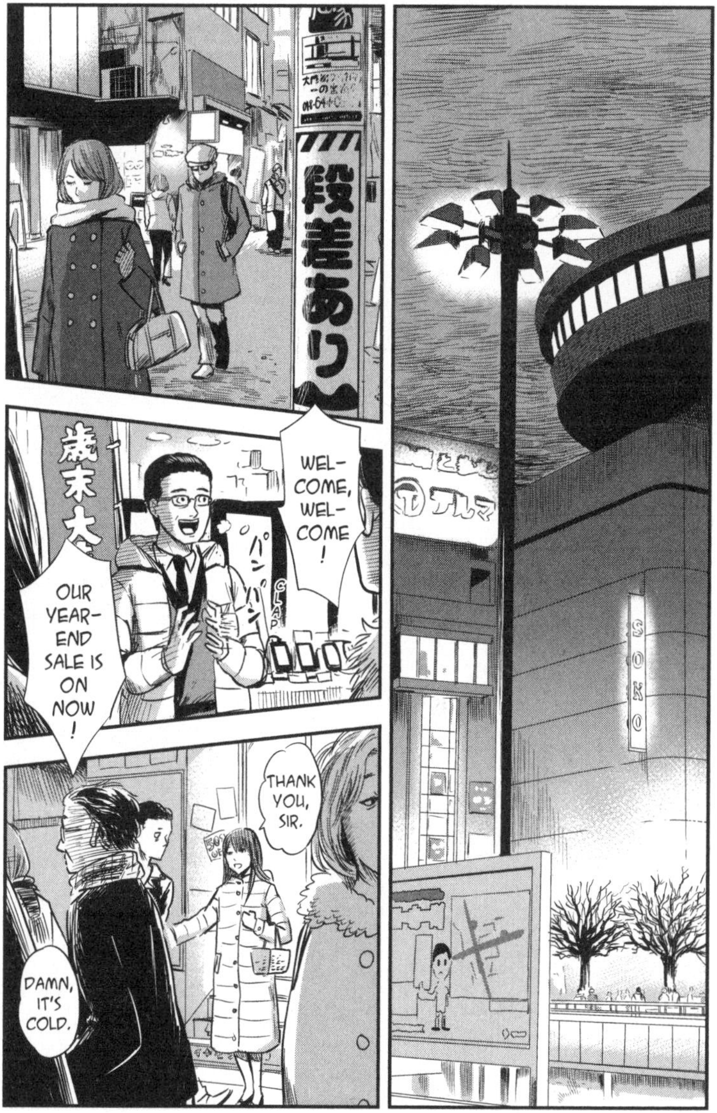

アルマ
SOKO
段差あり
WEL-COME, WEL-COME!
OUR YEAR-END SALE IS ON NOW!
パンパン
CLAP
THANK YOU, SIR.
DAMN, IT'S COLD.

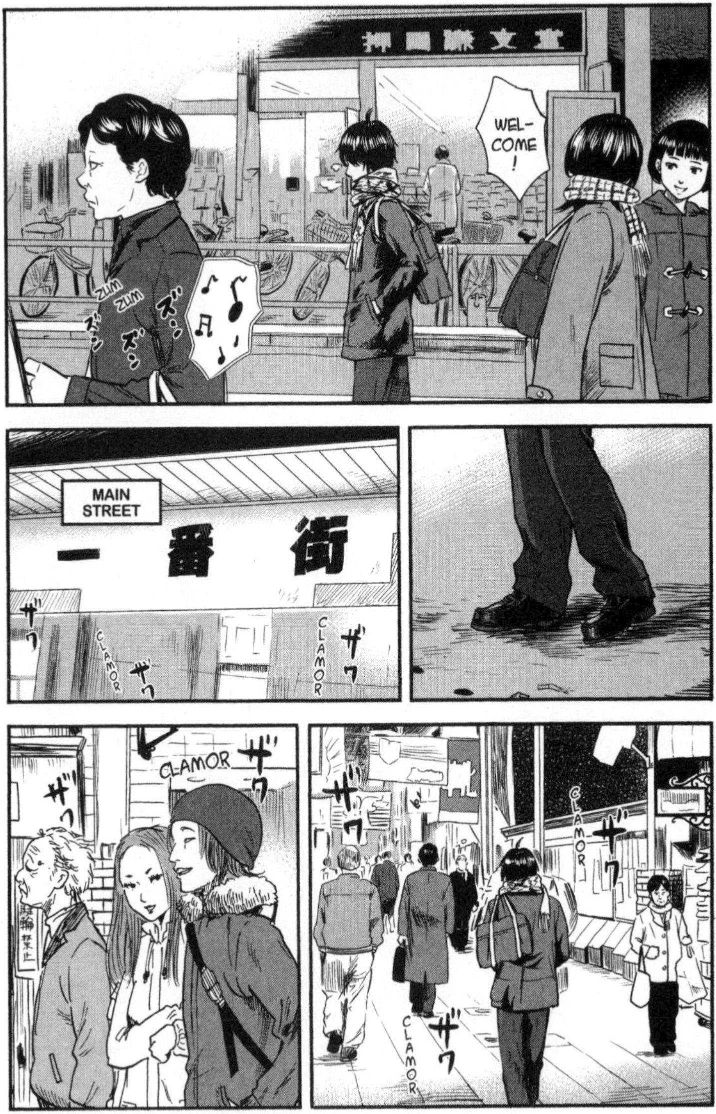
WEL-
COME
!
ZUM
ZUM
ズン
ズン
ズン
MAIN
STREET
一番街
ザワ
CLAMOR
ザワ
CLAMOR
ザワ
ザワ
ザワ
CLAMOR
ザワ
CLAMOR
CLAMOR
ザワ
ザワ
駐輪禁止

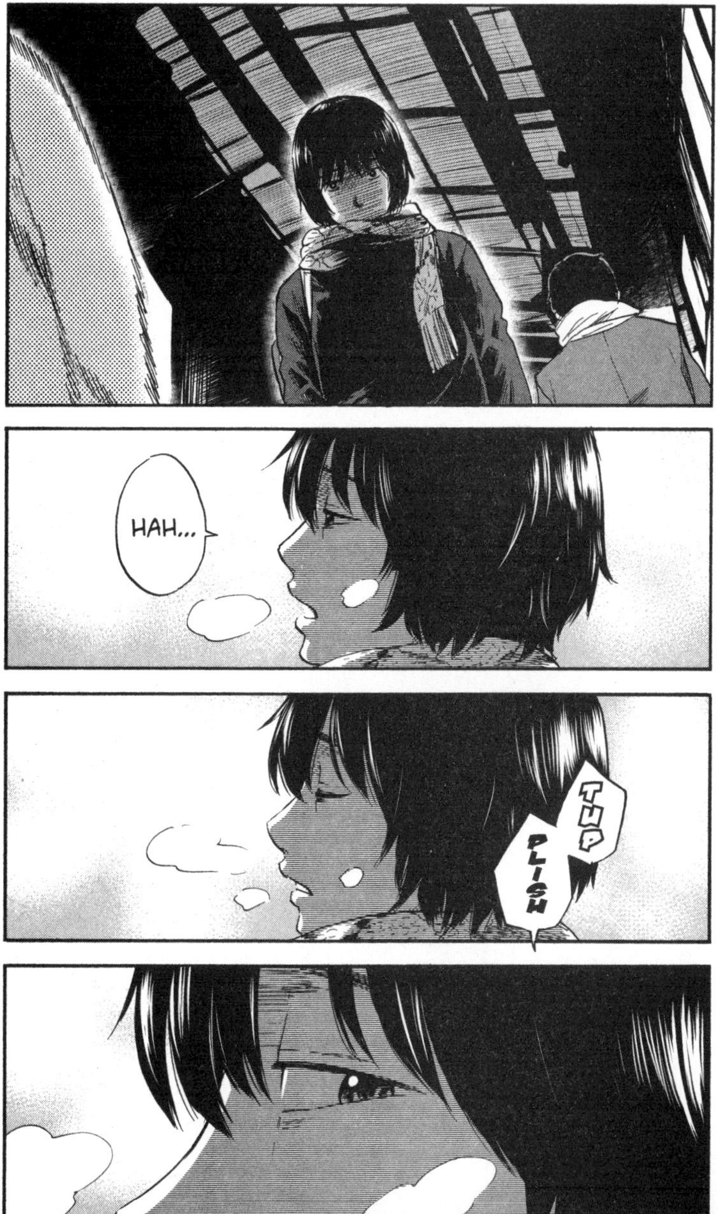
HAH...
TUP
PLISH

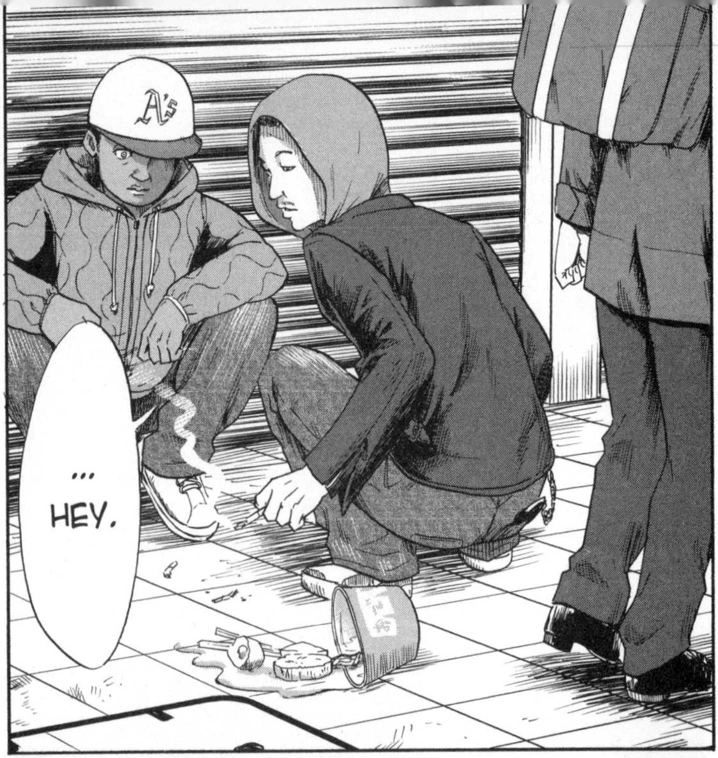
... HEY.
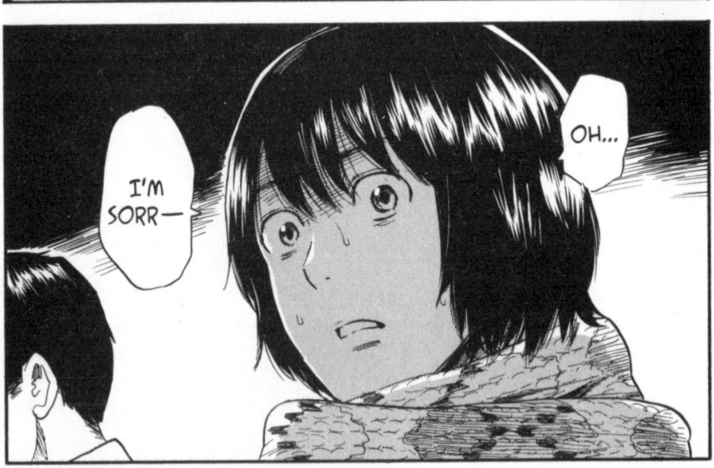
OH...
I'M SORR—

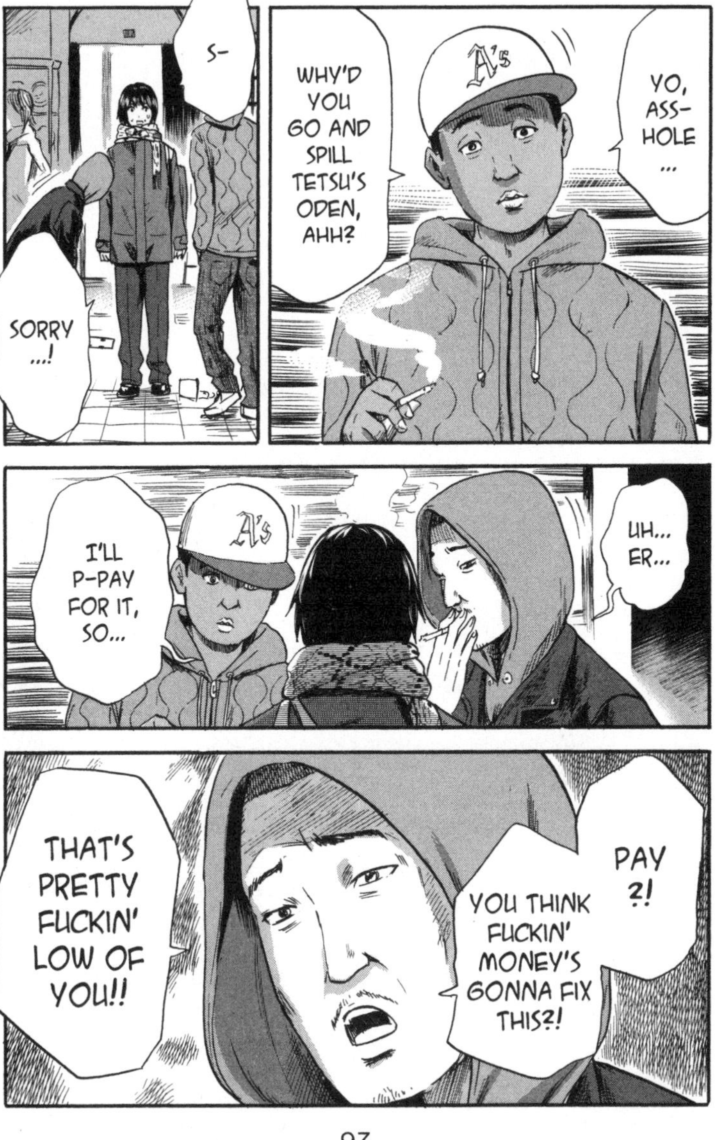
YO, ASS-HOLE...
WHY'D YOU GO AND SPILL TETSU'S ODEN, AHH?
S-
SORRY...!
UH... ER...
I'LL P-PAY FOR IT, SO...
PAY?!
YOU THINK FUCKIN' MONEY'S GONNA FIX THIS?!
THAT'S PRETTY FUCKIN' LOW OF YOU!!

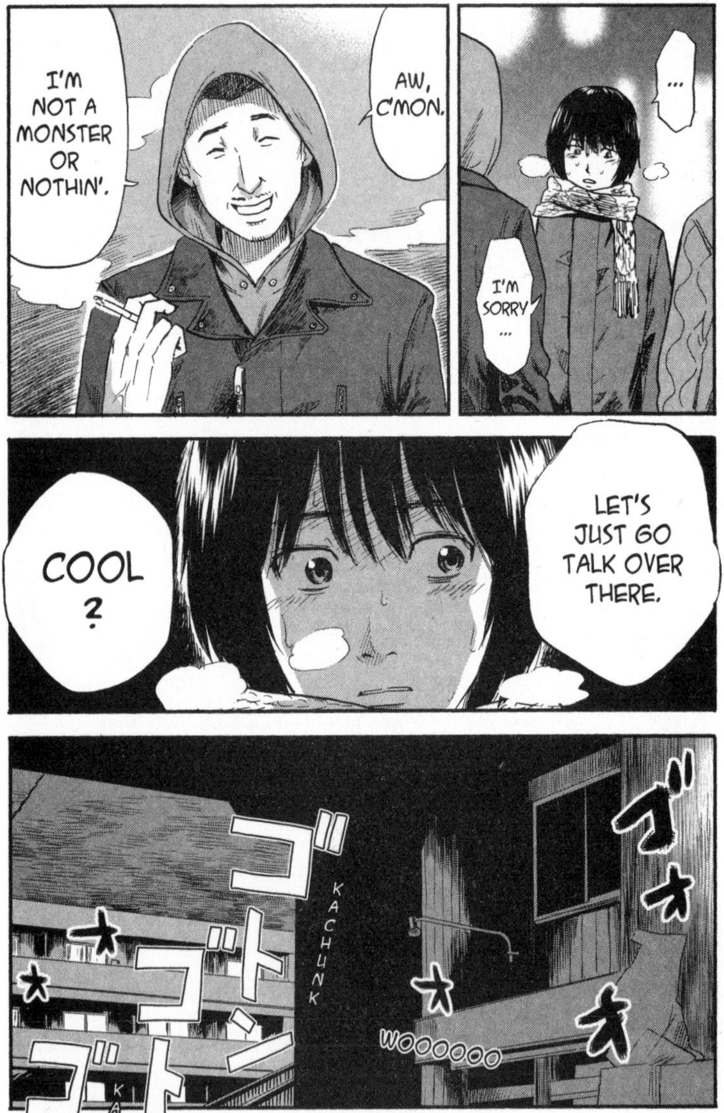
...
I'M SORRY ...
AW, C'MON.
I'M NOT A MONSTER OR NOTHIN'.
LET'S JUST GO TALK OVER THERE.
COOL?
WOOOOOO
KACHUNK
KACHUNK

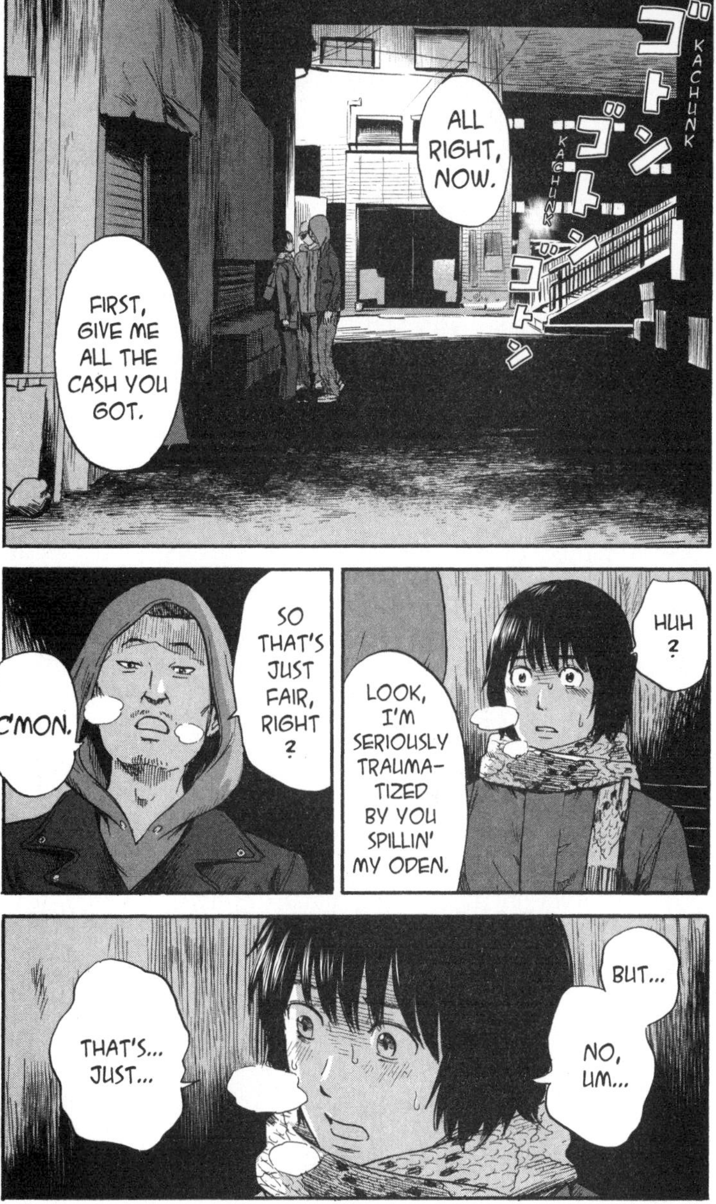
KACHUNK
KACHUNK
ALL RIGHT, NOW.
FIRST, GIVE ME ALL THE CASH YOU GOT.
HUH?
LOOK, I'M SERIOUSLY TRAUMA-TIZED BY YOU SPILLIN' MY ODEN.
SO THAT'S JUST FAIR, RIGHT?
C'MON.
BUT...
NO, UM...
THAT'S... JUST...

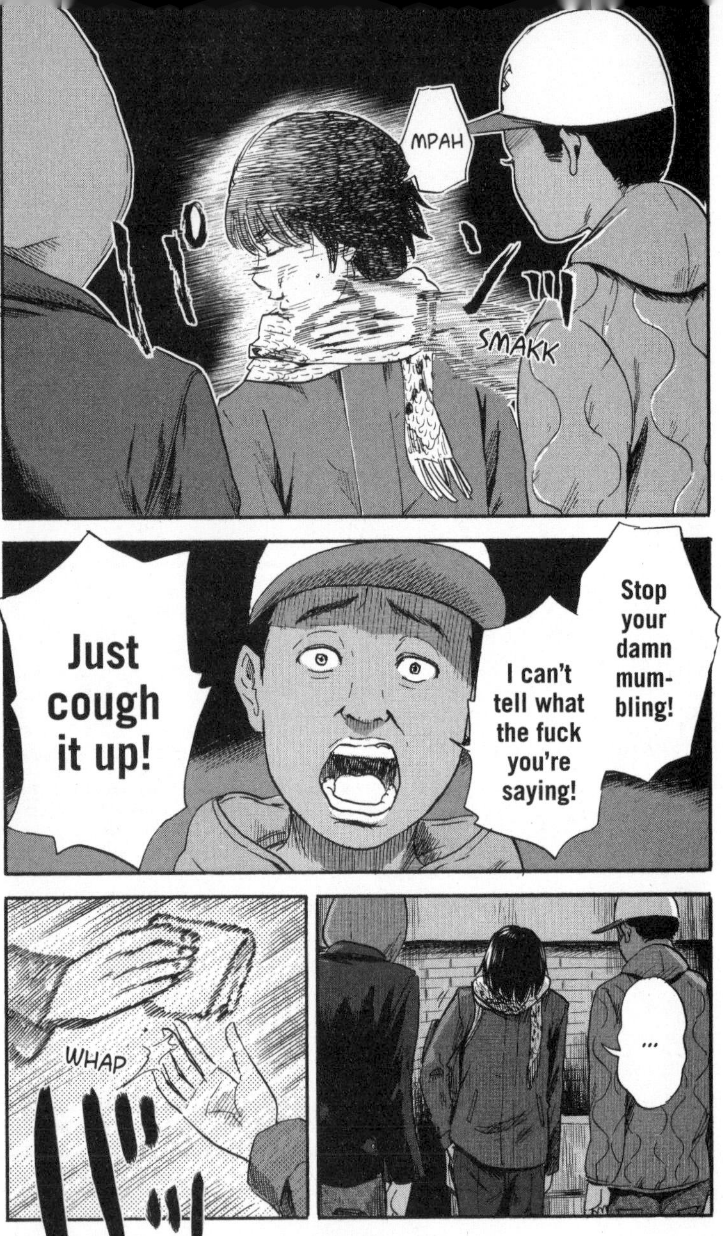
MPAH
SMAKK
Stop your damn mum- bling!
I can't tell what the fuck you're saying!
Just cough it up!
...
WHAP

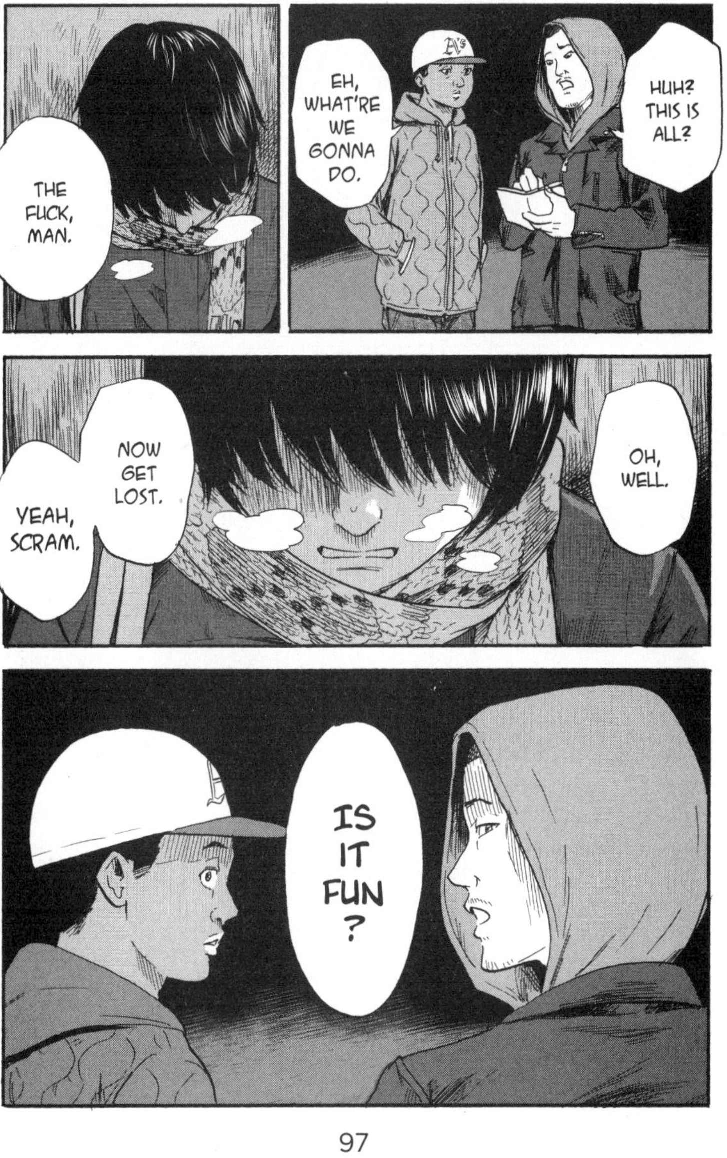
HUH? THIS IS ALL?
EH, WHAT'RE WE GONNA DO.
THE FUCK, MAN.
OH, WELL.
NOW GET LOST.
YEAH, SCRAM.
IS IT FUN?

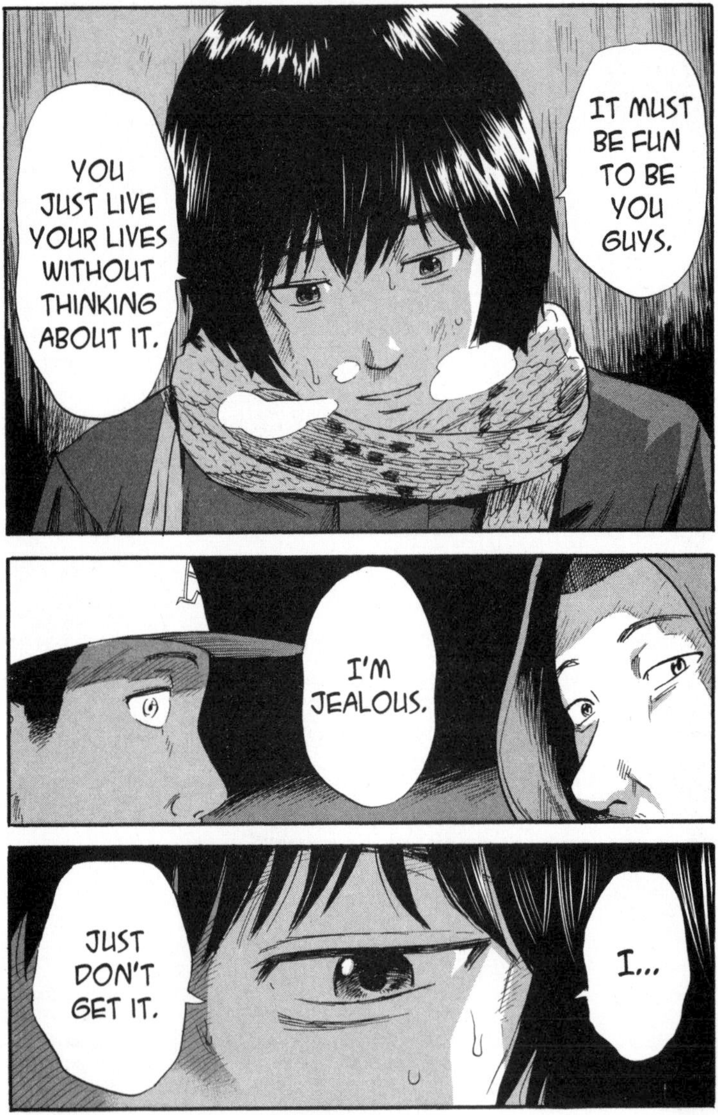
IT MUST BE FUN TO BE YOU GUYS.
YOU JUST LIVE YOUR LIVES WITHOUT THINKING ABOUT IT.
I'M JEALOUS.
I...
JUST DON'T GET IT.

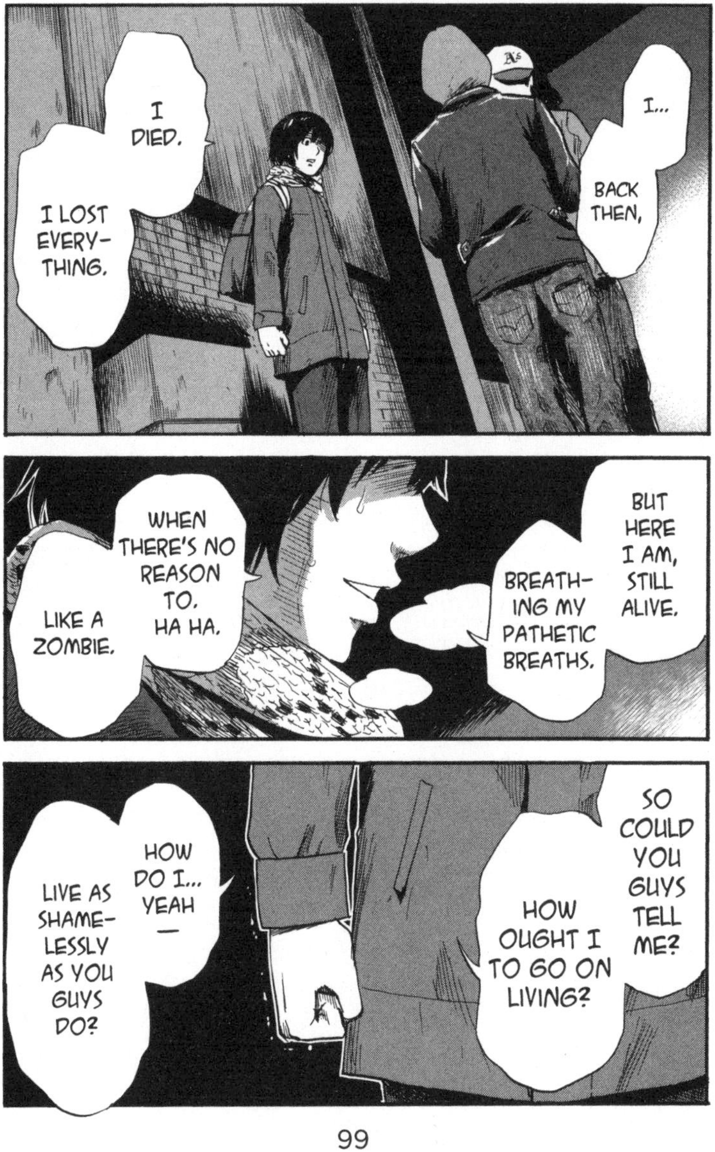

I... BACK THEN,
I DIED.
I LOST EVERYTHING.
BUT HERE I AM, STILL ALIVE.
BREATHING MY PATHETIC BREATHS.
WHEN THERE'S NO REASON TO. HA HA.
LIKE A ZOMBIE.
SO COULD YOU GUYS TELL ME?
HOW OUGHT I TO GO ON LIVING?
HOW DO I... YEAH —
LIVE AS SHAMELESSLY AS YOU GUYS DO?

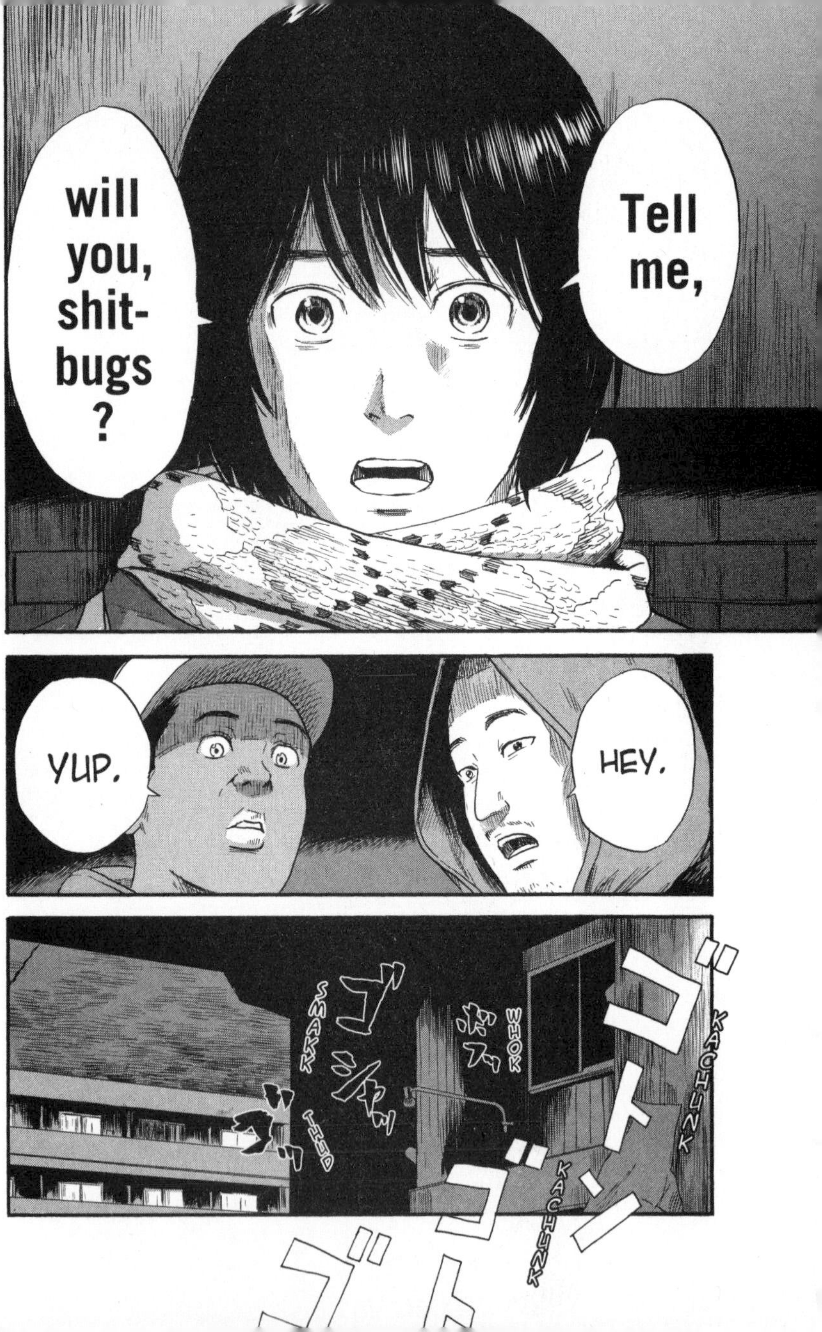
Tell me,
will you, shit-bugs?
HEY.
YUP.
KACHUNK
KACHUNK
WHOK
SMAKK
THUD

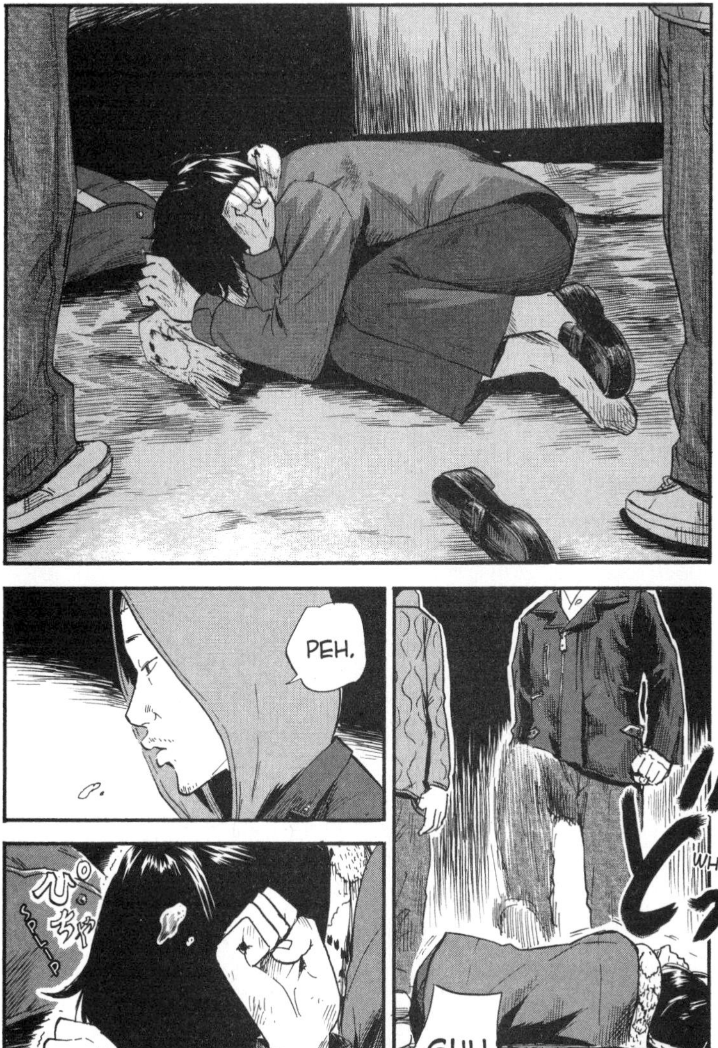
WHUMP
GUH —
PEH.

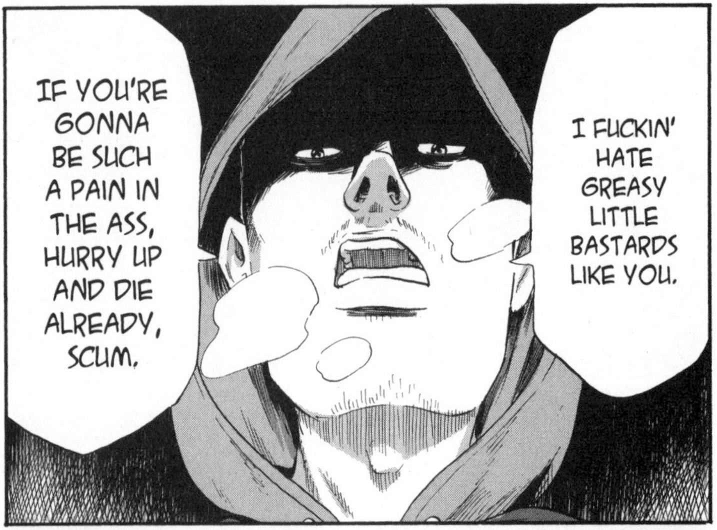
I FUCKIN' HATE GREASY LITTLE BASTARDS LIKE YOU.
IF YOU'RE GONNA BE SUCH A PAIN IN THE ASS, HURRY UP AND DIE ALREADY, SCUM.
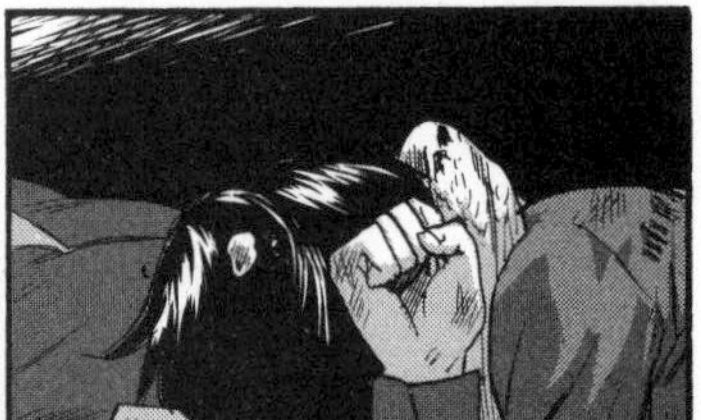
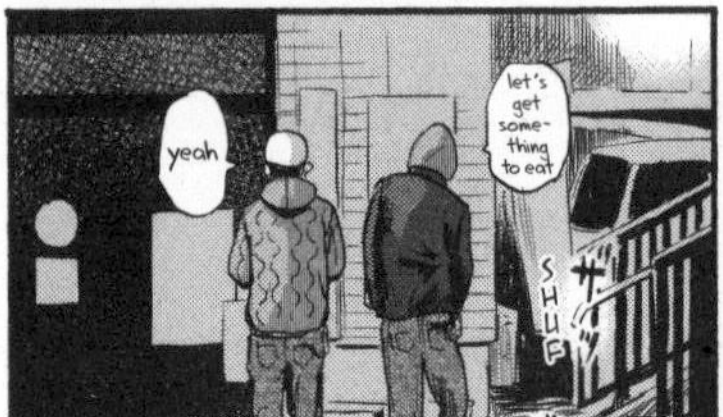
let's get some-thing to eat
yeah
SHUF
SHUF
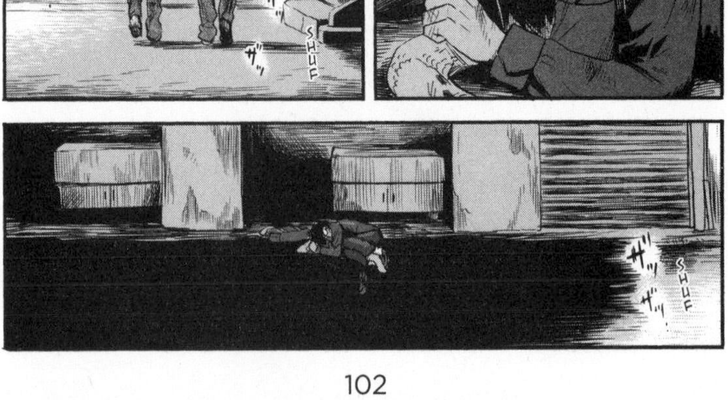
SHUF

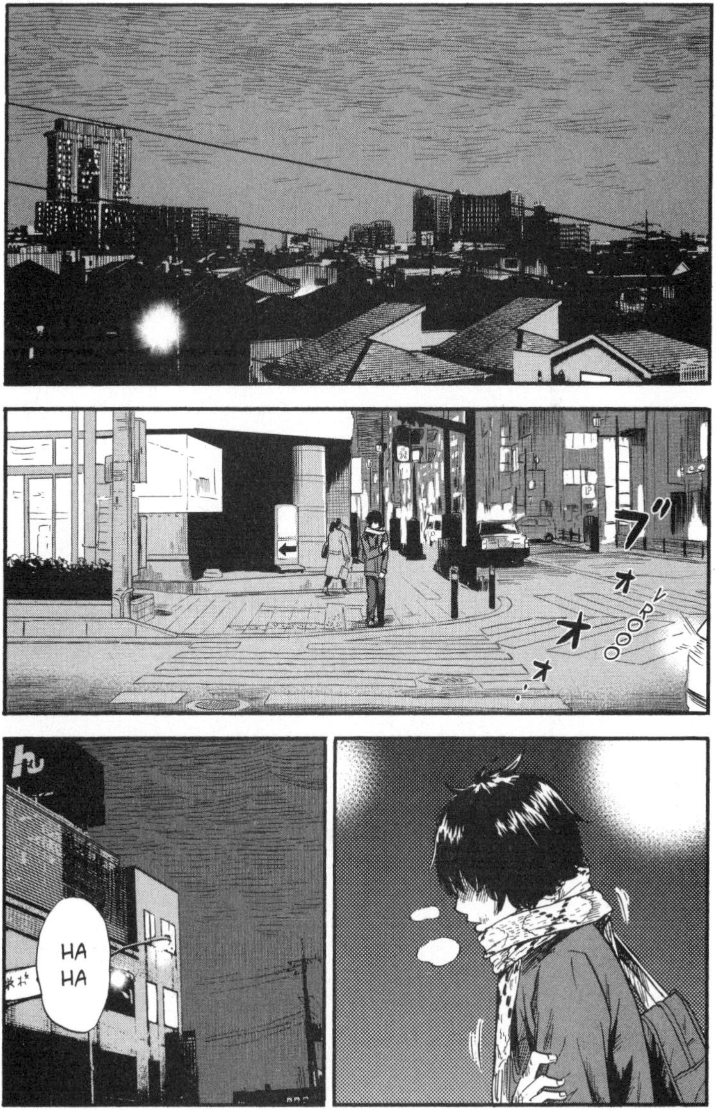
ブオオオ
VROOOO
HA HA

HE'S RIGHT.

YEAH.

GUESS I OUGHTTA CROAK.

I...

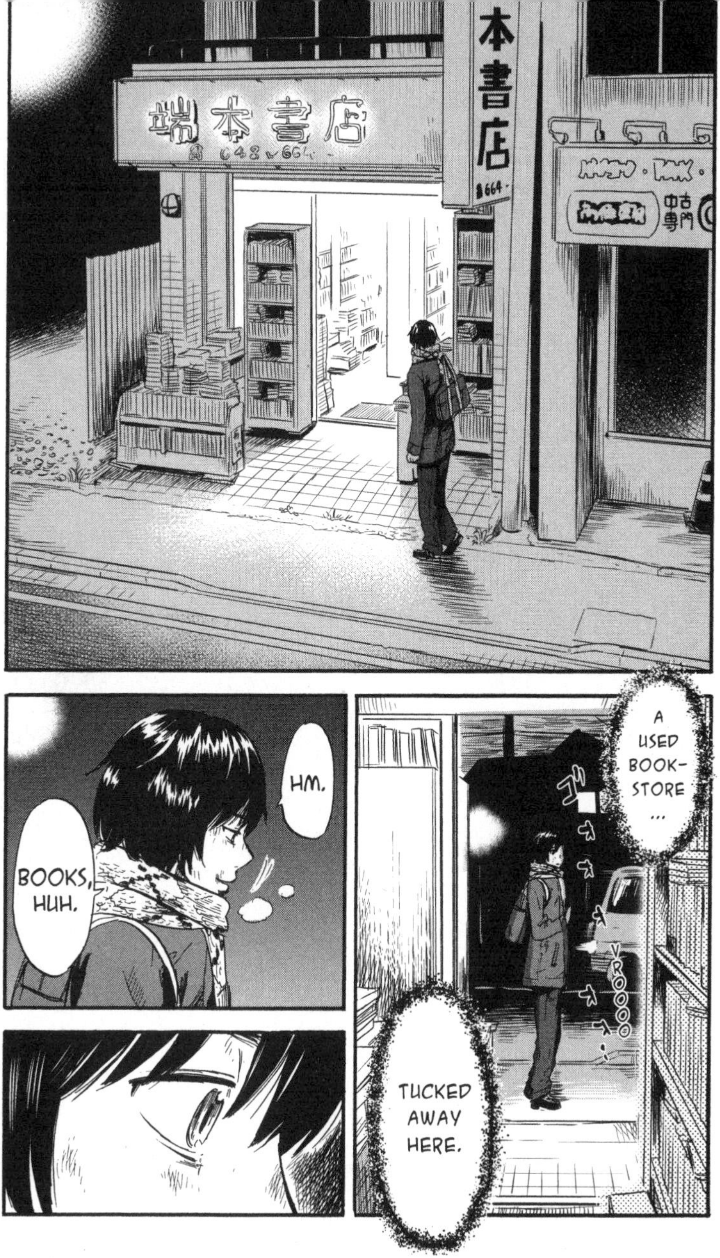

端本書店
本書店
A USED BOOK-STORE...
VROOOO
TUCKED AWAY HERE.
HM.
BOOKS, HUH.

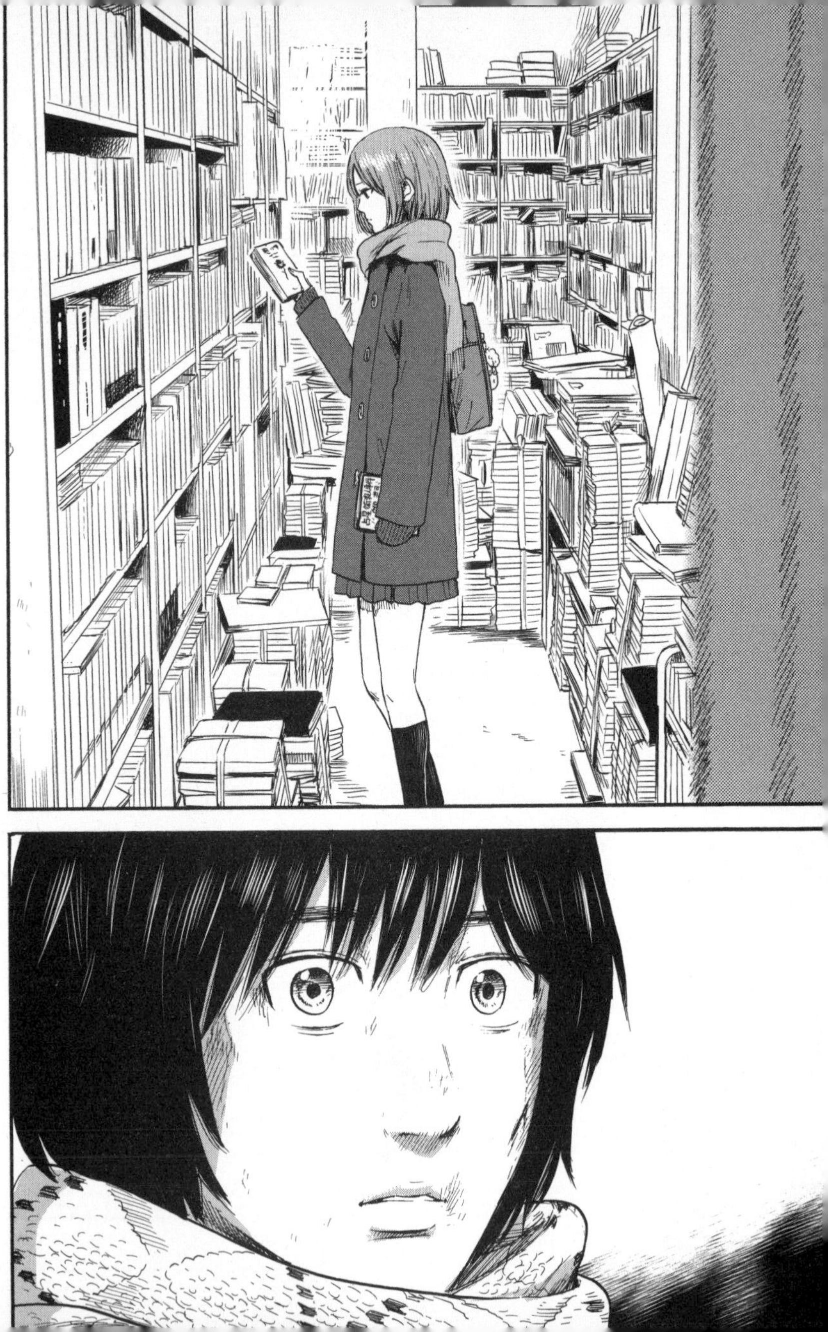

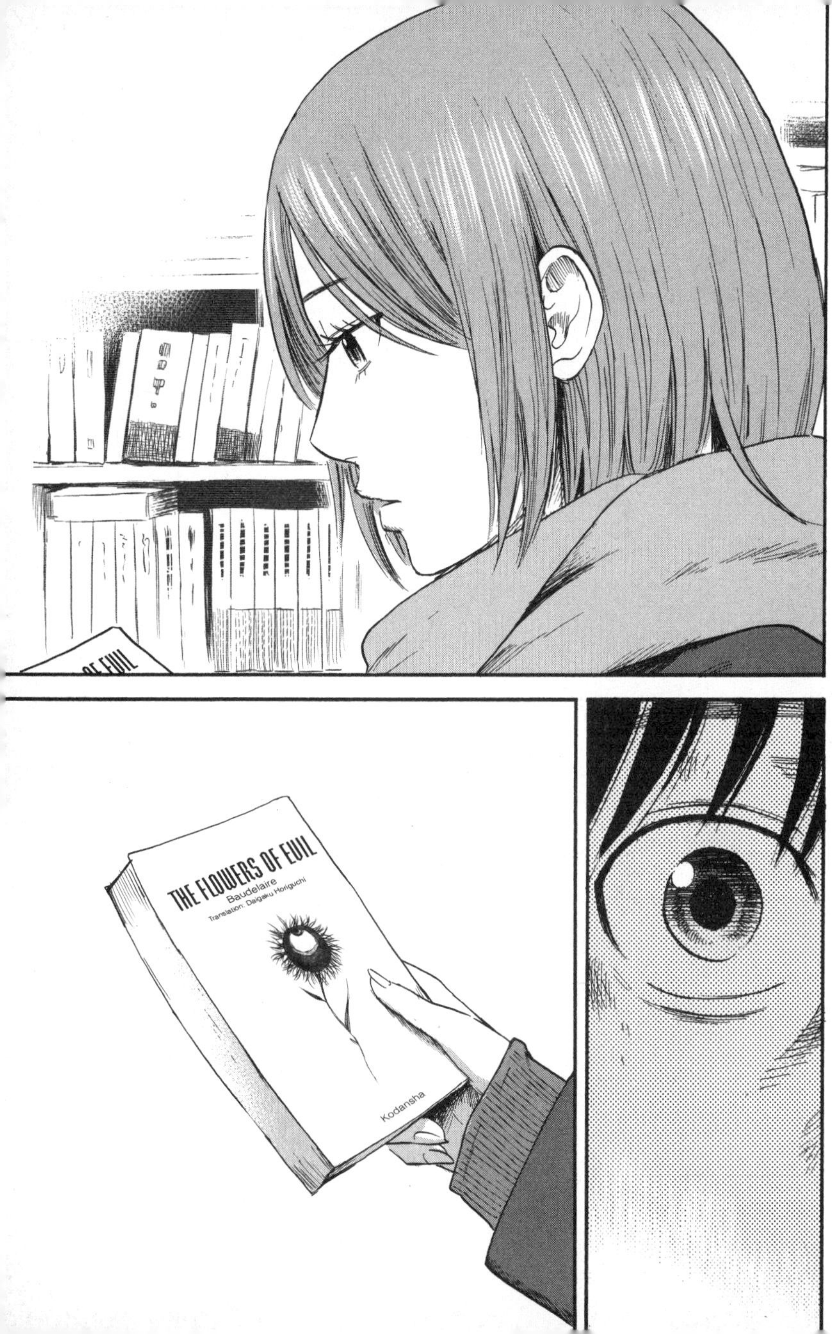
OF EVIL
THE FLOWERS OF EVIL
Baudelaire
Translation: Daigaku Horiguchi
Kodansha

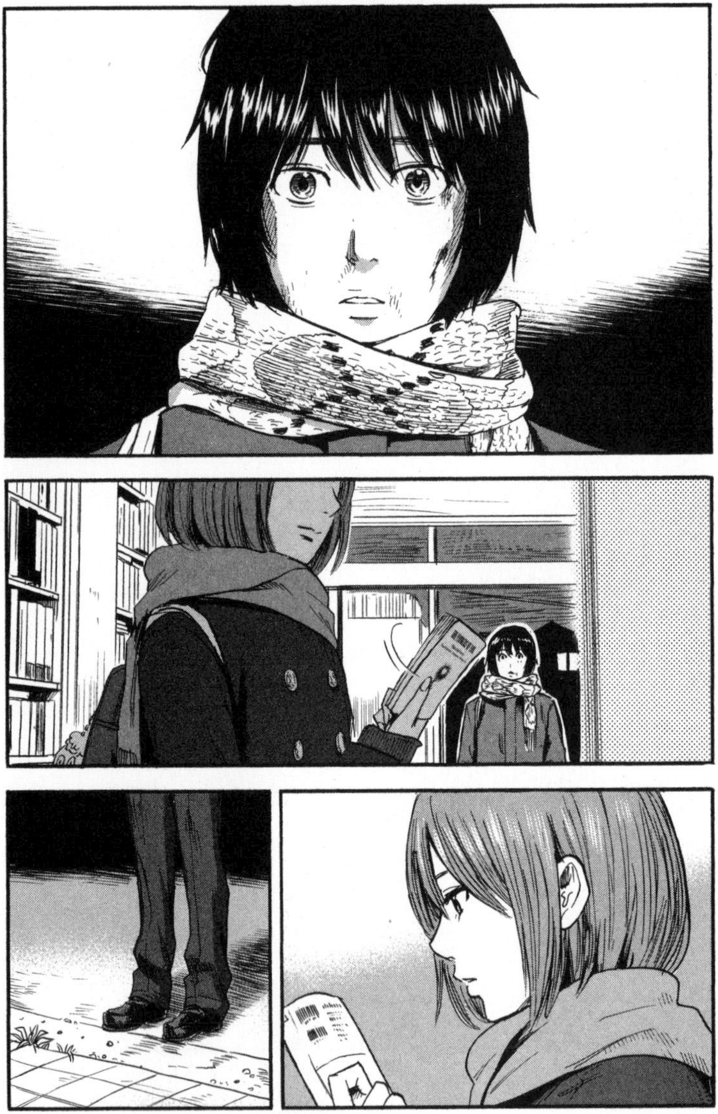

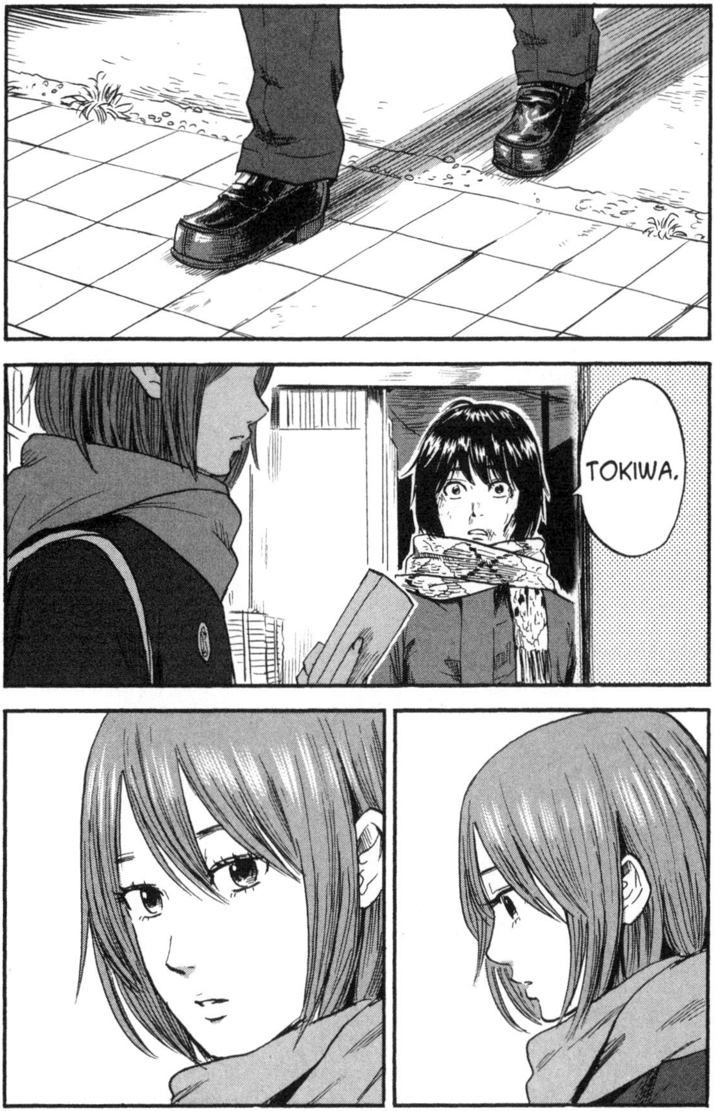
TOKIWA.

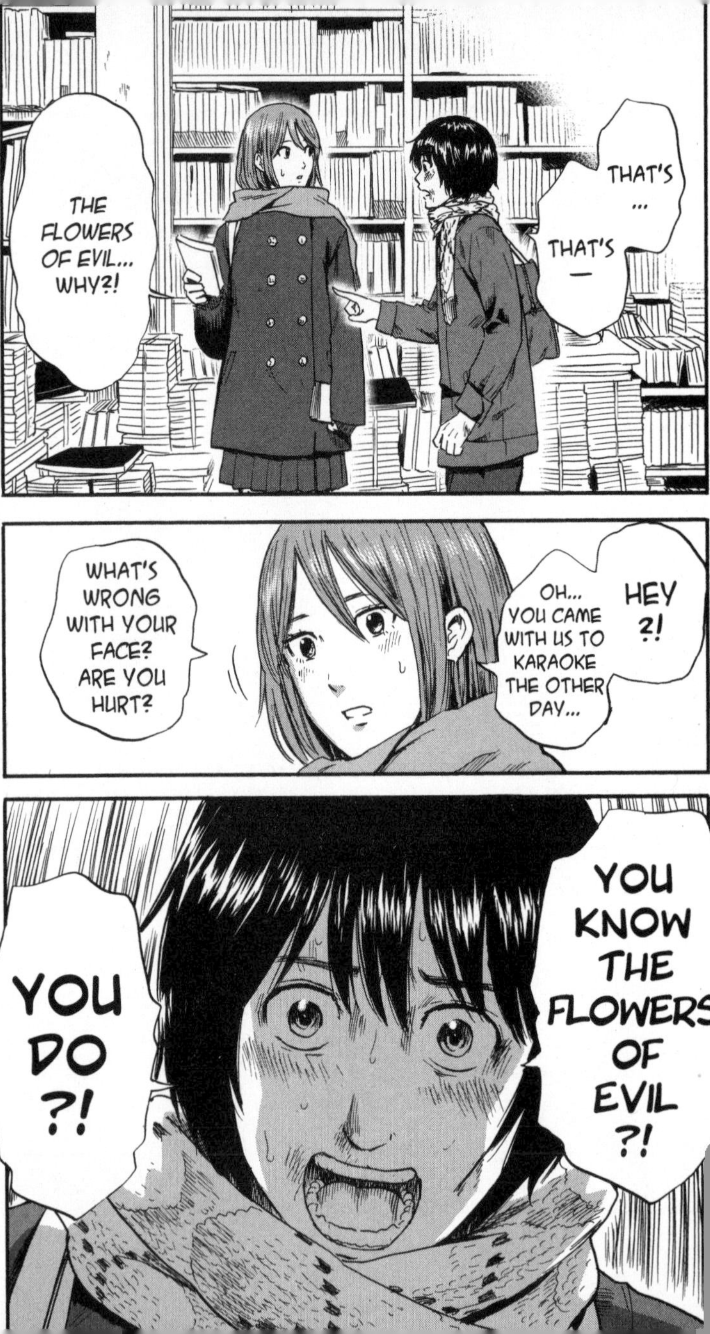
THAT'S ... THAT'S —
THE FLOWERS OF EVIL... WHY?!
HEY ?!
OH... YOU CAME WITH US TO KARAOKE THE OTHER DAY...
WHAT'S WRONG WITH YOUR FACE? ARE YOU HURT?
YOU KNOW THE FLOWERS OF EVIL ?!
YOU DO ?!

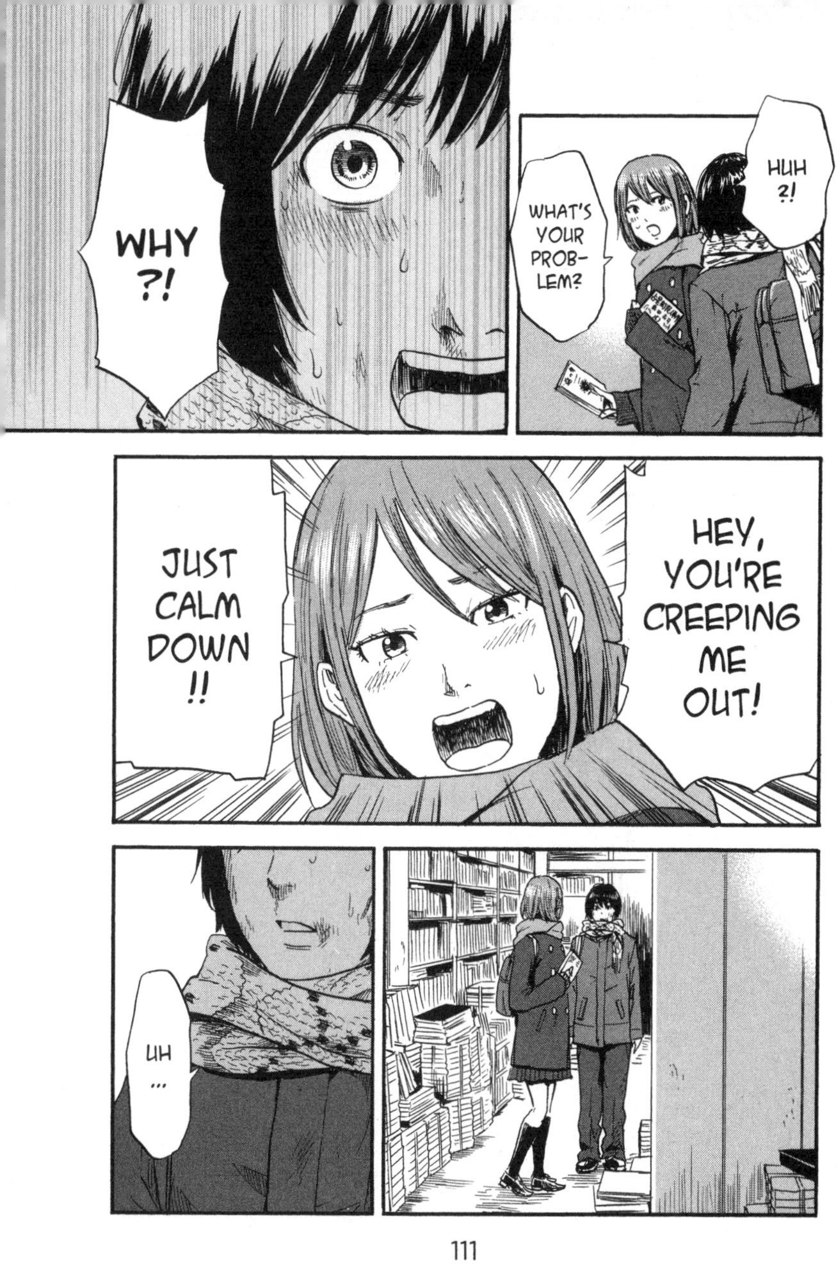
HUH ?!
WHAT'S YOUR PROB-LEM?
WHY ?!
HEY, YOU'RE CREEPING ME OUT!
JUST CALM DOWN !!
UH ...

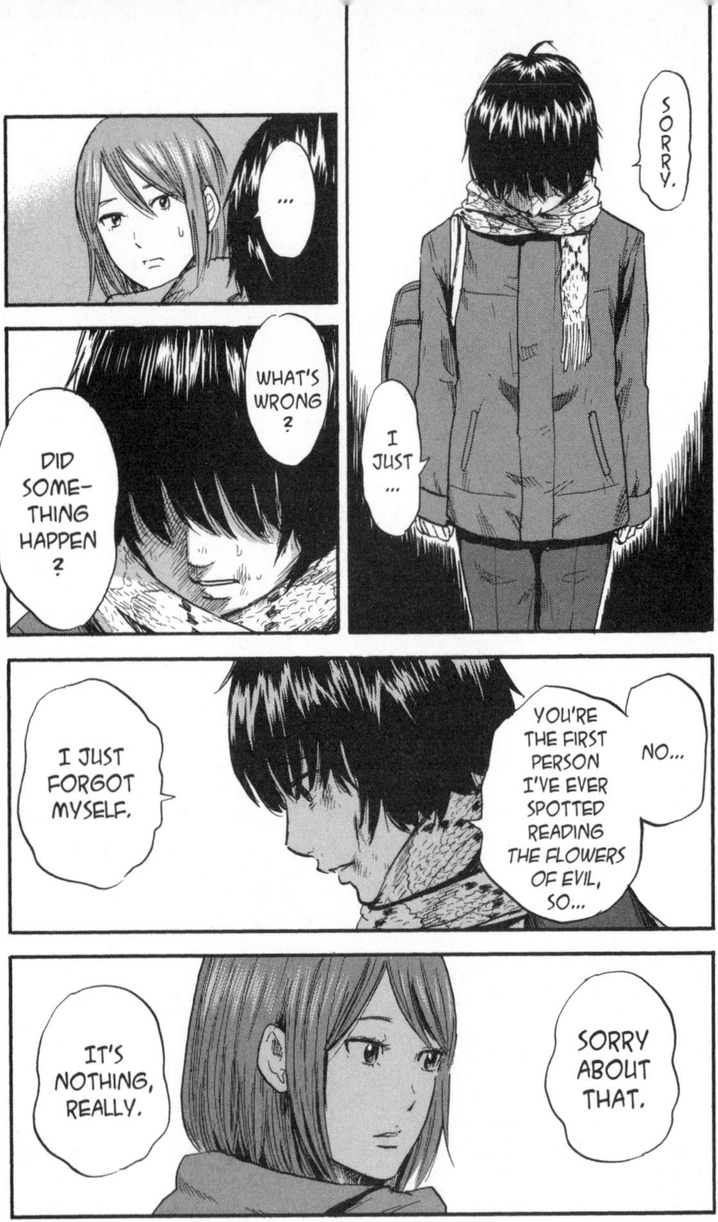
SORRY.
I JUST ...
...
WHAT'S WRONG?
DID SOMETHING HAPPEN?
NO...
YOU'RE THE FIRST PERSON I'VE EVER SPOTTED READING THE FLOWERS OF EVIL, SO...
I JUST FORGOT MYSELF.
SORRY ABOUT THAT.
IT'S NOTHING, REALLY.

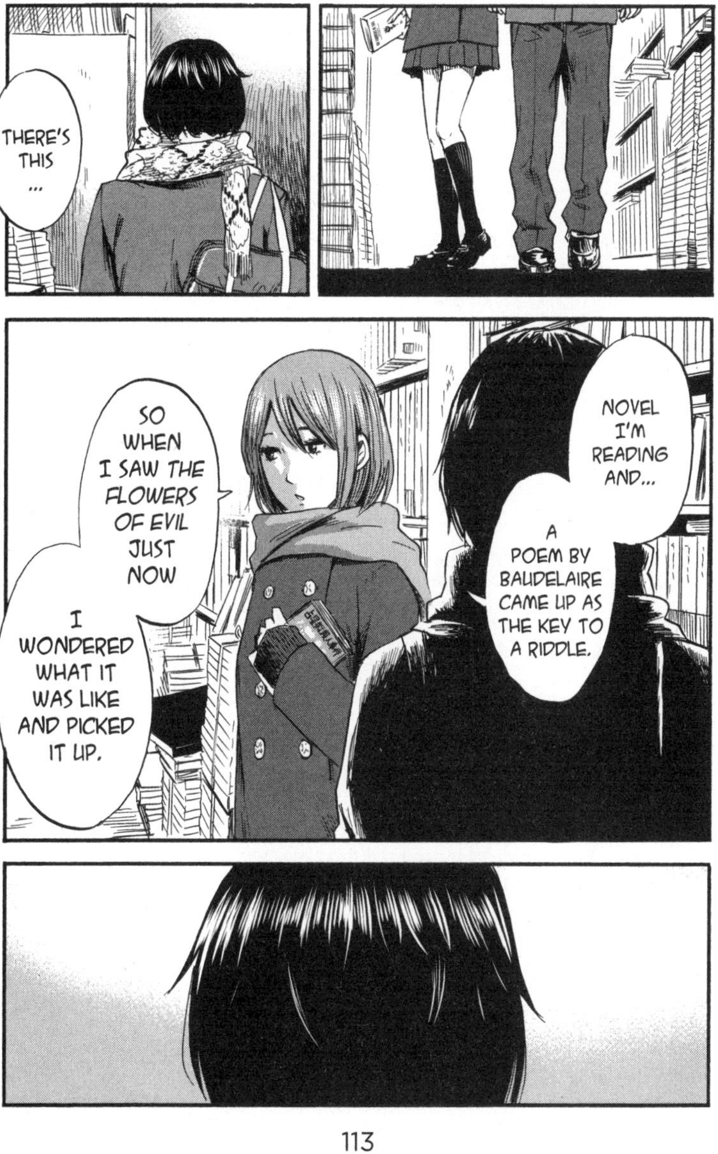
THERE'S THIS ...
NOVEL I'M READING AND...
A POEM BY BAUDELAIRE CAME UP AS THE KEY TO A RIDDLE.
SO WHEN I SAW THE FLOWERS OF EVIL JUST NOW
I WONDERED WHAT IT WAS LIKE AND PICKED IT UP.

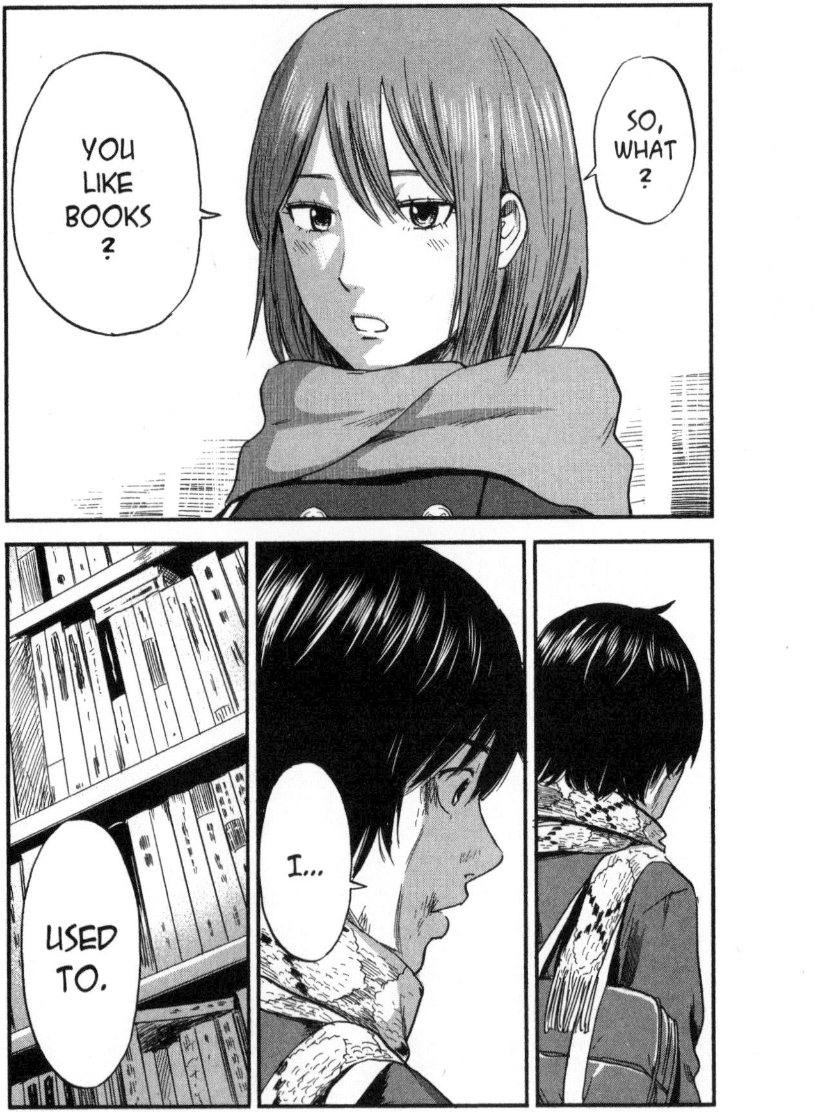
SO, WHAT?
YOU LIKE BOOKS?
I...
USED TO.

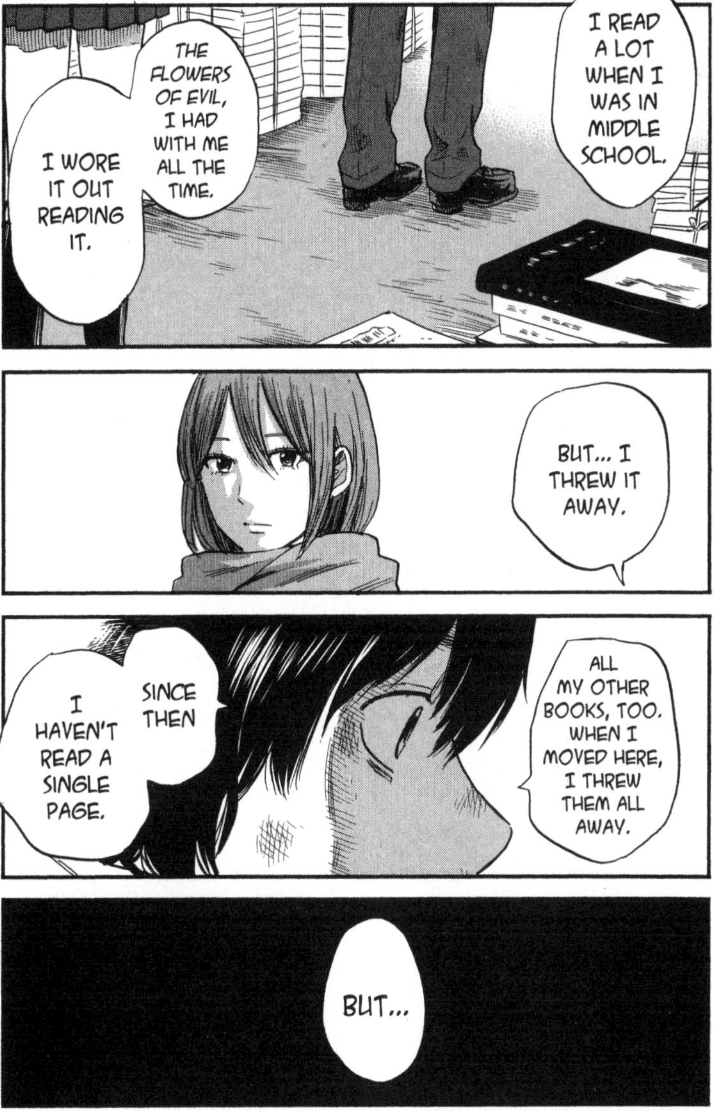
I READ A LOT WHEN I WAS IN MIDDLE SCHOOL.
THE FLOWERS OF EVIL, I HAD WITH ME ALL THE TIME.
I WORE IT OUT READING IT.
BUT... I THREW IT AWAY.
ALL MY OTHER BOOKS, TOO. WHEN I MOVED HERE, I THREW THEM ALL AWAY.
SINCE THEN I HAVEN'T READ A SINGLE PAGE.
BUT...

JUST NOW I WONDERED WHAT IT WOULD BE LIKE
IF I TRIED READING AGAIN.
I'LL LEND IT TO YOU
IF YOU WANT.
HUH?

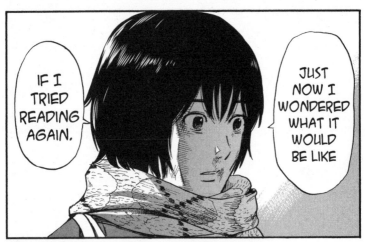

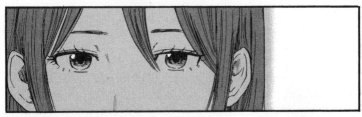

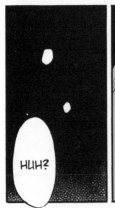

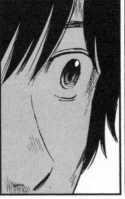

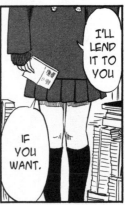

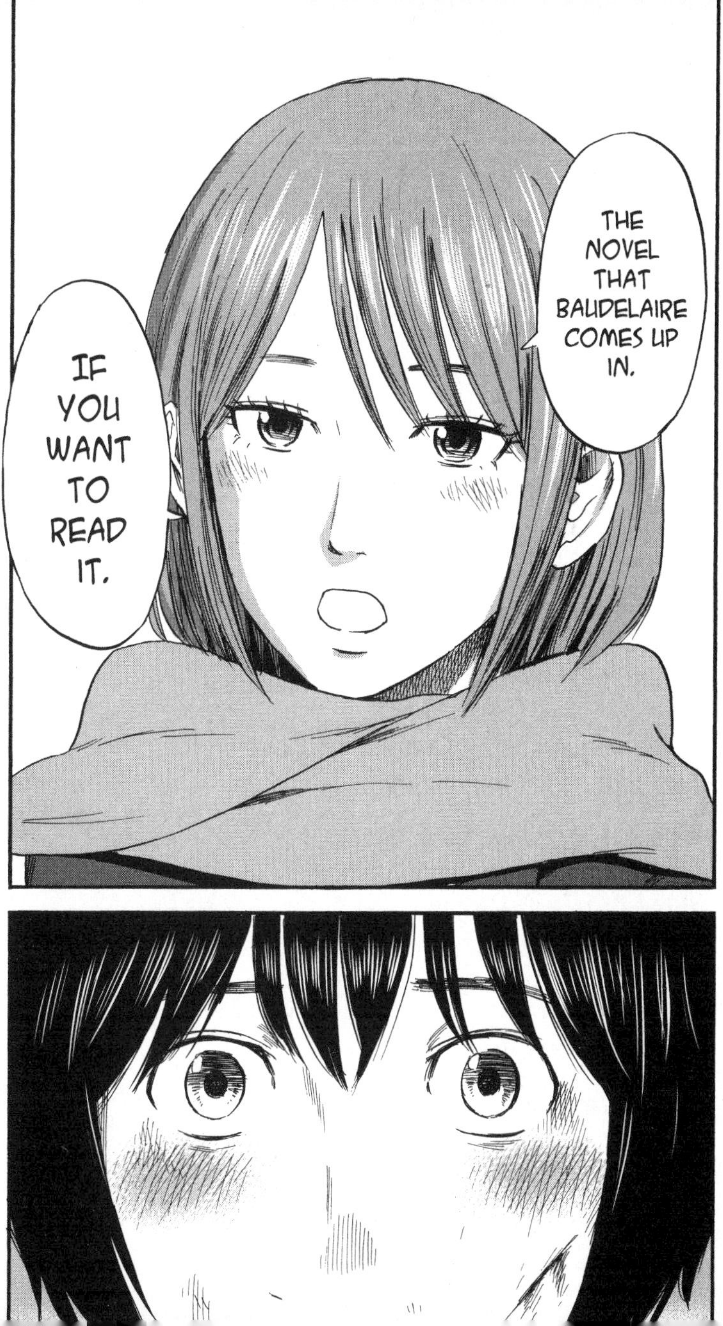
THE NOVEL THAT BAUDELAIRE COMES UP IN.
IF YOU WANT TO READ IT.

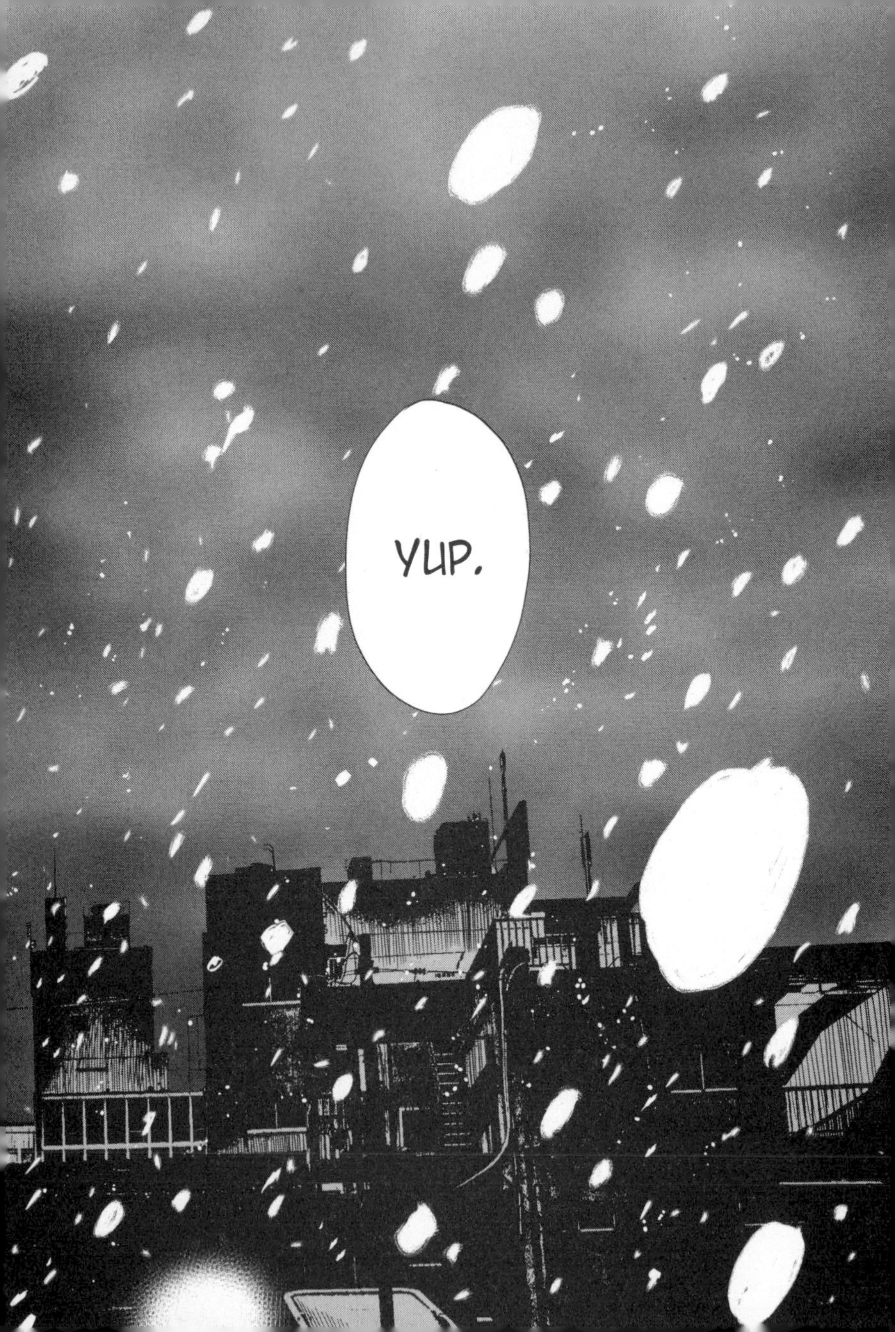
YUP.

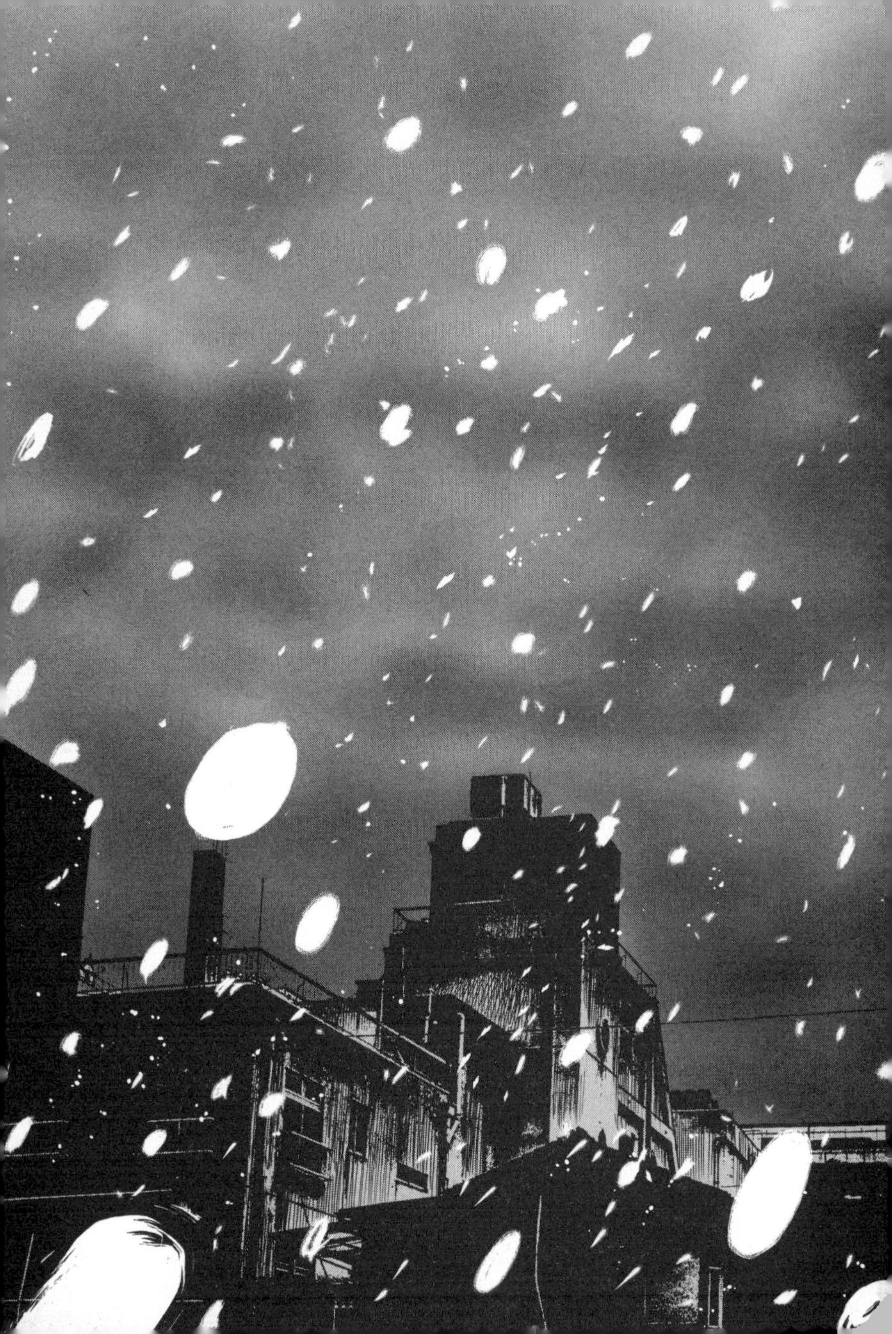

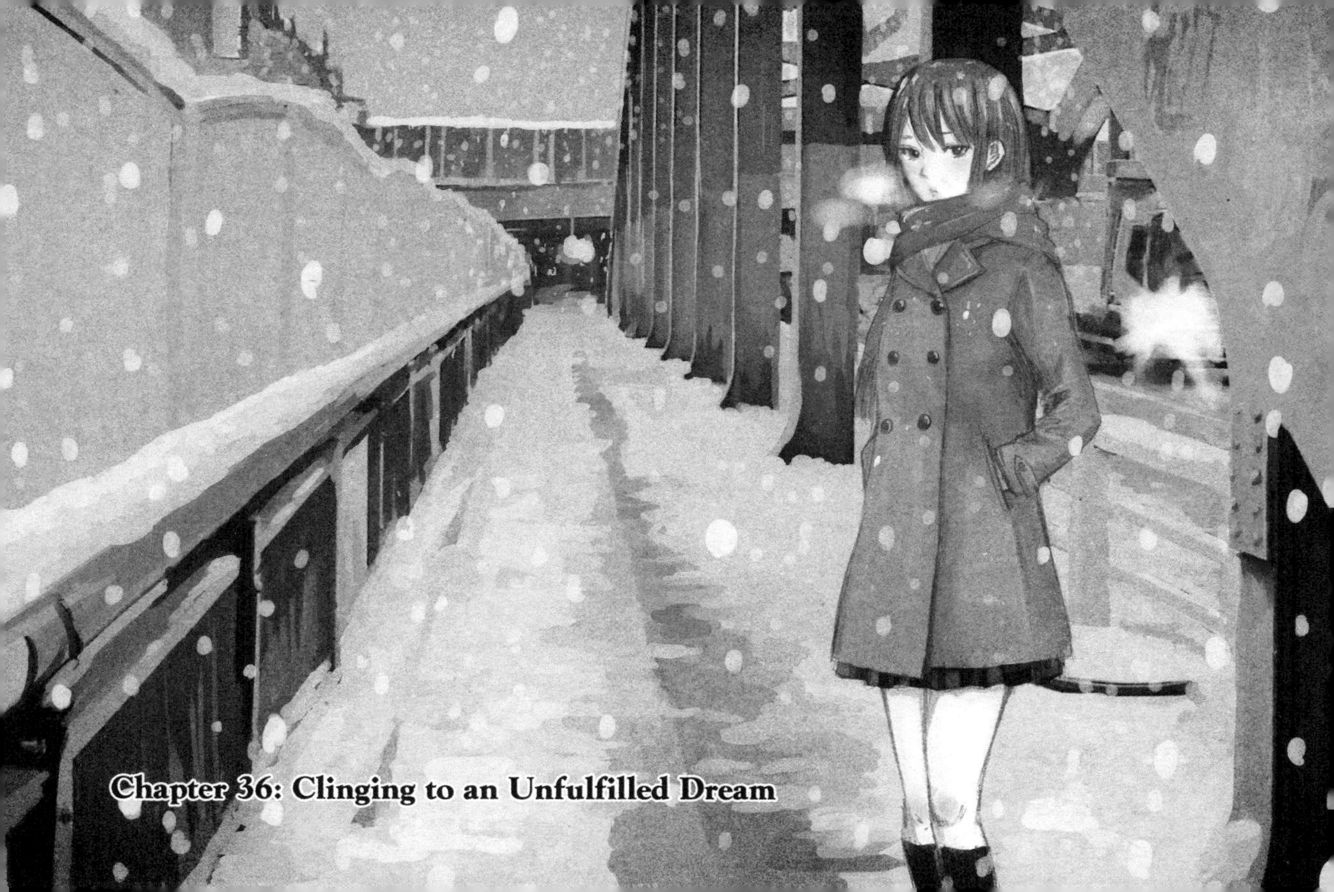
Chapter 36: Clinging to an Unfulfilled Dream

The Flowers
of Evil

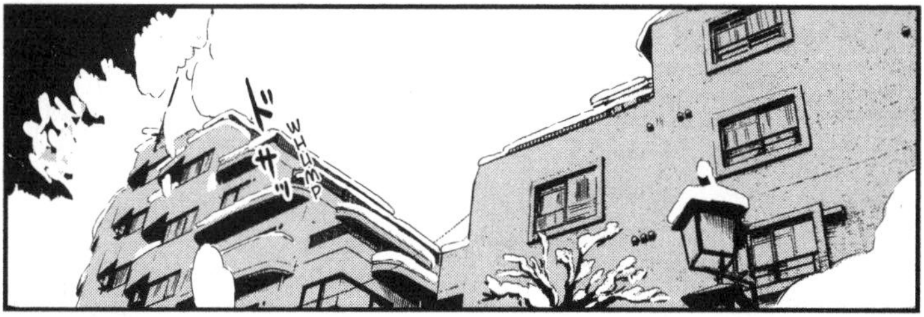
ドサッ
WHUMP
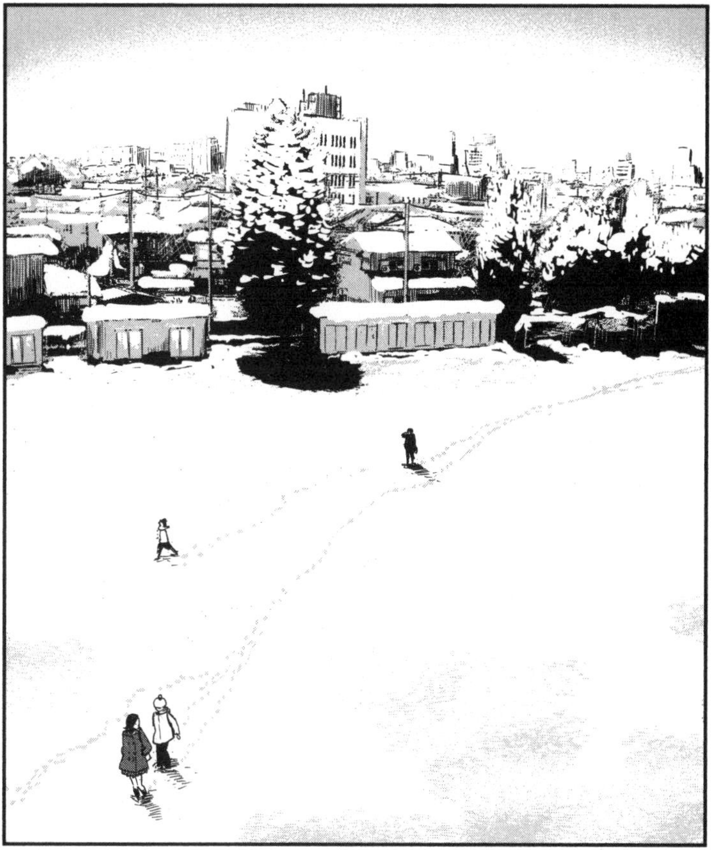

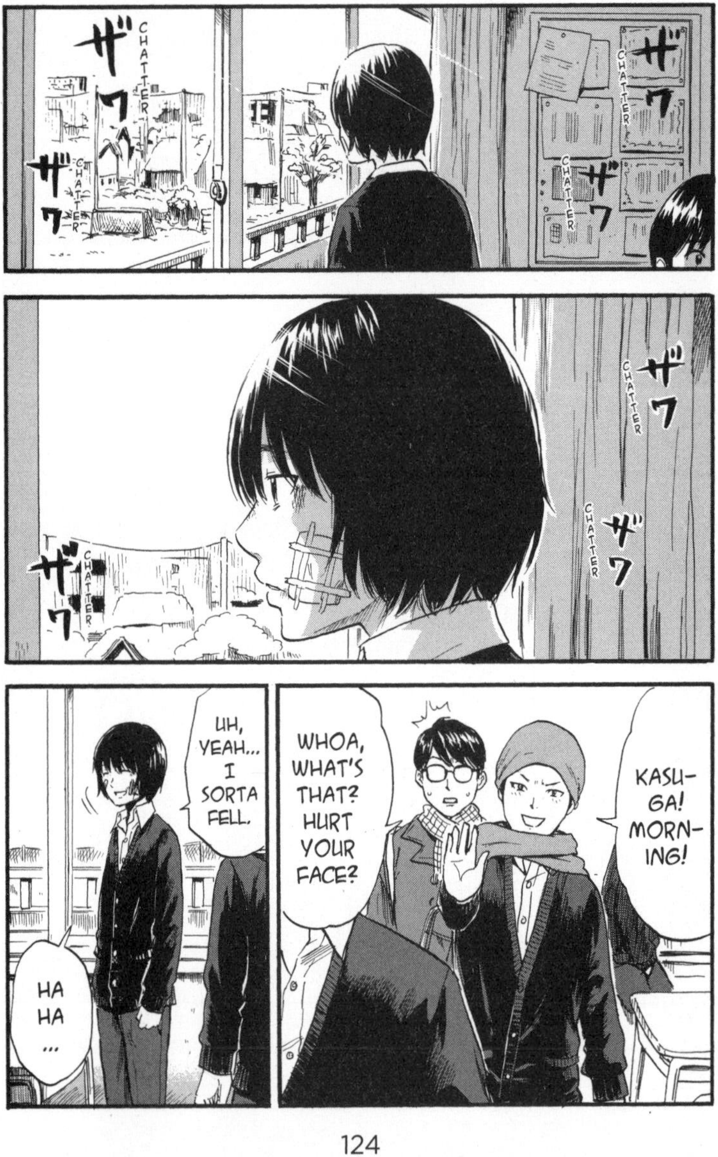
ザワ CHATTER
ザワ CHATTER
ザワ CHATTER
ザワ CHATTER
ザワ CHATTER
ザワ CHATTER
ザワ CHATTER
KASU-GA! MORN-ING!
WHOA, WHAT'S THAT? HURT YOUR FACE?
UH, YEAH... I SORTA FELL.
HA HA ...

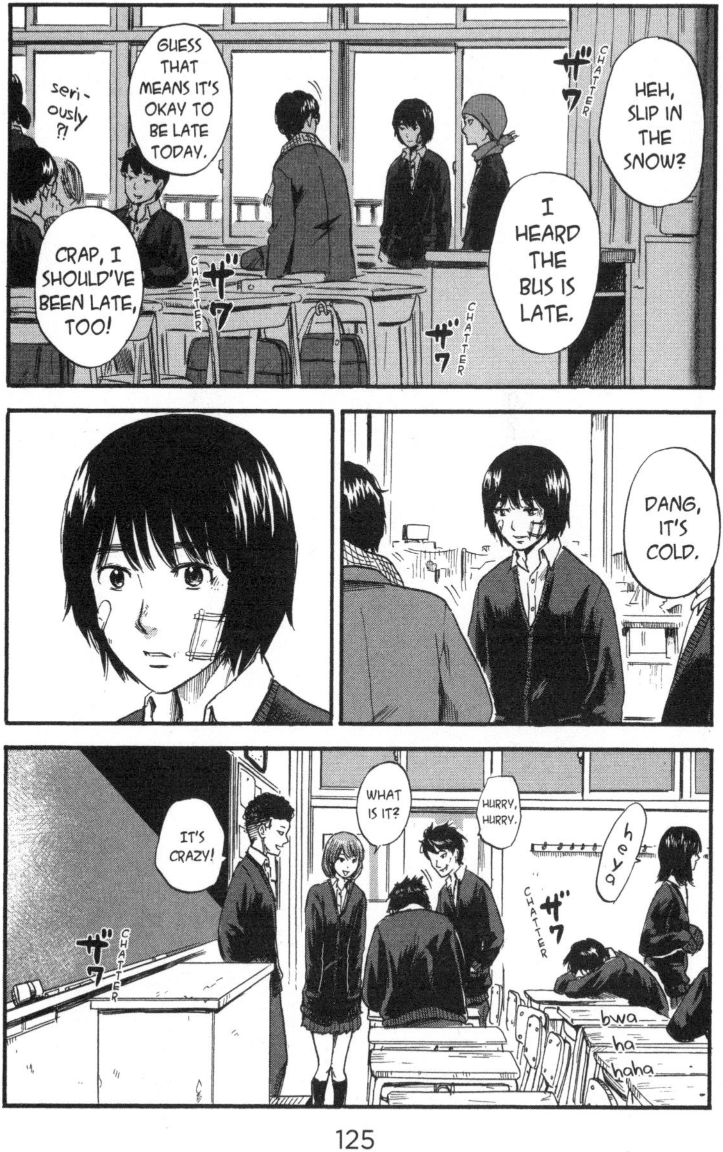
HEH, SLIP IN THE SNOW?
ザワ CHATTER
I HEARD THE BUS IS LATE.
ザワ CHATTER
GUESS THAT MEANS IT'S OKAY TO BE LATE TODAY.
seri-ously ?!
ザワ CHATTER
CRAP, I SHOULD'VE BEEN LATE, TOO!
DANG, IT'S COLD.
heya
ザワ CHATTER
HURRY, HURRY.
WHAT IS IT?
IT'S CRAZY!
ザワ CHATTER
bwa ha haha

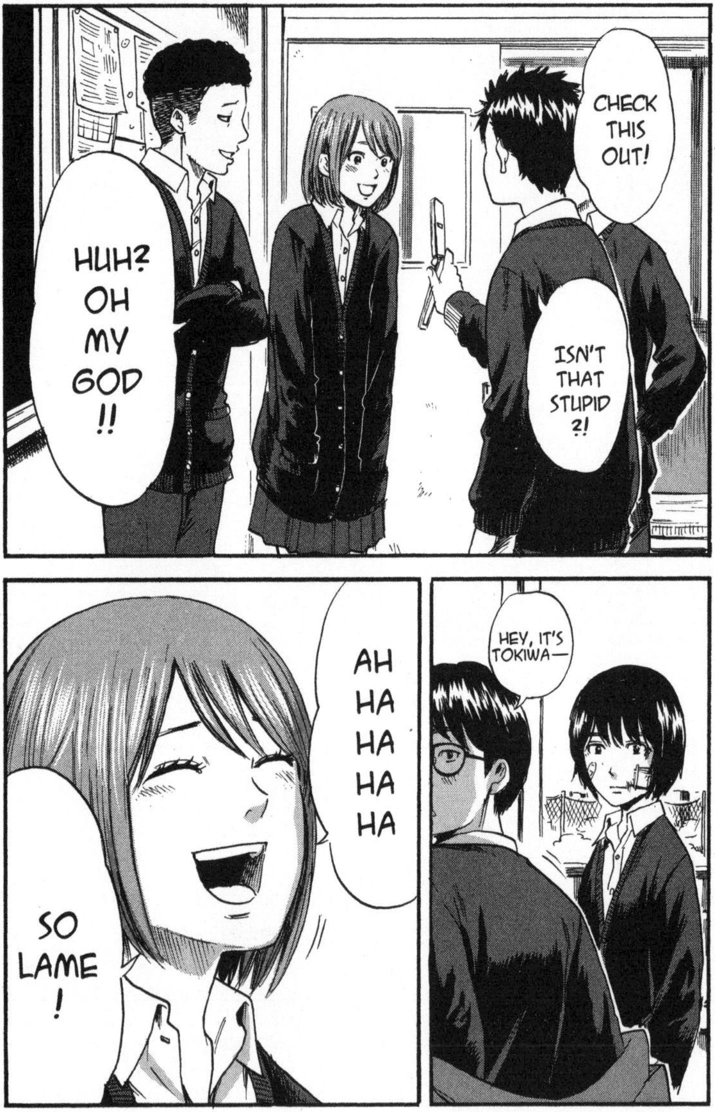
CHECK THIS OUT!
ISN'T THAT STUPID?!
HUH? OH MY GOD!!
HEY, IT'S TOKIWA—
AH HA HA HA HA
SO LAME!

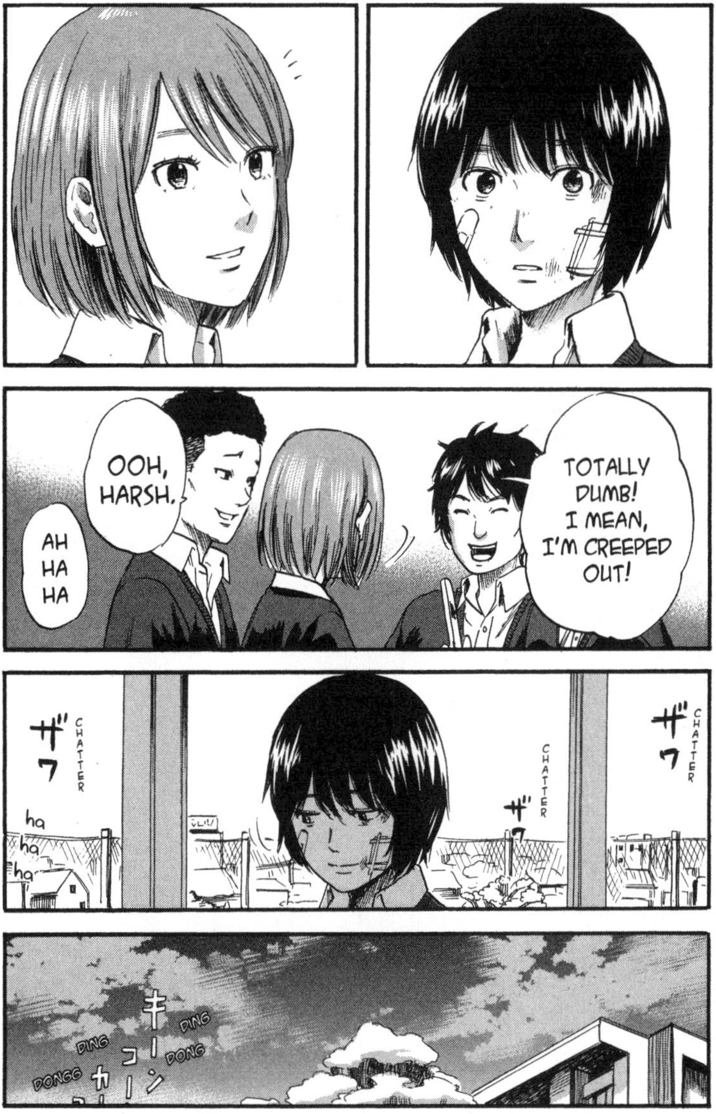
TOTALLY DUMB! I MEAN, I'M CREEPED OUT!
OOH, HARSH.
AH HA HA
ザワ
CHATTER
ザワ
CHATTER
ザワ
CHATTER
ha ha ha
キーン
コーン
カー
DING DONG
DING DONGG

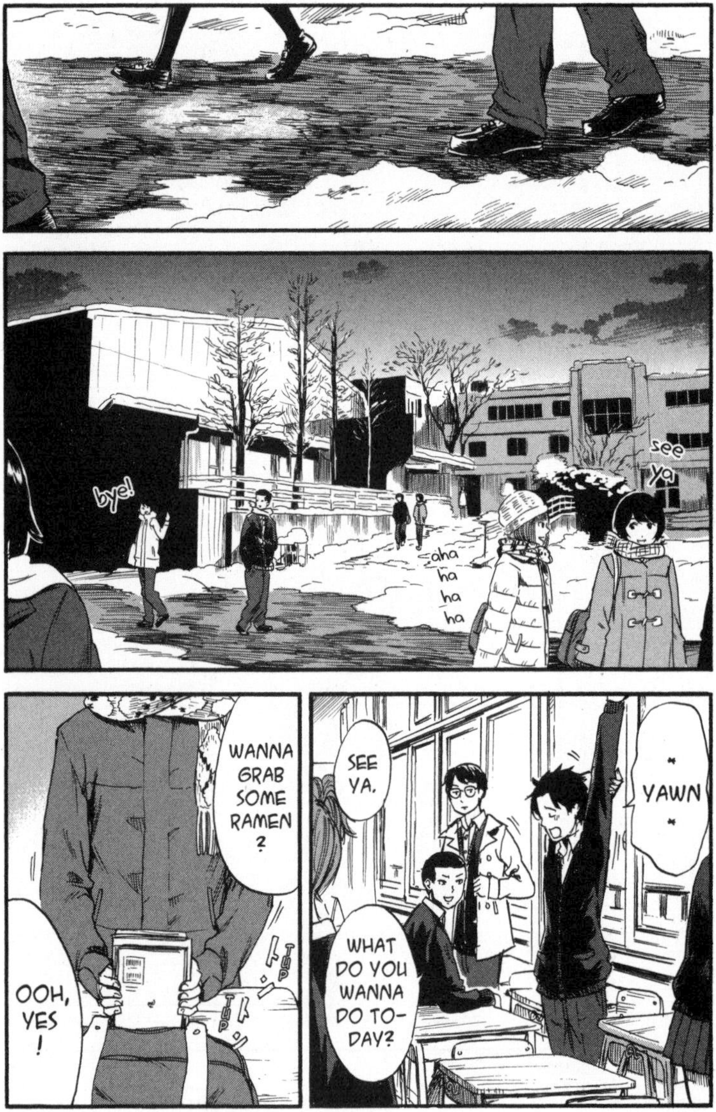
see ya
aha ha ha ha
bye!
YAWN
SEE YA.
WHAT DO YOU WANNA DO TO-DAY?
WANNA GRAB SOME RAMEN?
TUP
TUP
OOH, YES!

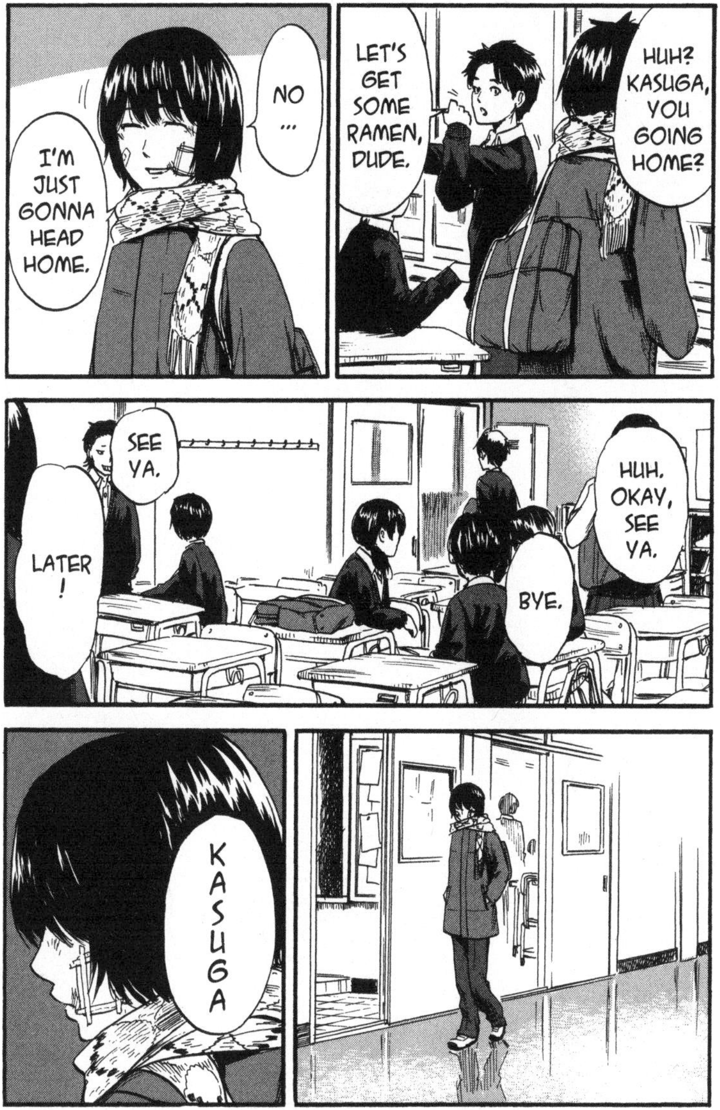
HUH? KASUGA, YOU GOING HOME?
LET'S GET SOME RAMEN, DUDE.
NO ...
I'M JUST GONNA HEAD HOME.
HUH. OKAY, SEE YA.
BYE.
SEE YA.
LATER!
KASUGA

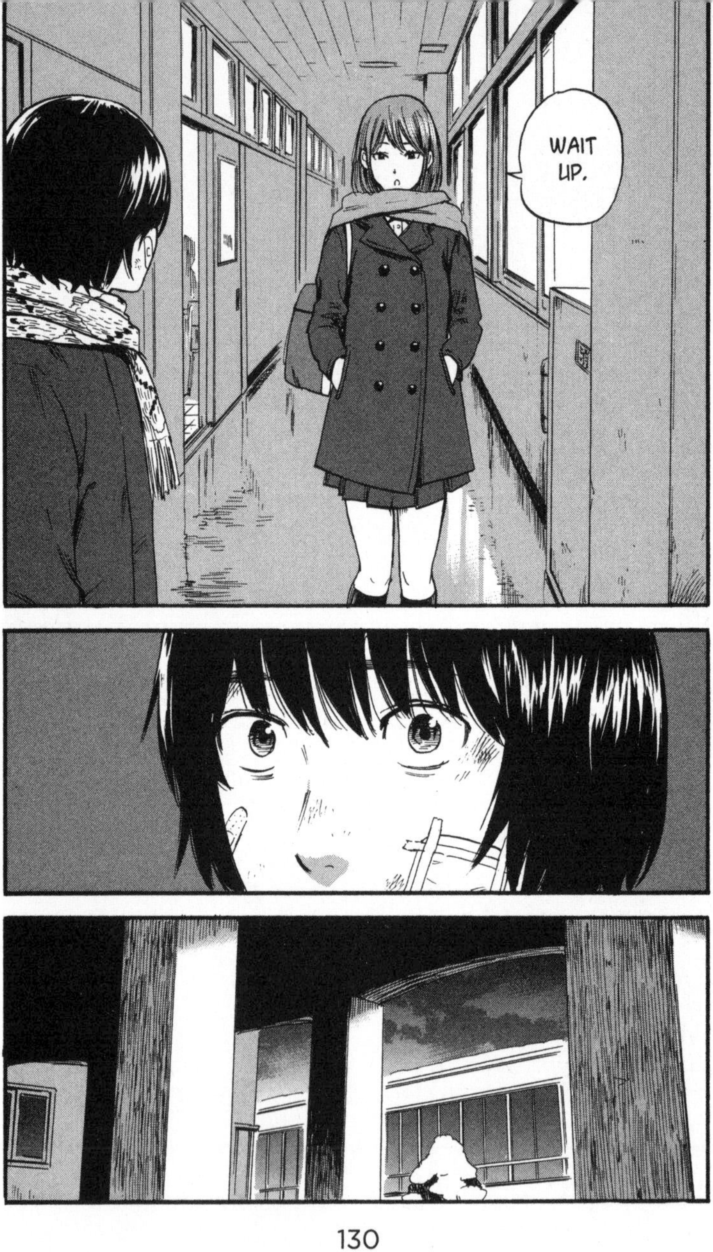
WAIT UP.

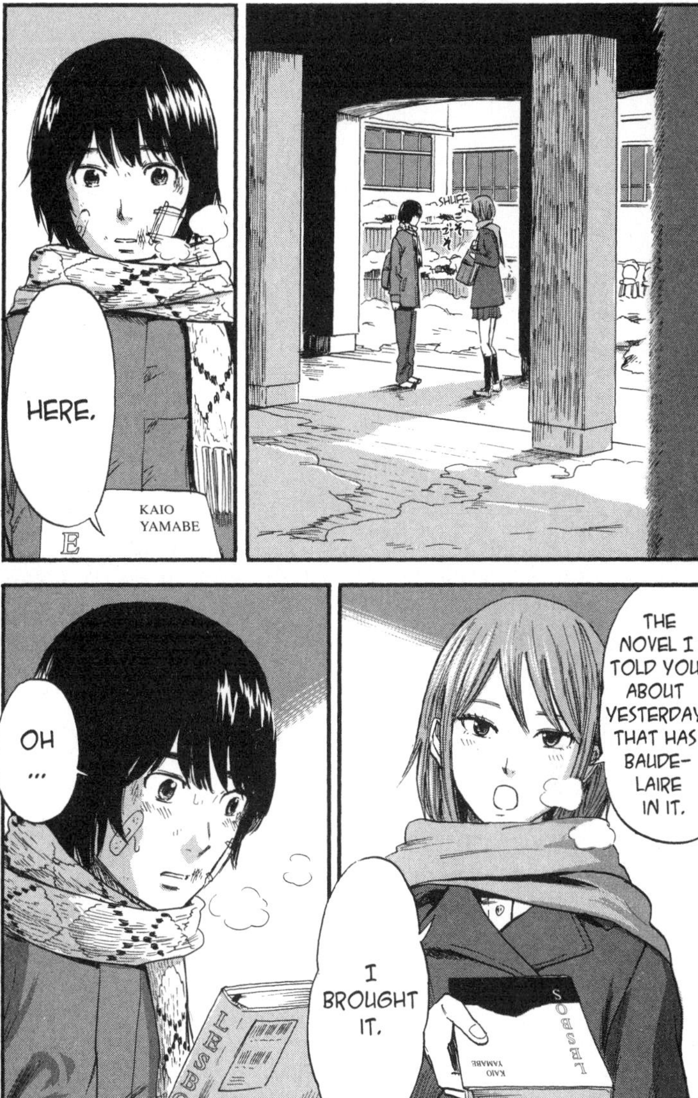

SHUFF
HERE.
KAIO YAMABE
THE NOVEL I TOLD YOU ABOUT YESTERDAY THAT HAS BAUDE-LAIRE IN IT.
I BROUGHT IT.
OH ...

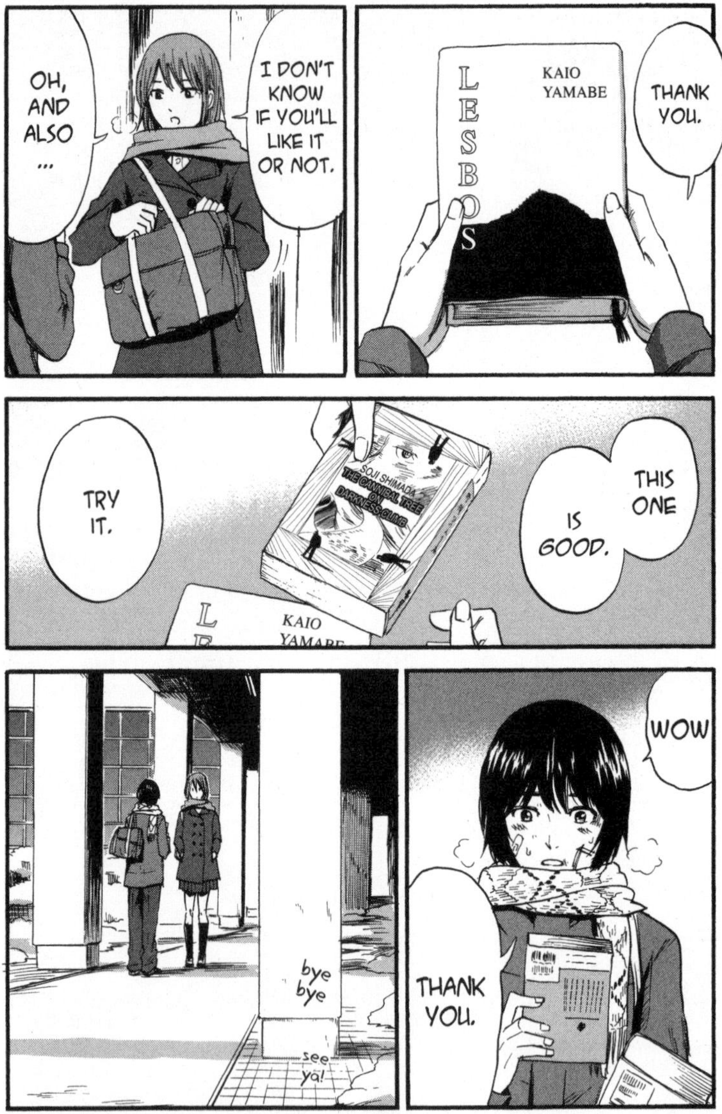
KAIO YAMABE
LESBOS
THANK YOU.
I DON'T KNOW IF YOU'LL LIKE IT OR NOT.
OH, AND ALSO ...
THIS ONE IS GOOD.
SOJI SHIMADA
THE CANNIBAL TREE ON DARKNESS CLIMB
KAIO YAMABE
TRY IT.
WOW
THANK YOU.
bye bye
see ya!

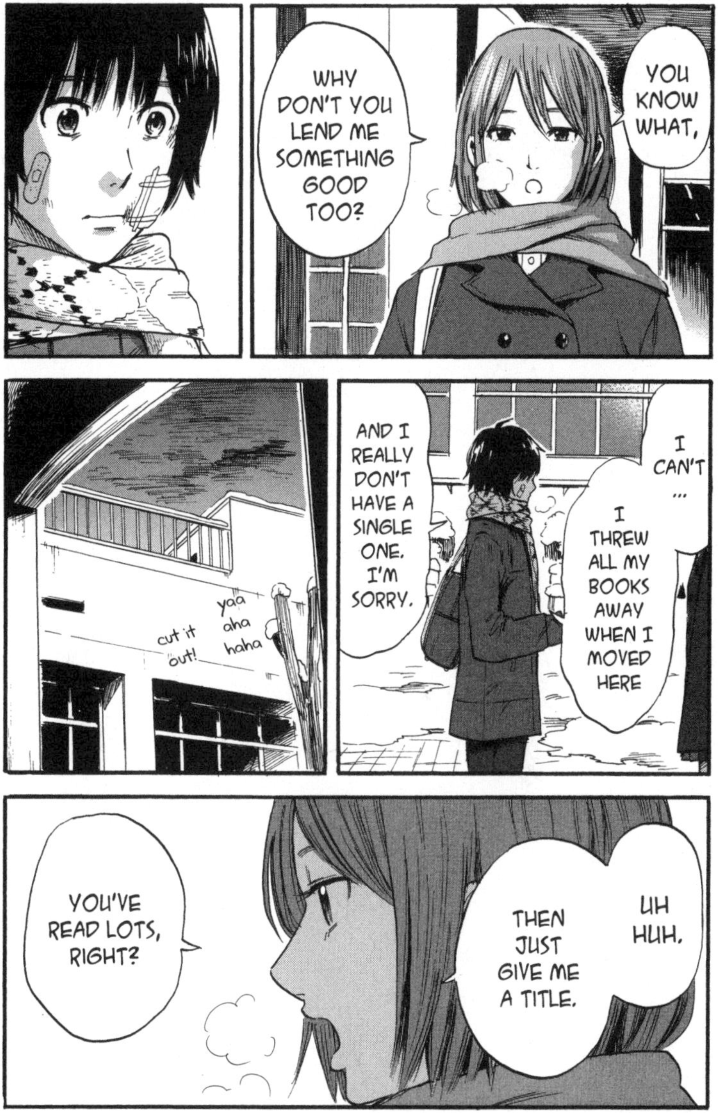
YOU KNOW WHAT,
WHY DON'T YOU LEND ME SOMETHING GOOD TOO?
I CAN'T ...
I THREW ALL MY BOOKS AWAY WHEN I MOVED HERE
AND I REALLY DON'T HAVE A SINGLE ONE. I'M SORRY.
yaa aha haha
cut it out!
UH HUH.
THEN JUST GIVE ME A TITLE.
YOU'VE READ LOTS, RIGHT?

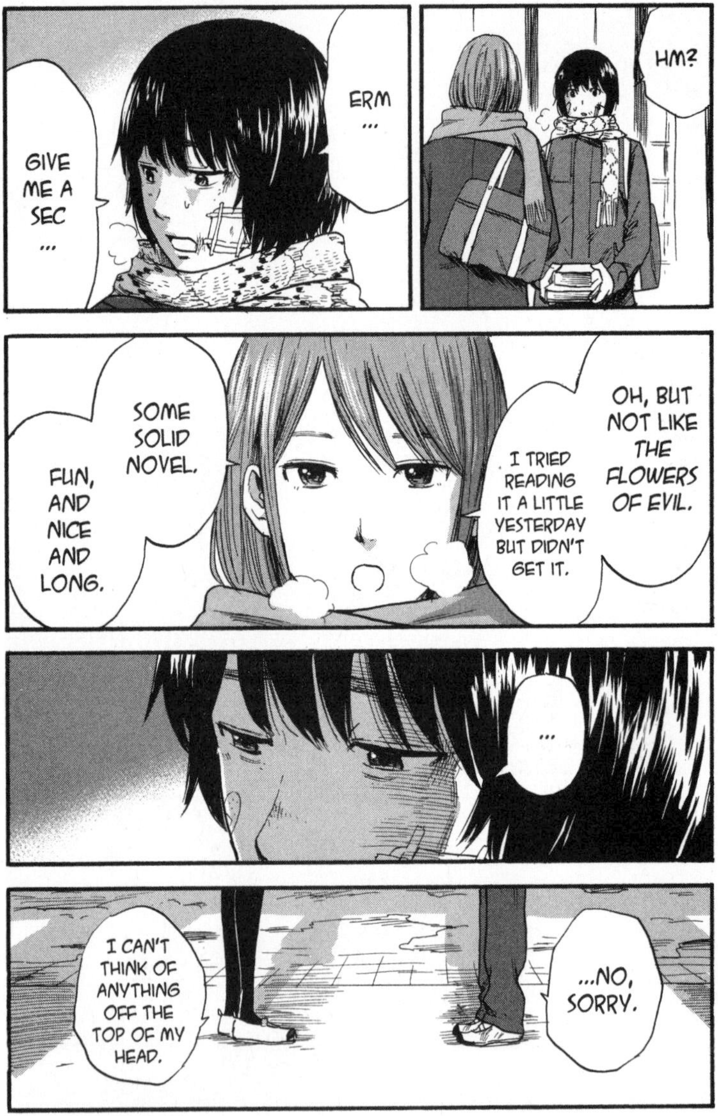
HM?
ERM ...
GIVE ME A SEC ...
OH, BUT NOT LIKE THE FLOWERS OF EVIL.
I TRIED READING IT A LITTLE YESTERDAY BUT DIDN'T GET IT.
SOME SOLID NOVEL.
FUN, AND NICE AND LONG.
...
...NO, SORRY.
I CAN'T THINK OF ANYTHING OFF THE TOP OF MY HEAD.

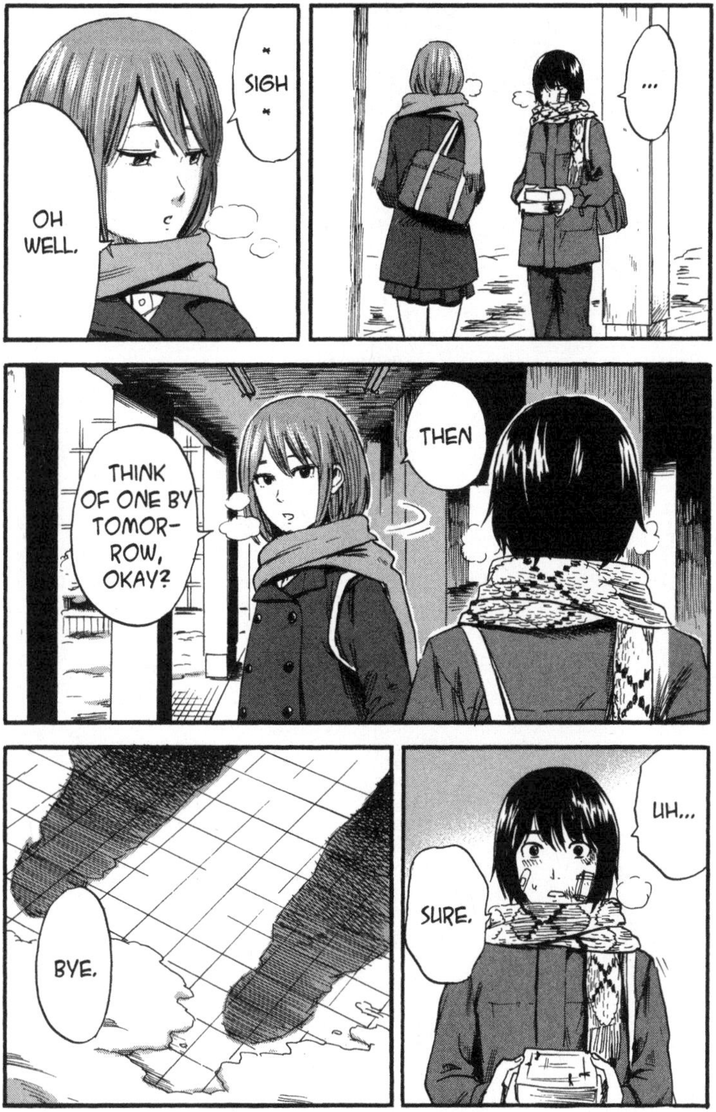
...
* SIGH *
OH WELL.
THEN
THINK OF ONE BY TOMORROW, OKAY?
UH...
SURE.
BYE.

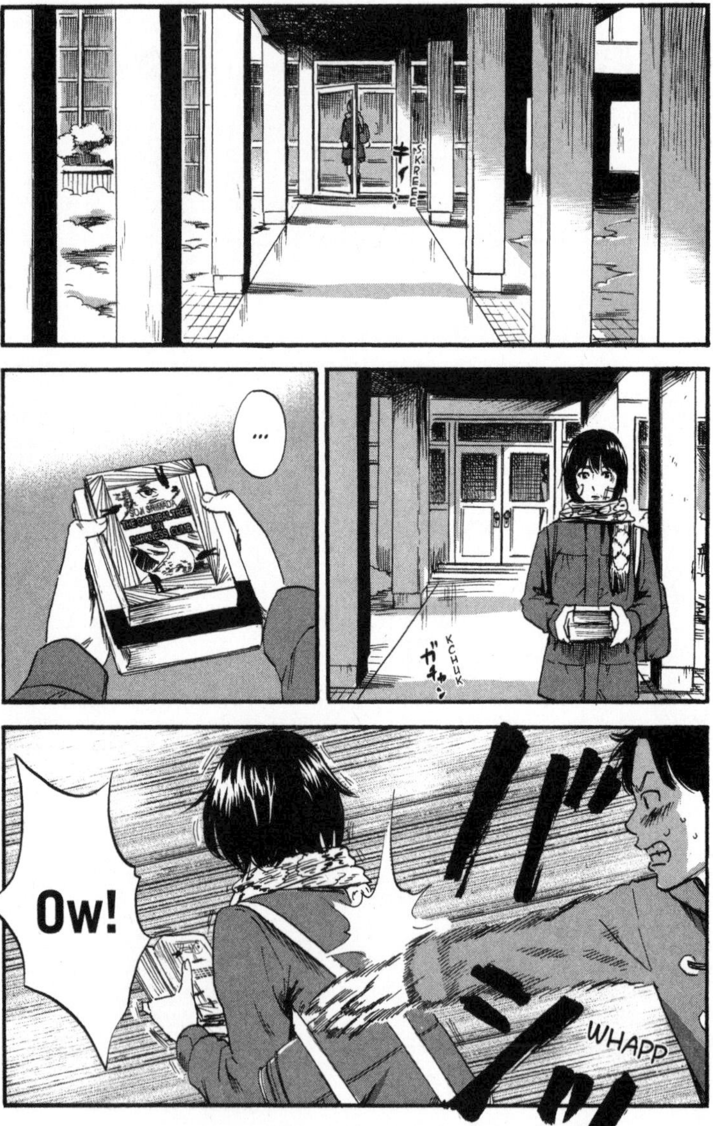
SKREEE
キィ…
KCHUK
ガチャン
...
SOJI SHIMADA
THE CANNIBAL TREE
ON
DARKNESS CLUB
Ow!
WHAPP

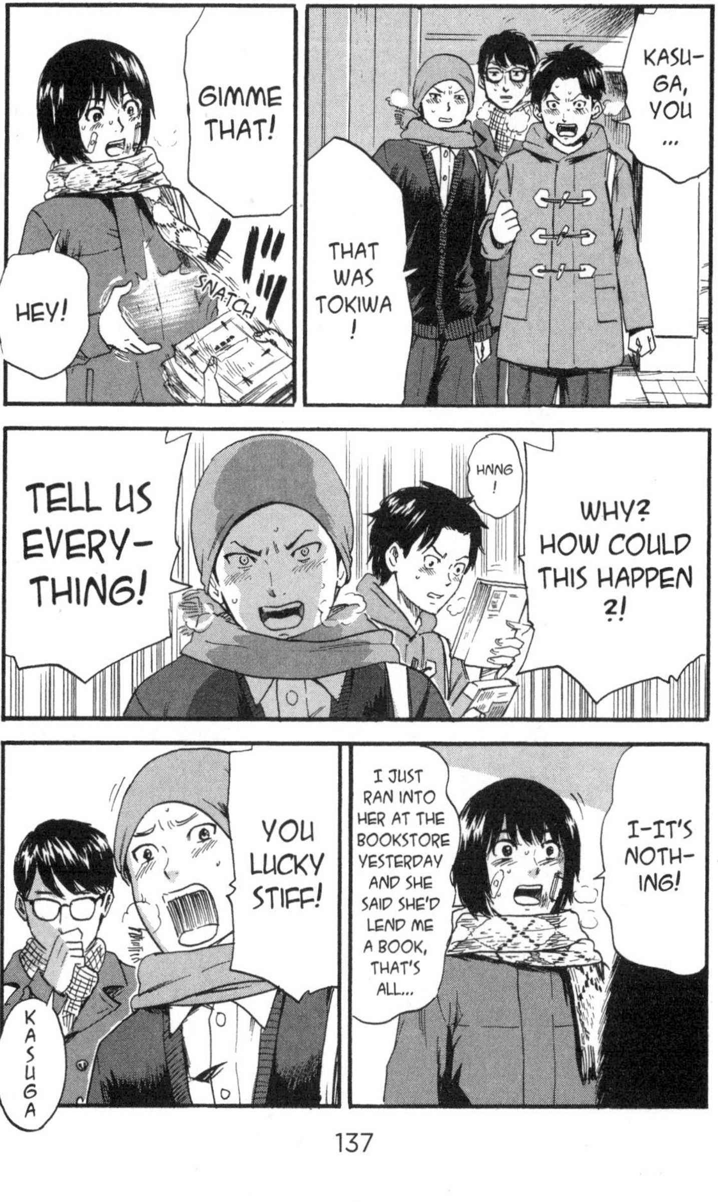
KASU-GA, YOU ...
THAT WAS TOKIWA!
GIMME THAT!
SNATCH
HEY!
WHY? HOW COULD THIS HAPPEN?!
HNNG!
TELL US EVERY-THING!
I-IT'S NOTH-ING!
I JUST RAN INTO HER AT THE BOOKSTORE YESTERDAY AND SHE SAID SHE'D LEND ME A BOOK, THAT'S ALL...
YOU LUCKY STIFF!
KASUGA

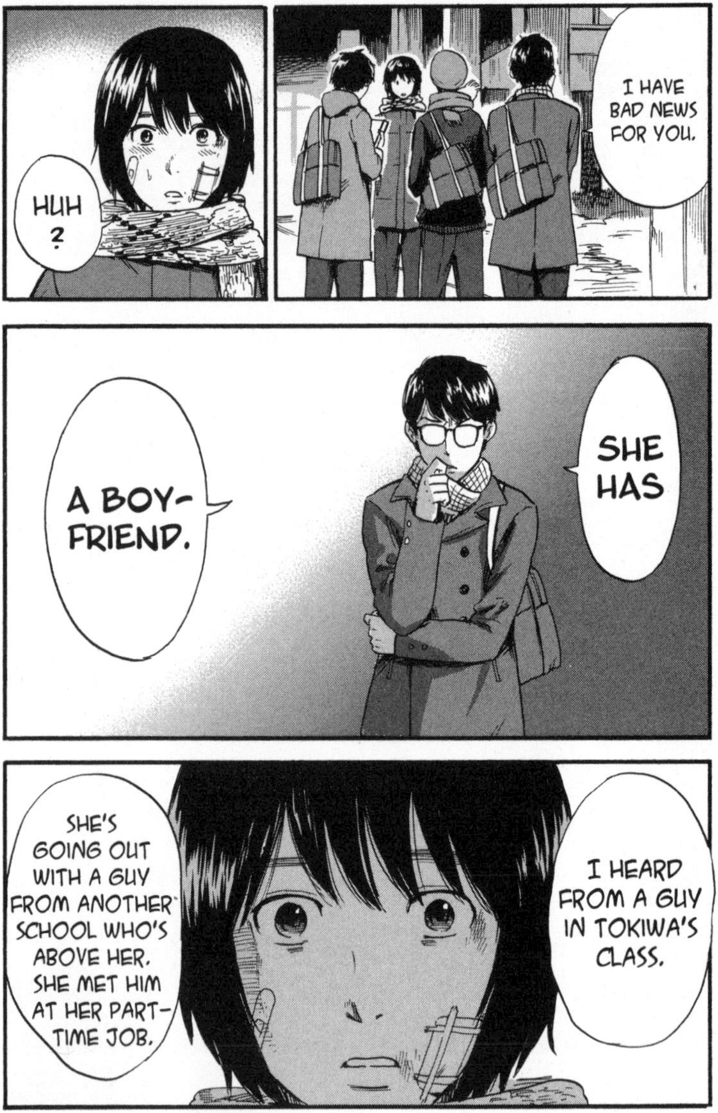
I HAVE BAD NEWS FOR YOU.
HUH ?
SHE HAS
A BOY-FRIEND.
I HEARD FROM A GUY IN TOKIWA'S CLASS.
SHE'S GOING OUT WITH A GUY FROM ANOTHER SCHOOL WHO'S ABOVE HER. SHE MET HIM AT HER PART-TIME JOB.

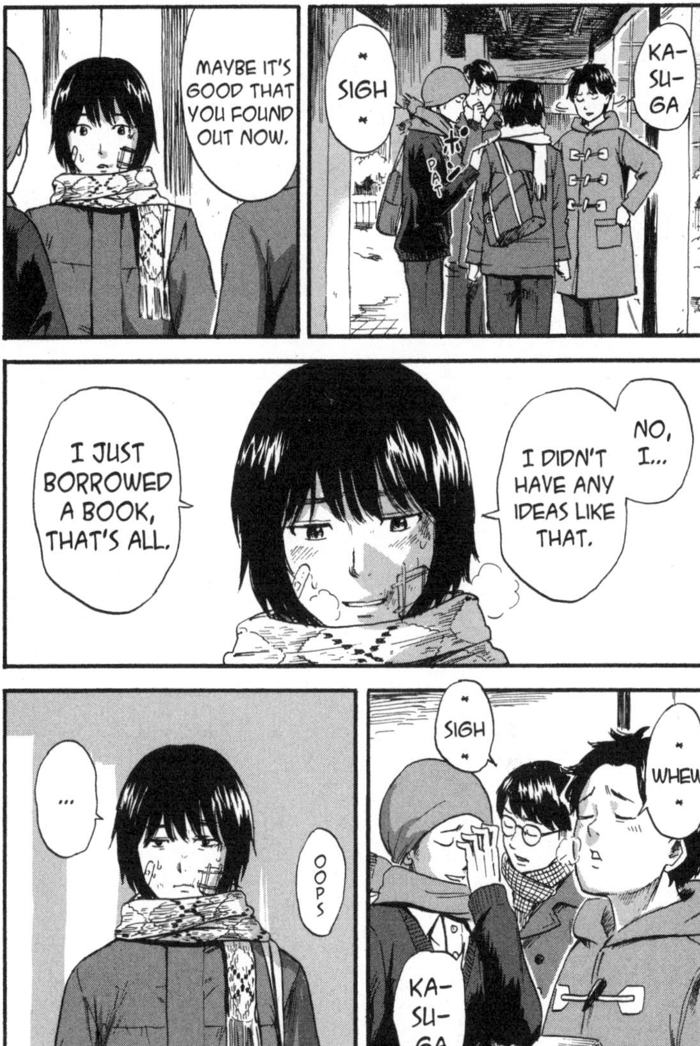
KA-SU-GA
SIGH
PAT
MAYBE IT'S GOOD THAT YOU FOUND OUT NOW.
NO, I...
I DIDN'T HAVE ANY IDEAS LIKE THAT.
I JUST BORROWED A BOOK, THAT'S ALL.
WHEW
SIGH
KA-SU-GA
OOPS
...

ビュ
SHOOOOOOOO
ウ
ウ
ウ
ウ
ぎし
KREAK
ジャーー
FSSSSSH
カチャカチャ
KLAK
KLAK

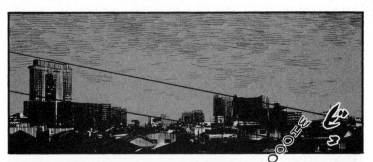

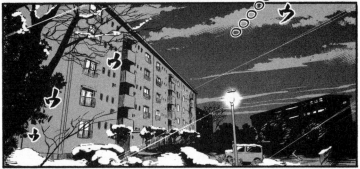

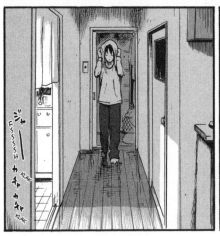

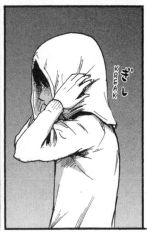

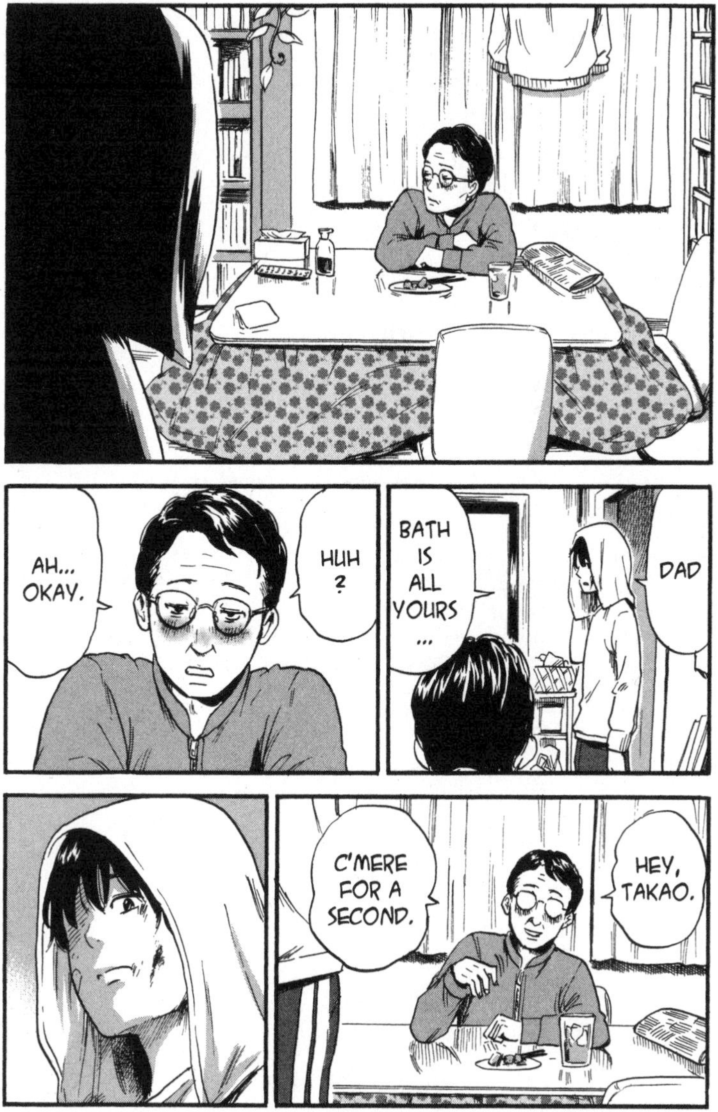
DAD
BATH IS ALL YOURS ...
HUH ?
AH... OKAY.
HEY, TAKAO.
C'MERE FOR A SECOND.

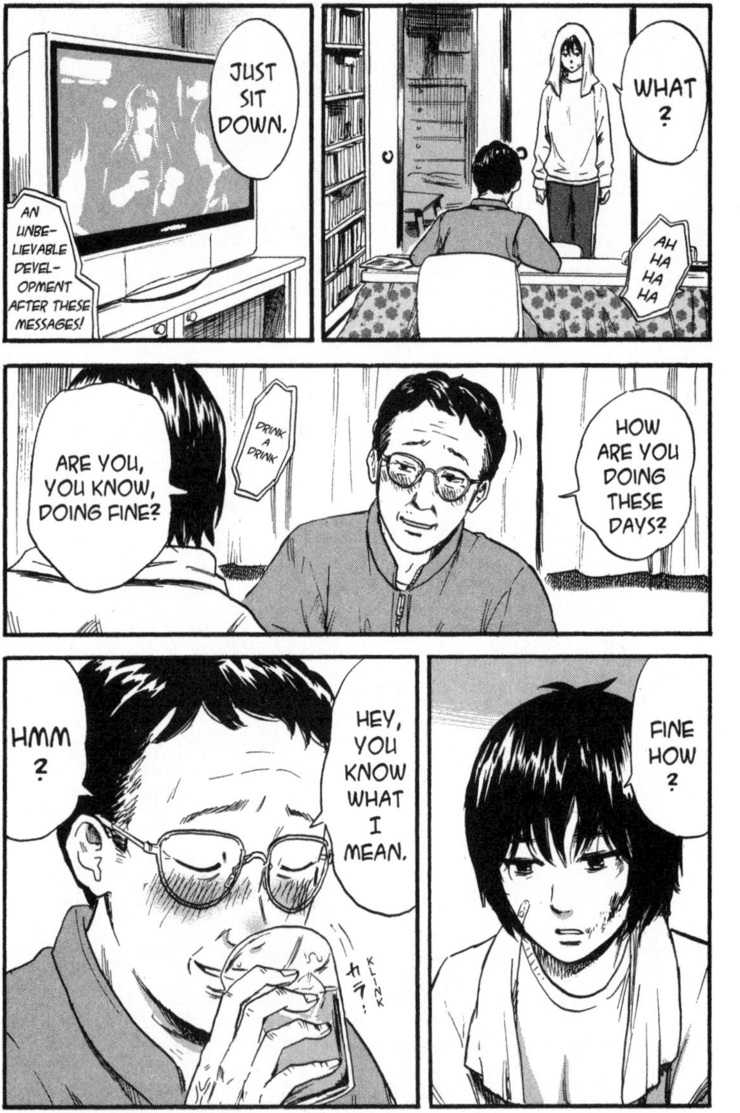
WHAT?
AH HA HA HA
JUST SIT DOWN.
AN UNBE-LIEVABLE DEVEL-OPMENT AFTER THESE MESSAGES!
HOW ARE YOU DOING THESE DAYS?
DRINK A DRINK
ARE YOU, YOU KNOW, DOING FINE?
FINE HOW?
HEY, YOU KNOW WHAT I MEAN.
KLINK
HMM?

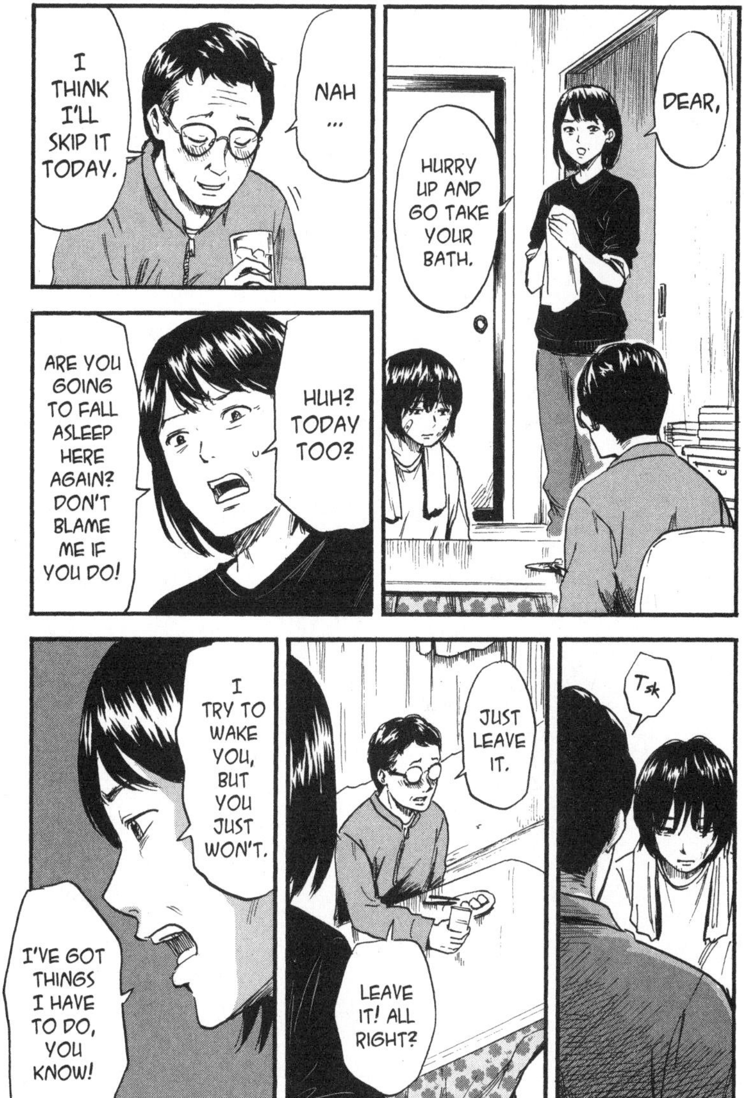
DEAR,
HURRY UP AND GO TAKE YOUR BATH.
NAH ...
I THINK I'LL SKIP IT TODAY.
HUH? TODAY TOO?
ARE YOU GOING TO FALL ASLEEP HERE AGAIN? DON'T BLAME ME IF YOU DO!
Tsk
JUST LEAVE IT.
LEAVE IT! ALL RIGHT?
I TRY TO WAKE YOU, BUT YOU JUST WON'T.
I'VE GOT THINGS I HAVE TO DO, YOU KNOW!

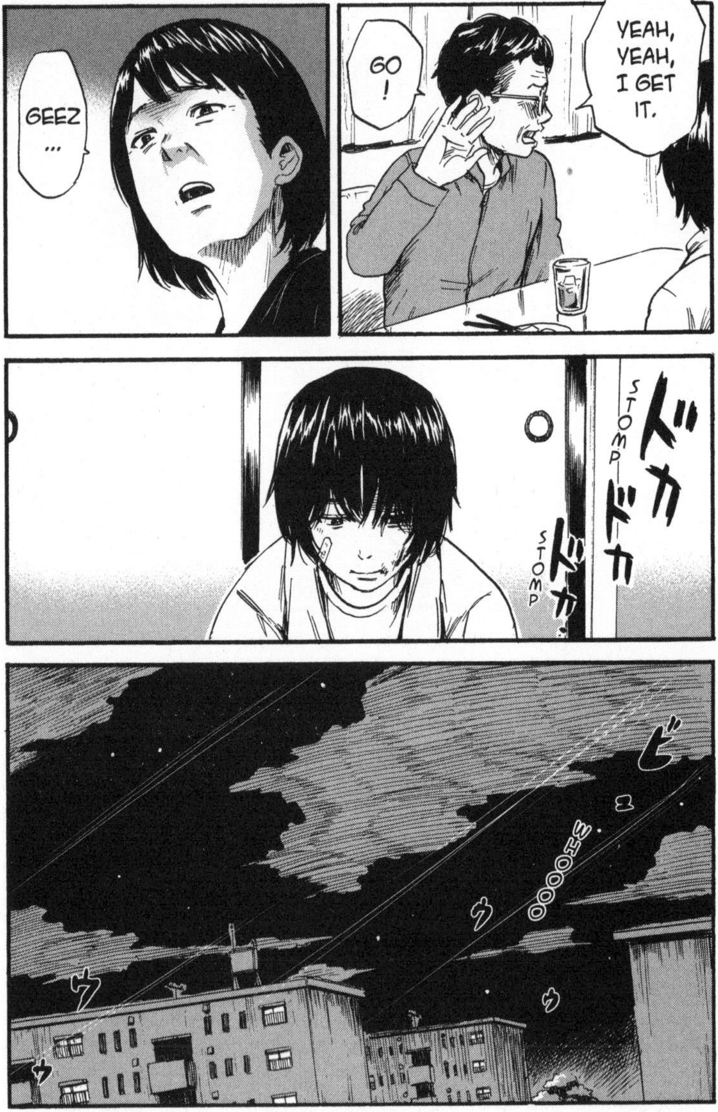
YEAH, YEAH, I GET IT.
GO!
GEEZ...
ドカ STOMP
ドカ... STOMP
ビュウウウウ
WHOOOOO

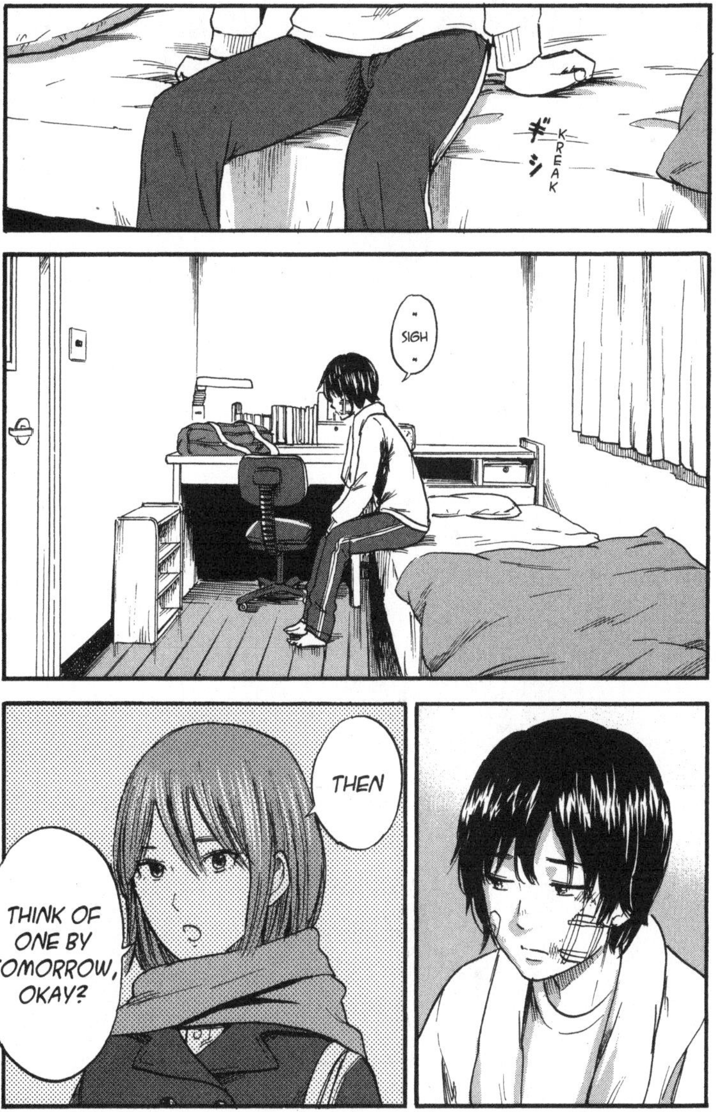
ギシ
KREAK
" SIGH "
THEN
THINK OF ONE BY TOMORROW, OKAY?

ギシ
KREAK
ごそ
SHUFF
LESBOS
KAIO YAMABE
パラ..
FLIPP
LESBO
KAIO YAMABE

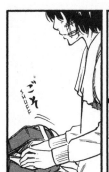

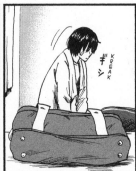

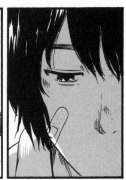

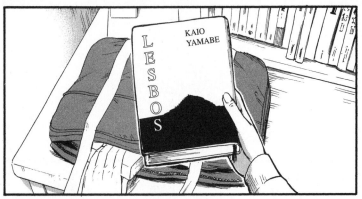

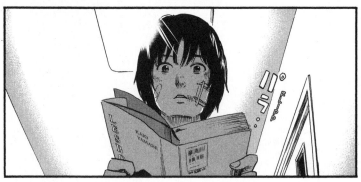

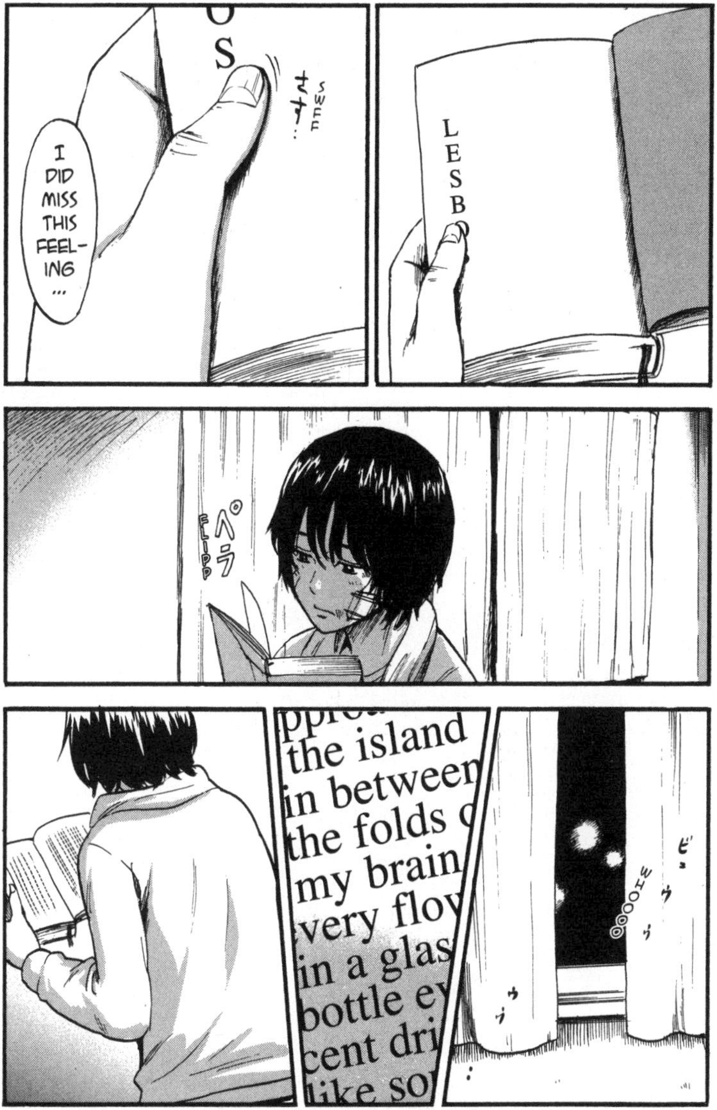
LESBO
S
さす…
SWEFF
I DID MISS THIS FEELING-ING...
ペラ
FLIPP
ビュウゥ
WHOOOO
the island
in between
the folds
my brain
very flov
in a glas
bottle ey
cent dri
like so

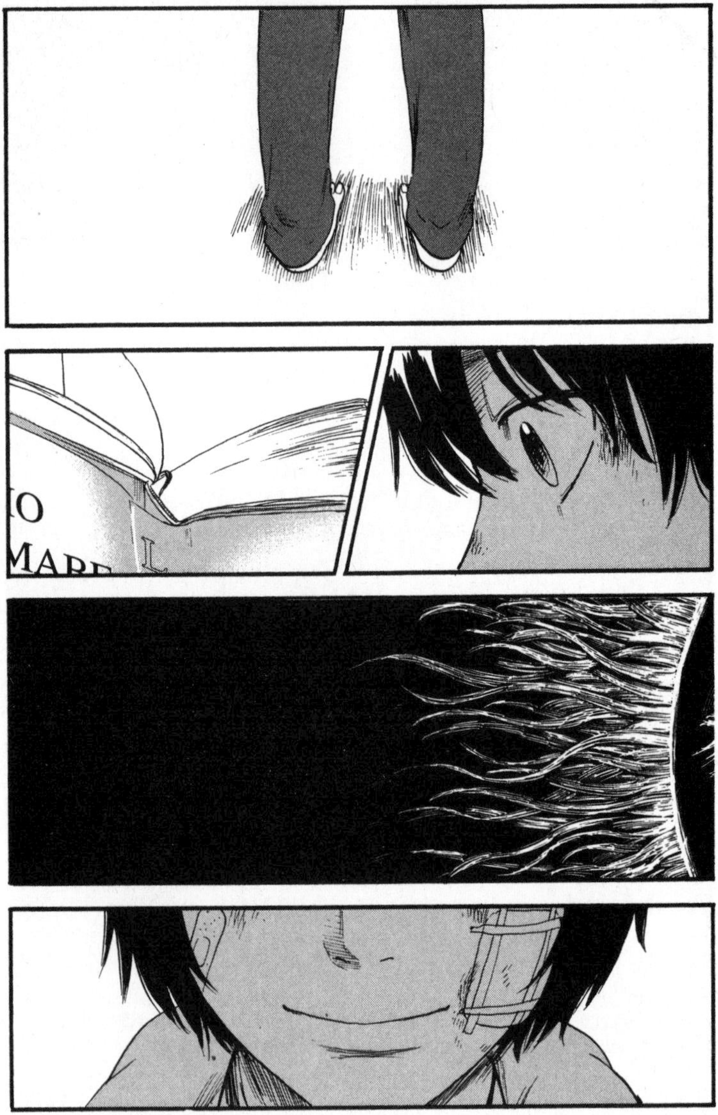
IO
MARE

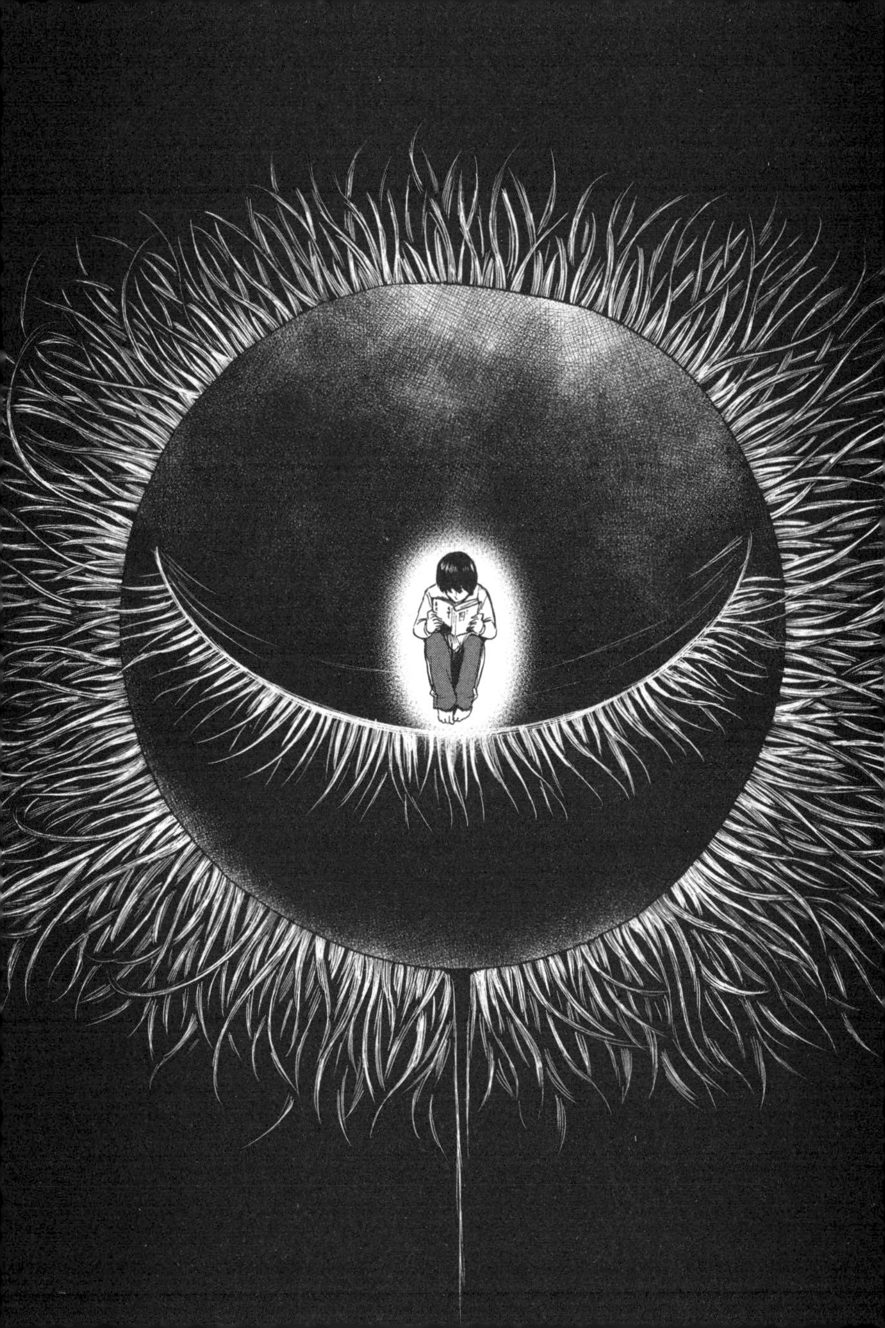

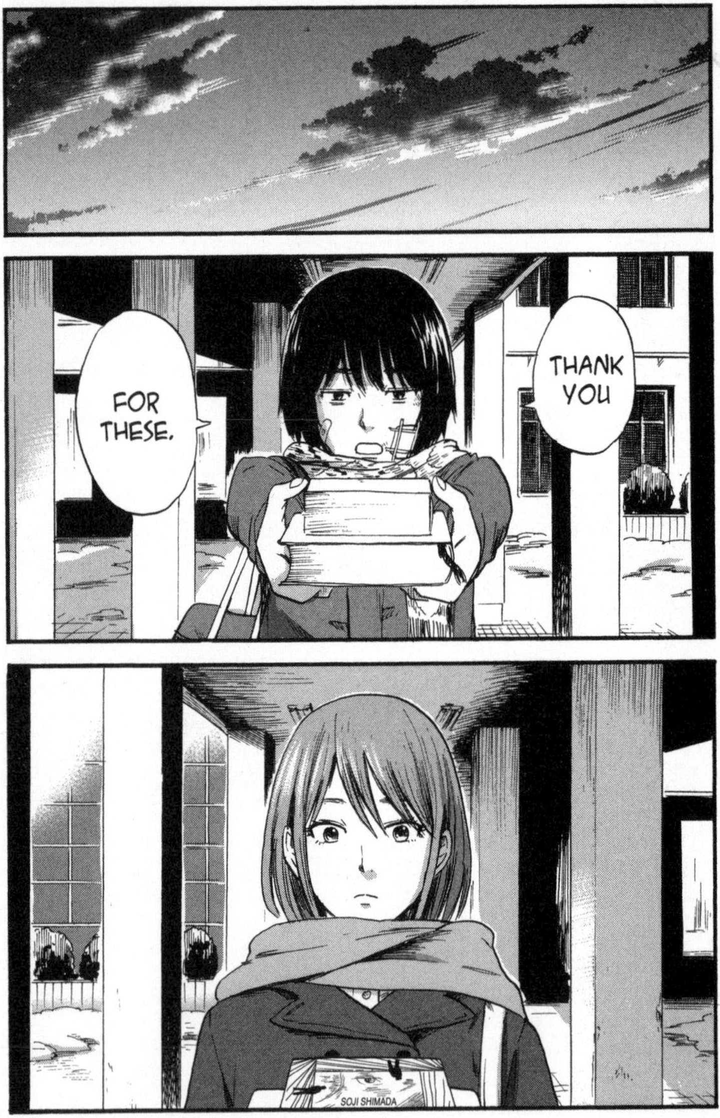
THANK YOU
FOR THESE.
SOJI SHIMADA

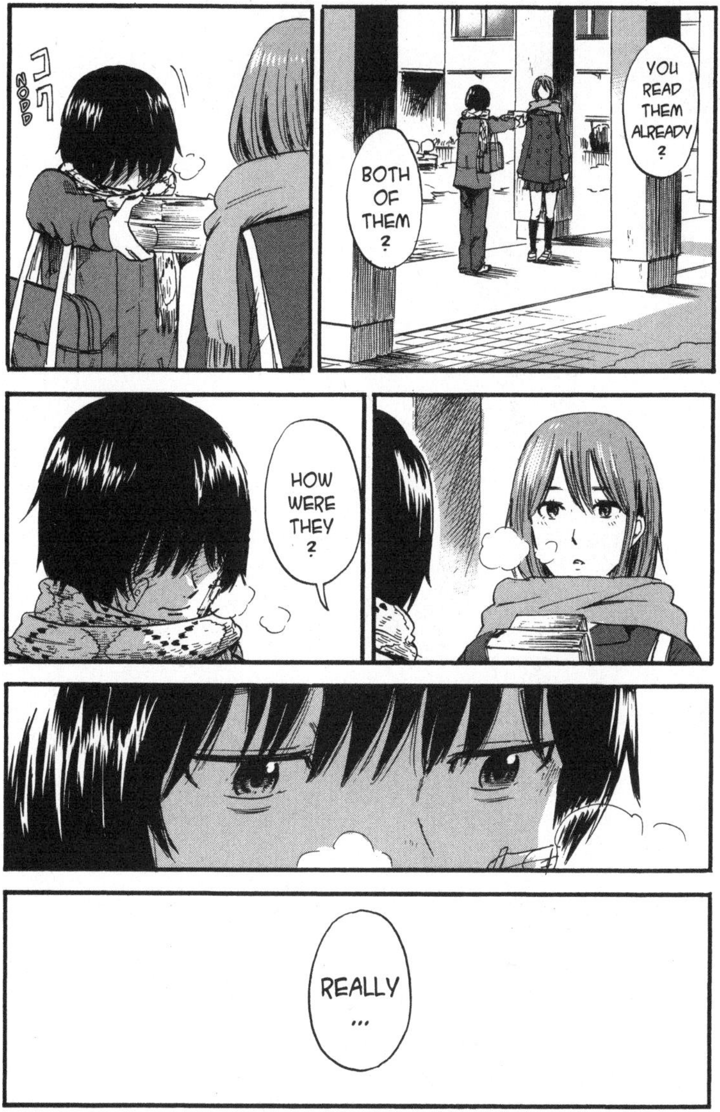
YOU READ THEM ALREADY?
BOTH OF THEM?
コク
NODD
HOW WERE THEY?
REALLY...

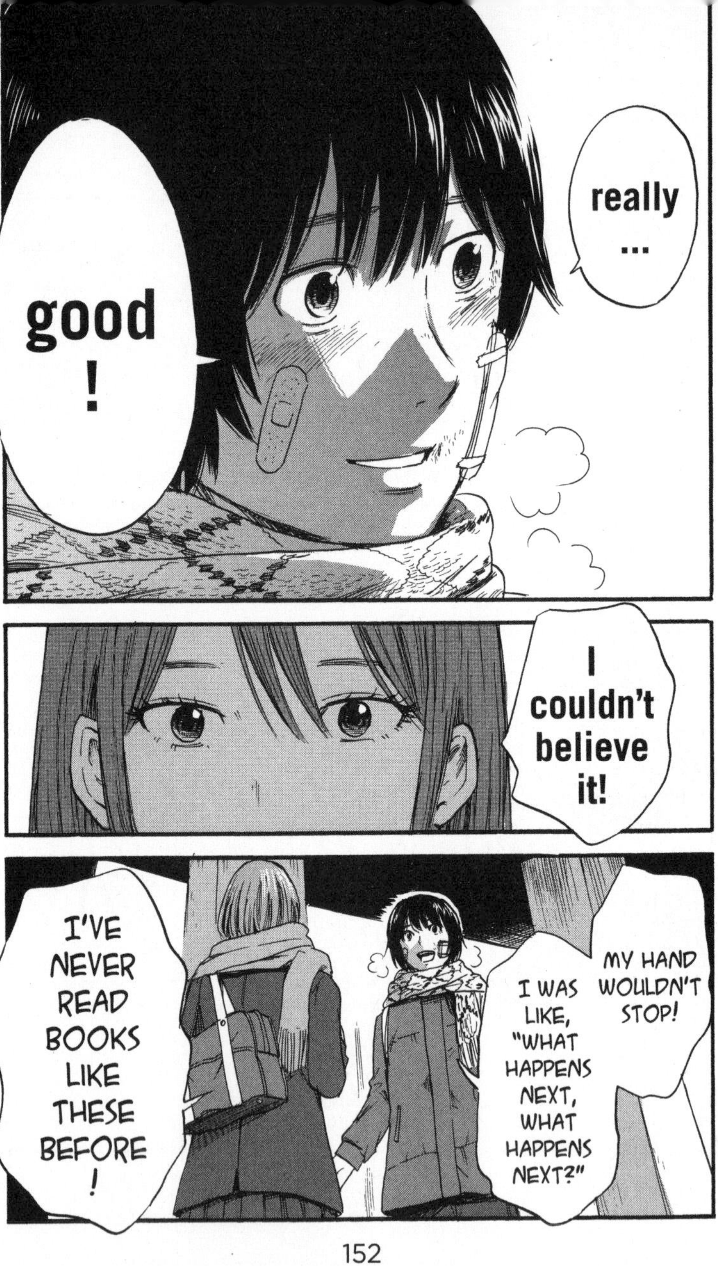
really ...
good !
I couldn't believe it!
MY HAND WOULDN'T STOP!
I WAS LIKE, "WHAT HAPPENS NEXT, WHAT HAPPENS NEXT?"
I'VE NEVER READ BOOKS LIKE THESE BEFORE !

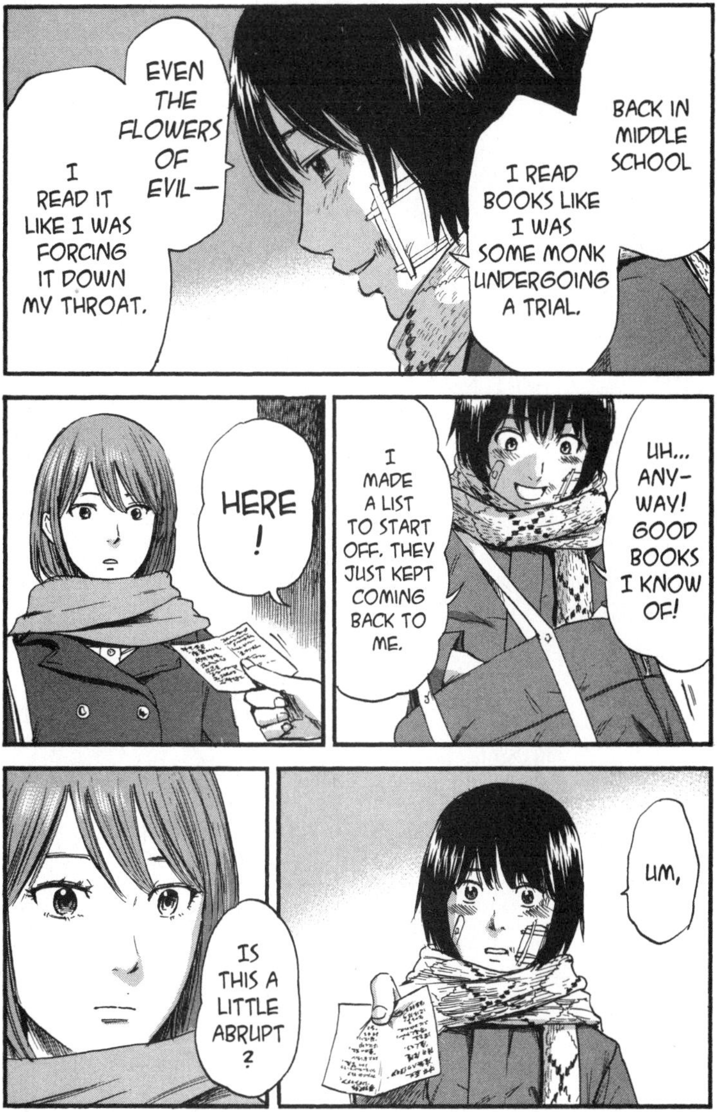
BACK IN MIDDLE SCHOOL
I READ BOOKS LIKE I WAS SOME MONK UNDERGOING A TRIAL.
EVEN THE FLOWERS OF EVIL—
I READ IT LIKE I WAS FORCING IT DOWN MY THROAT.
UH... ANY-WAY! GOOD BOOKS I KNOW OF!
I MADE A LIST TO START OFF. THEY JUST KEPT COMING BACK TO ME.
HERE!
UM,
IS THIS A LITTLE ABRUPT?

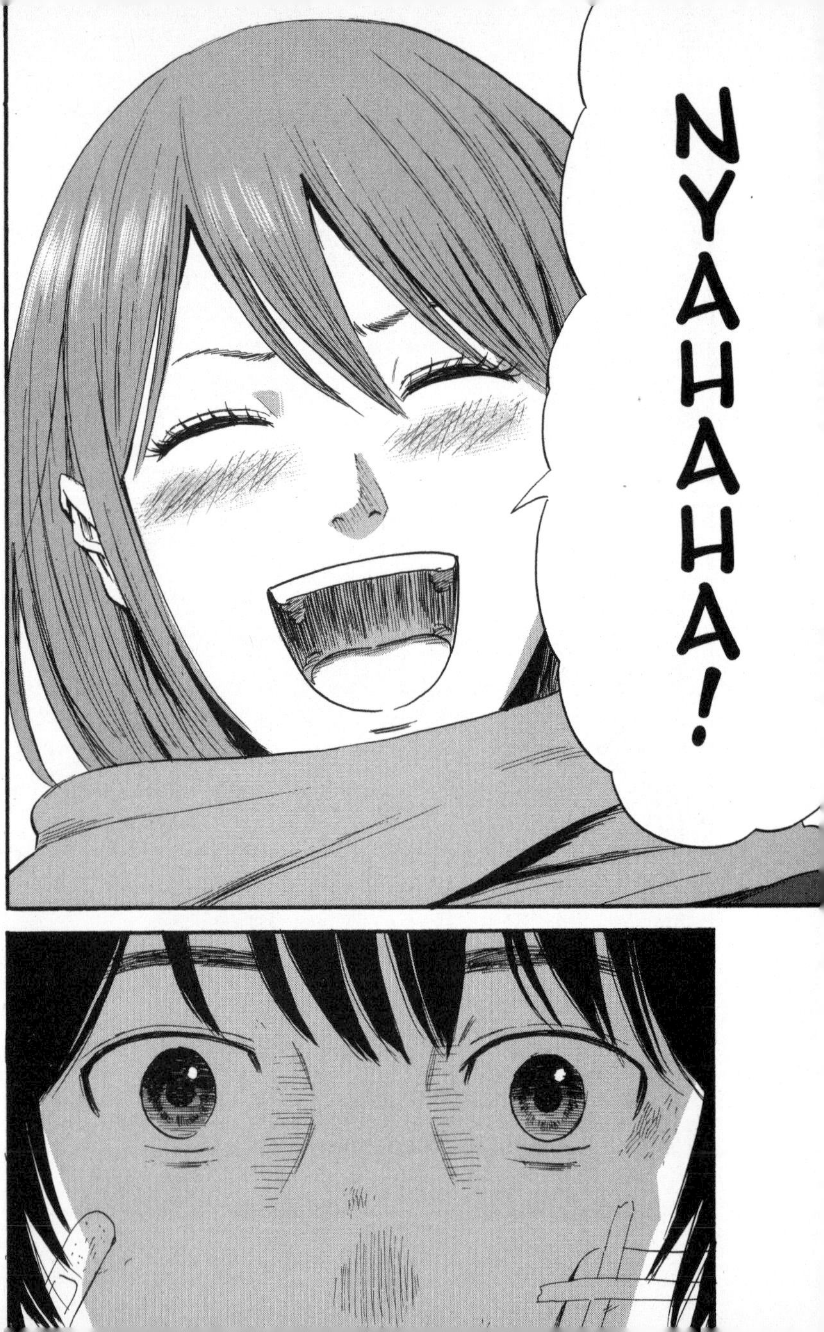
NYAHAHA!

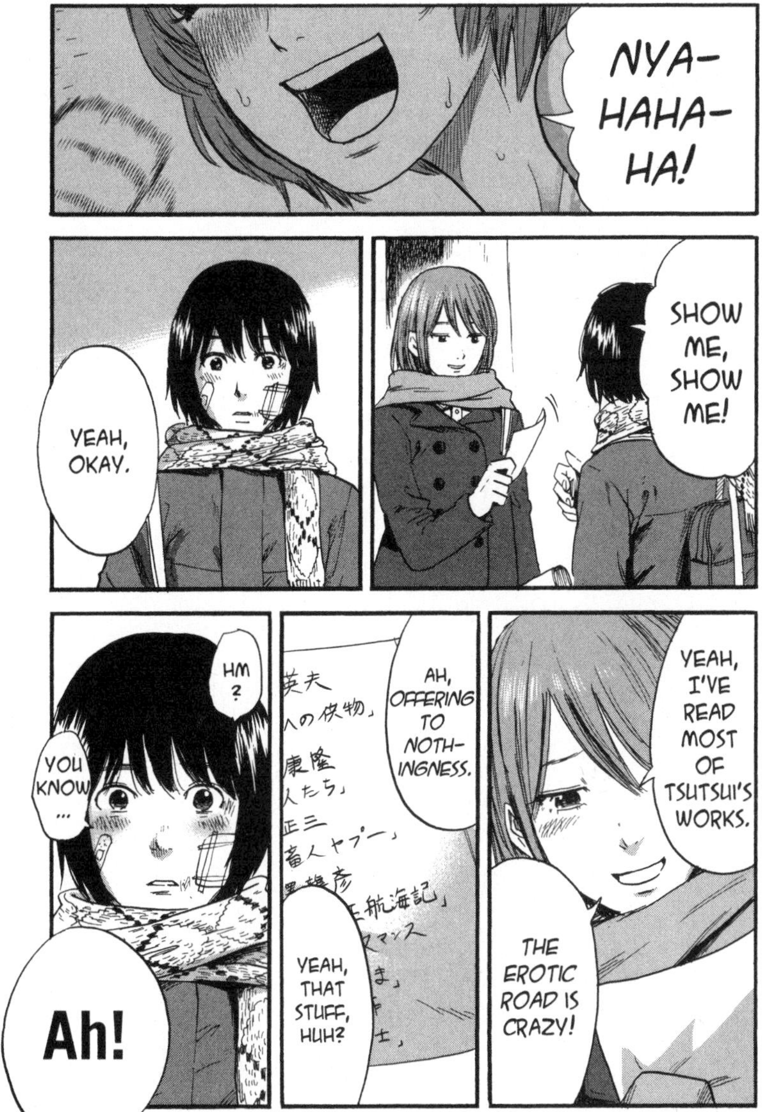
NYA-HAHAHA-HA!
SHOW ME, SHOW ME!
YEAH, OKAY.
YEAH, I'VE READ MOST OF TSUTSUI'S WORKS.
THE EROTIC ROAD IS CRAZY!
AH, OFFERING TO NOTHINGNESS.
YEAH, THAT STUFF, HUH?
HM?
YOU KNOW...
Ah!

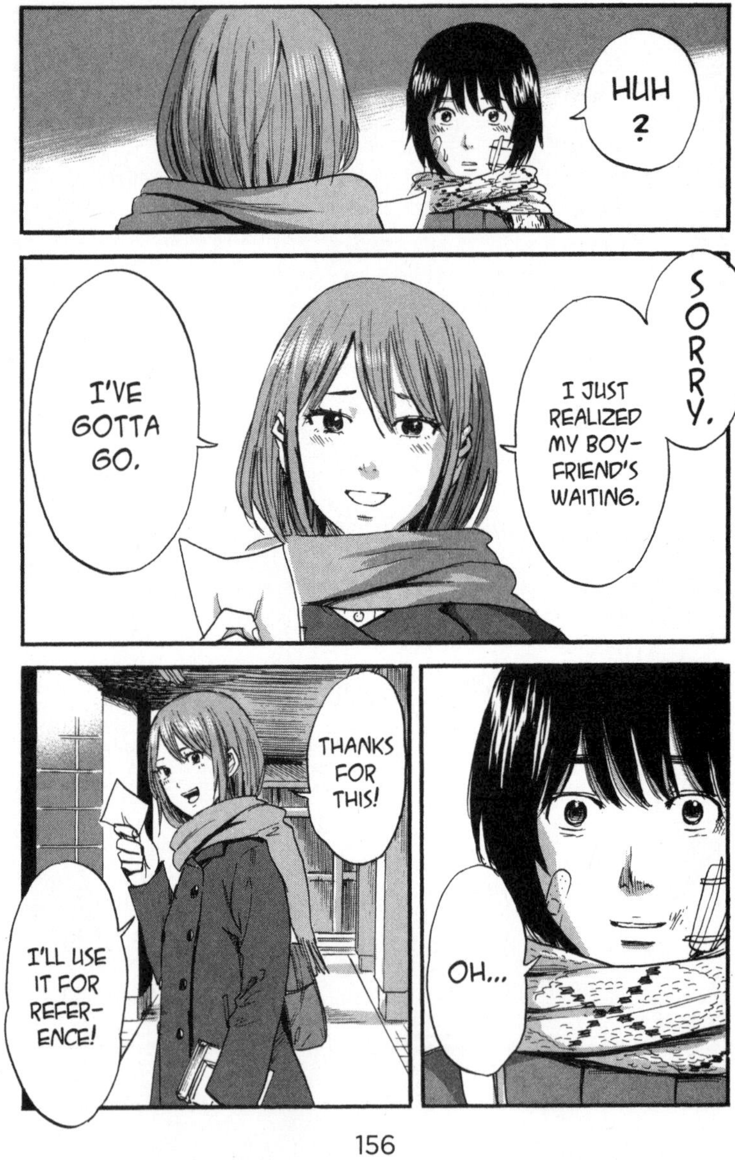
HUH?
SORRY.
I JUST REALIZED MY BOY-FRIEND'S WAITING.
I'VE GOTTA GO.
OH...
THANKS FOR THIS!
I'LL USE IT FOR REFER-ENCE!

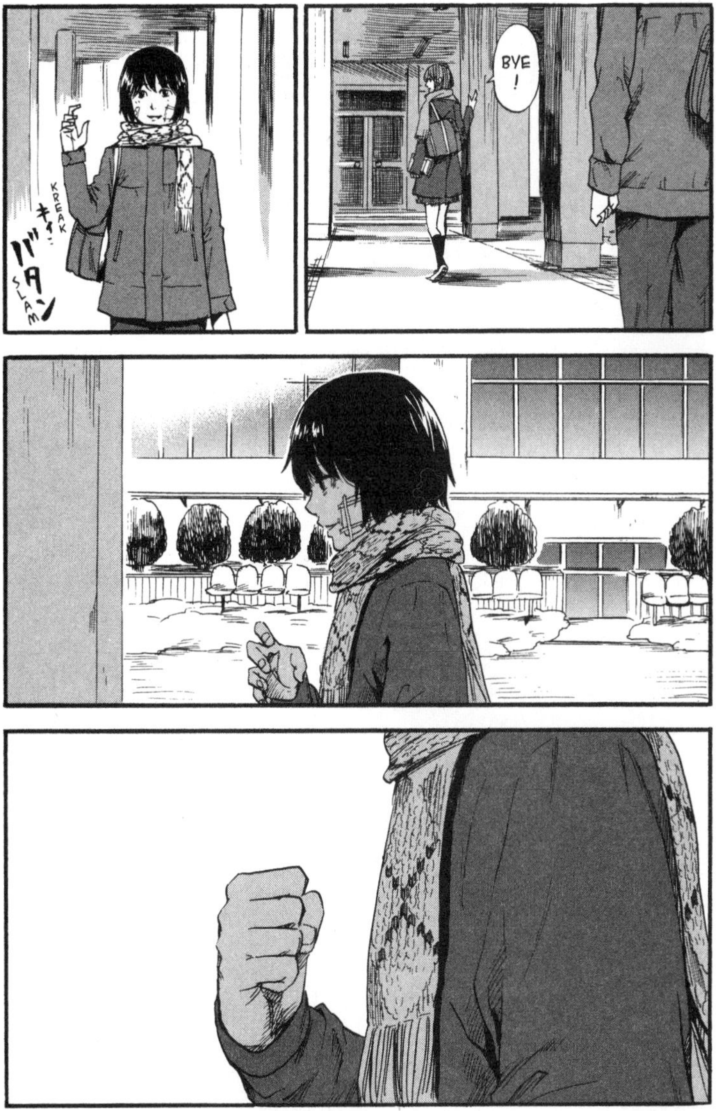
BYE!
KREAK
キィー
バタン
SLAM

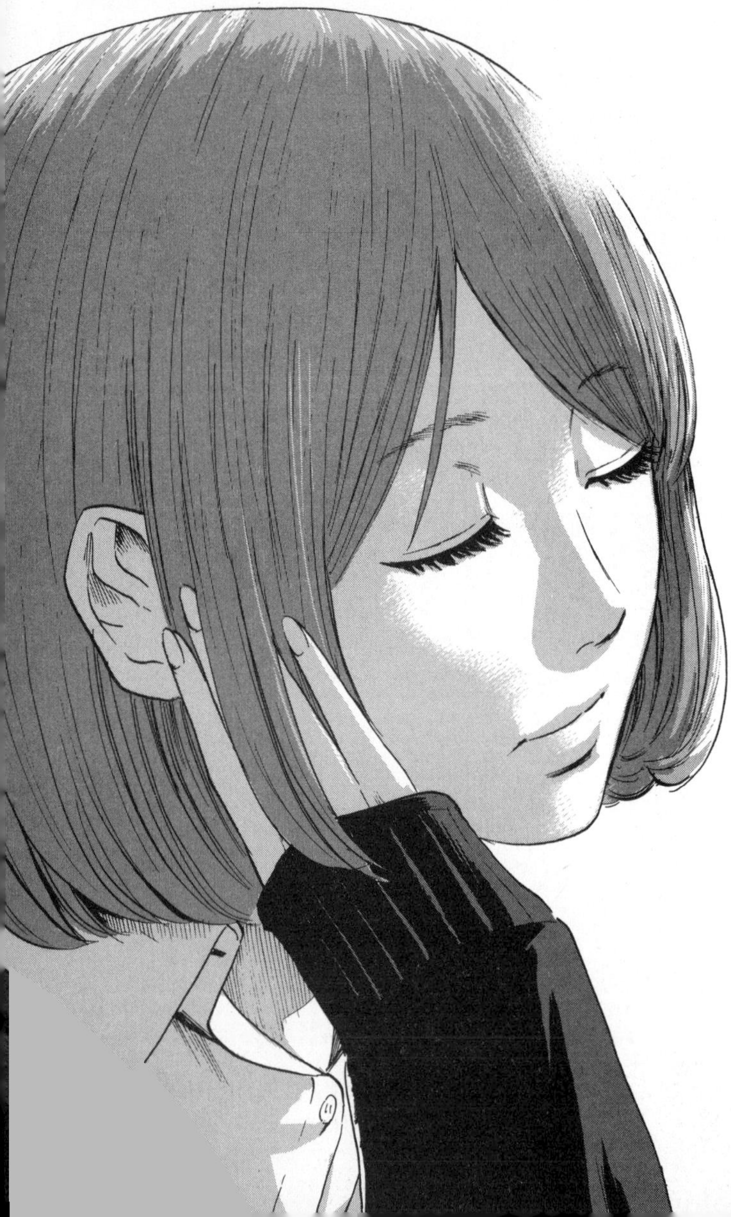

Chapter 37: Shafts of Winter Sunlight

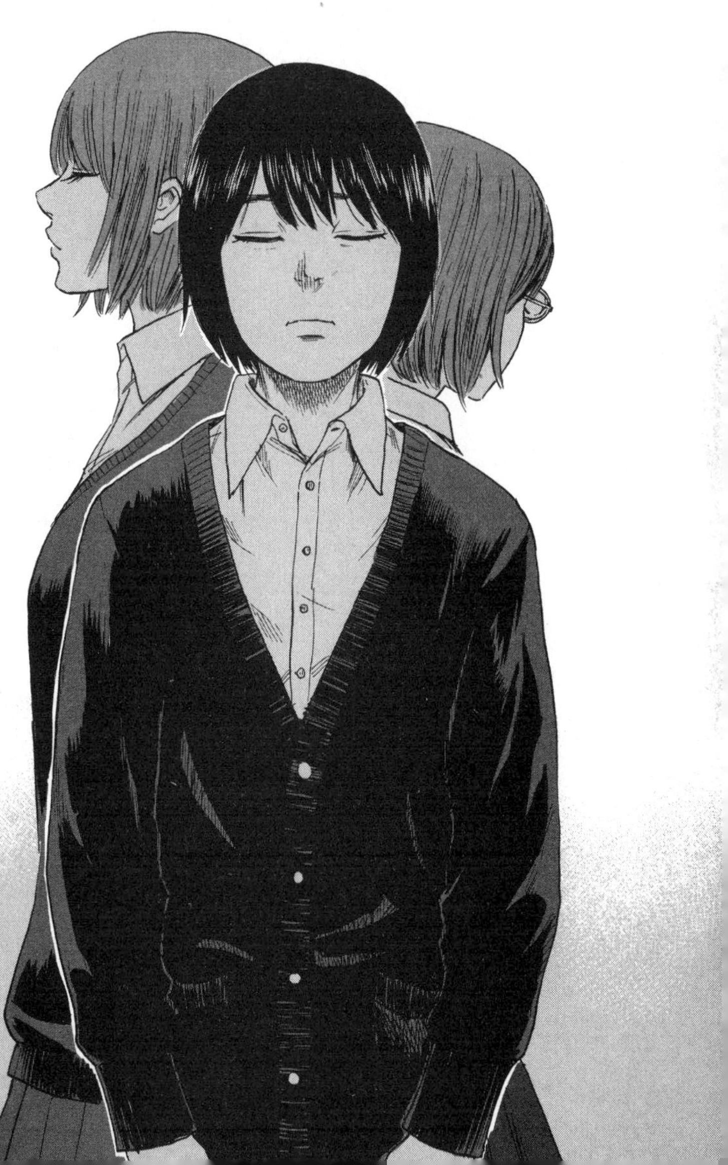

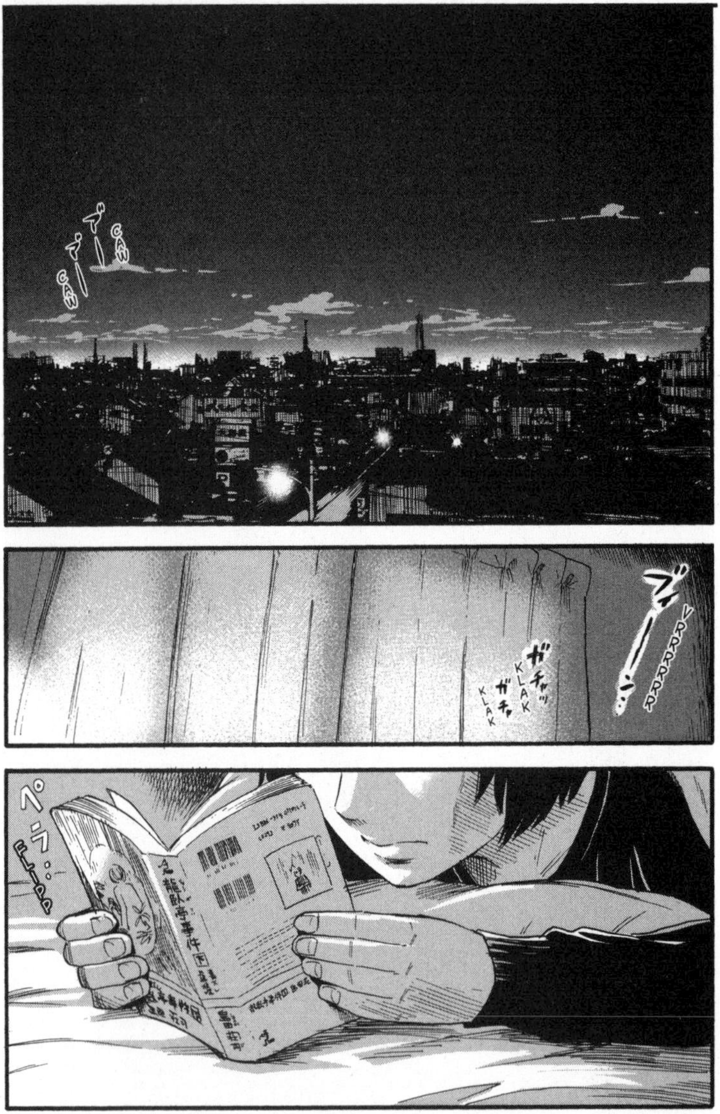
ア゛ー
CAW
ア゛ー
CAW
ブィー…!
VRRRRRRR
ガチャッ
KLAK
ガチャ
KLAK
ペラ…
FLIPP

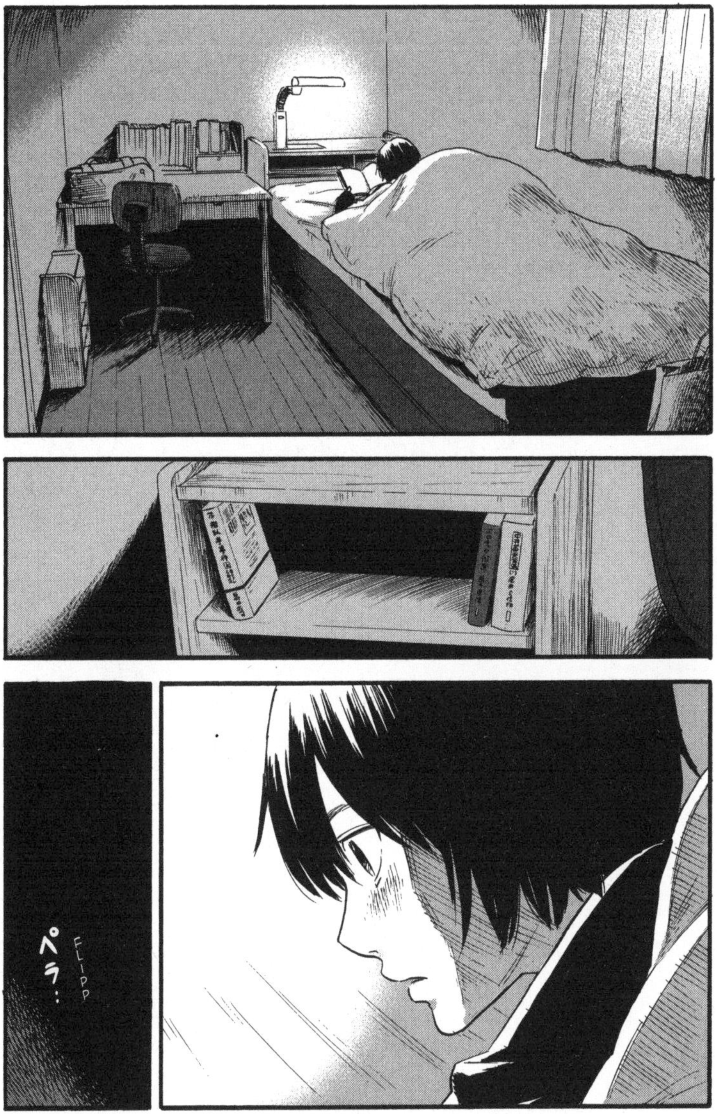
ペラ‥
FLIPP

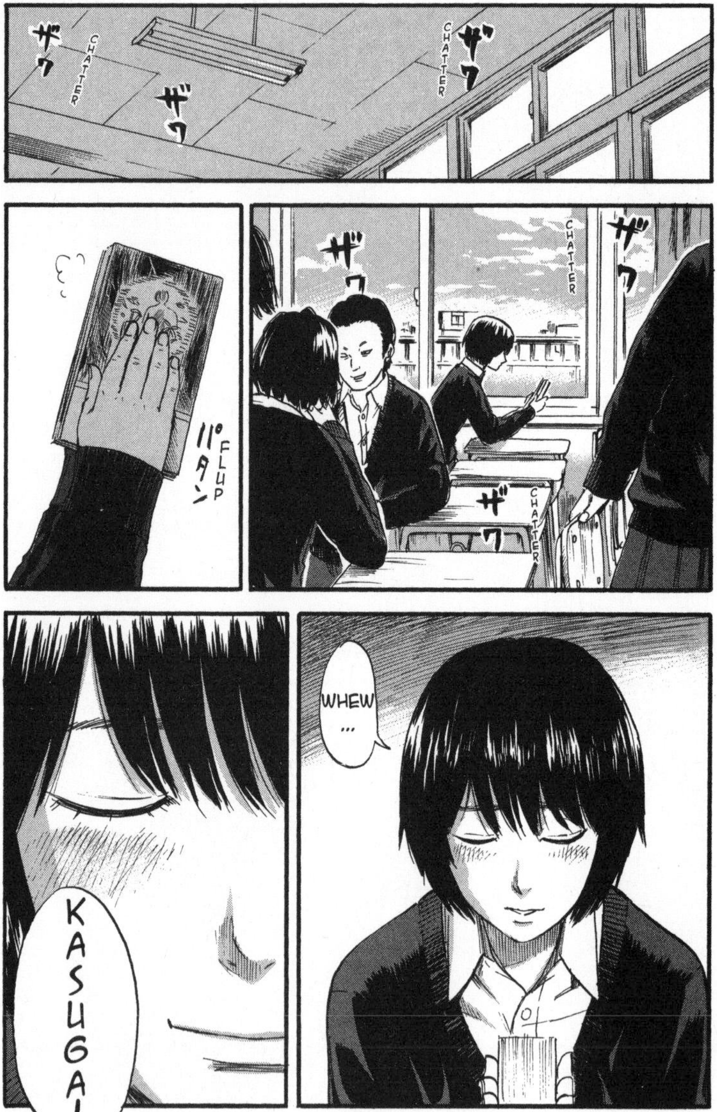
ザワ
CHATTER
ザワ
ザワ
CHATTER
ザワ
CHATTER
ザワ
ザワ
CHATTER
パタン
FLUP
WHEW ...
KASUGA!

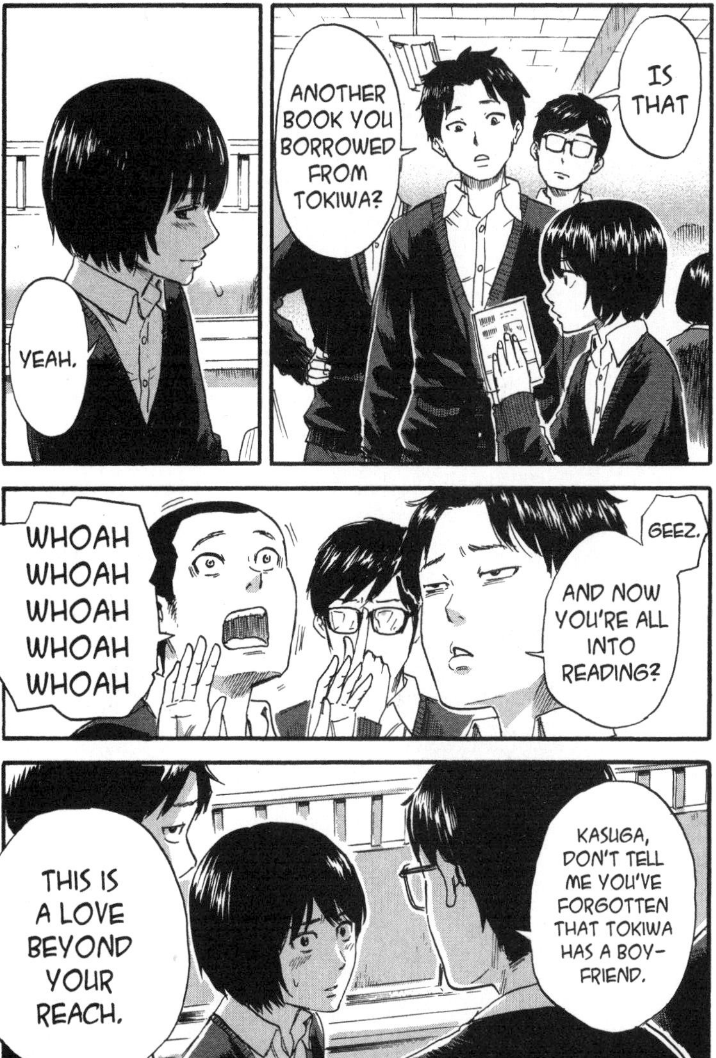
IS THAT
ANOTHER BOOK YOU BORROWED FROM TOKIWA?
YEAH.
GEEZ.
AND NOW YOU'RE ALL INTO READING?
WHOAH WHOAH WHOAH WHOAH WHOAH
KASUGA, DON'T TELL ME YOU'VE FORGOTTEN THAT TOKIWA HAS A BOY-FRIEND.
THIS IS A LOVE BEYOND YOUR REACH.

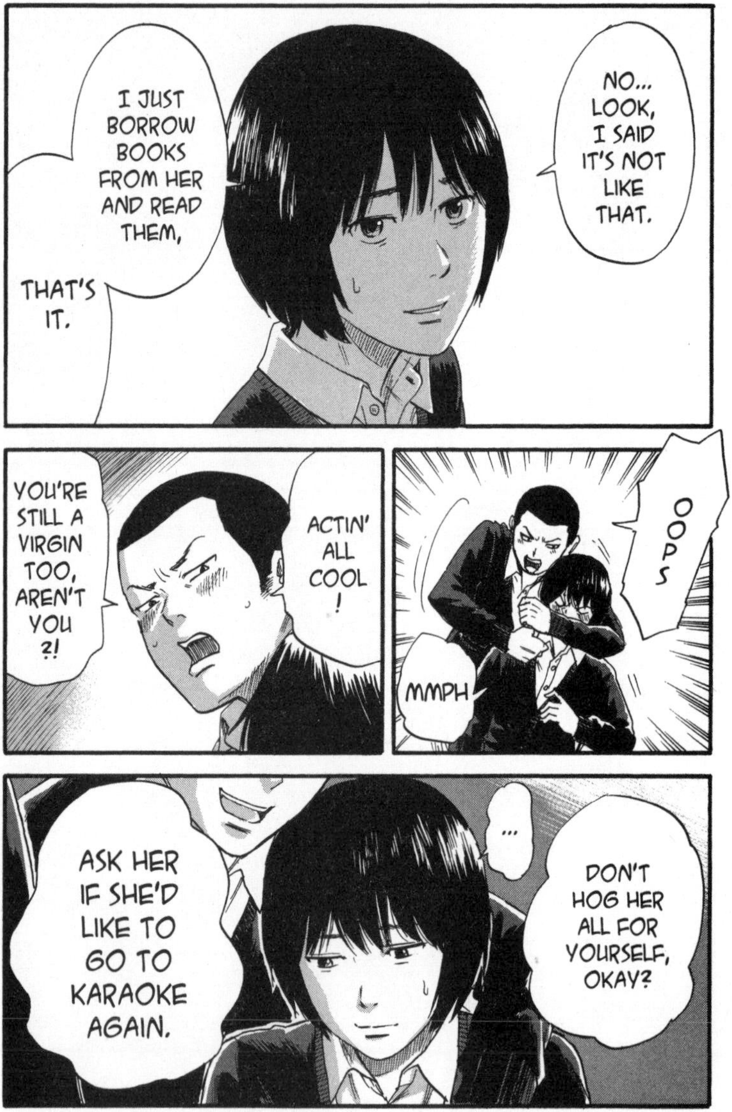
NO... LOOK, I SAID IT'S NOT LIKE THAT.
I JUST BORROW BOOKS FROM HER AND READ THEM,
THAT'S IT.
OOPS
MMPH
ACTIN' ALL COOL!
YOU'RE STILL A VIRGIN TOO, AREN'T YOU?!
...
DON'T HOG HER ALL FOR YOURSELF, OKAY?
ASK HER IF SHE'D LIKE TO GO TO KARAOKE AGAIN.

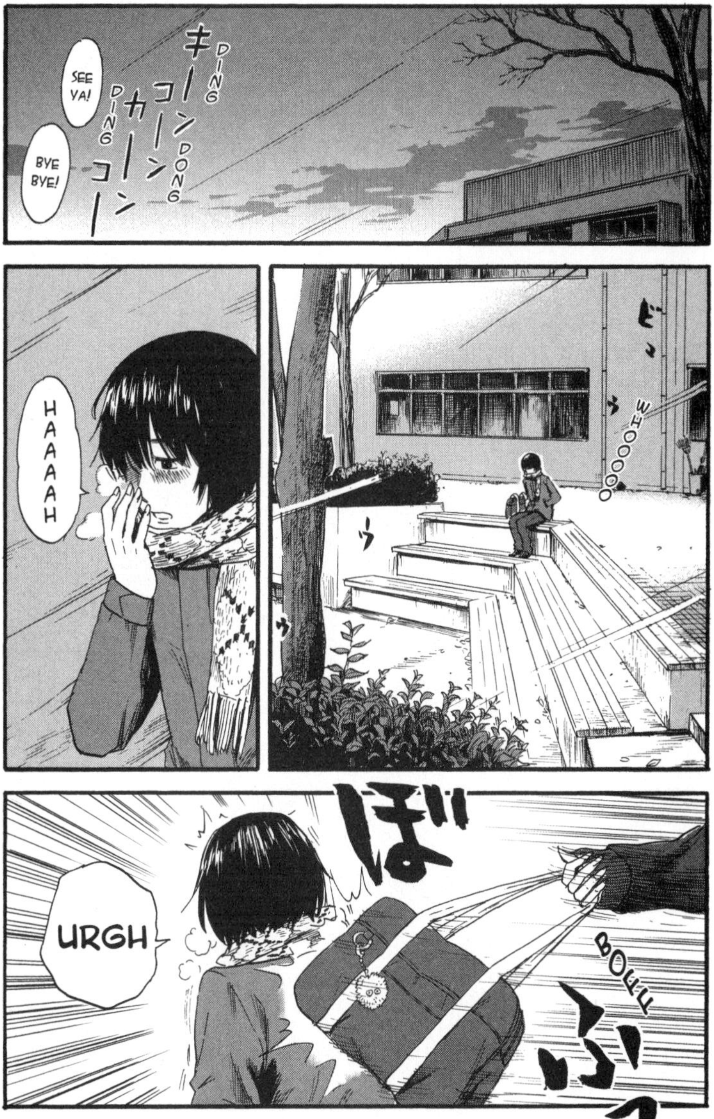
キーンコーンカーンコーン
DING DONG DING DONG
SEE YA!
BYE BYE!
WHOOOOOO
HAAAAAH
ぼ
BOUU
ぶへ
URGH

NYA HA HA HA HA.

"URGH."

DID YOU READ IT?

SO.

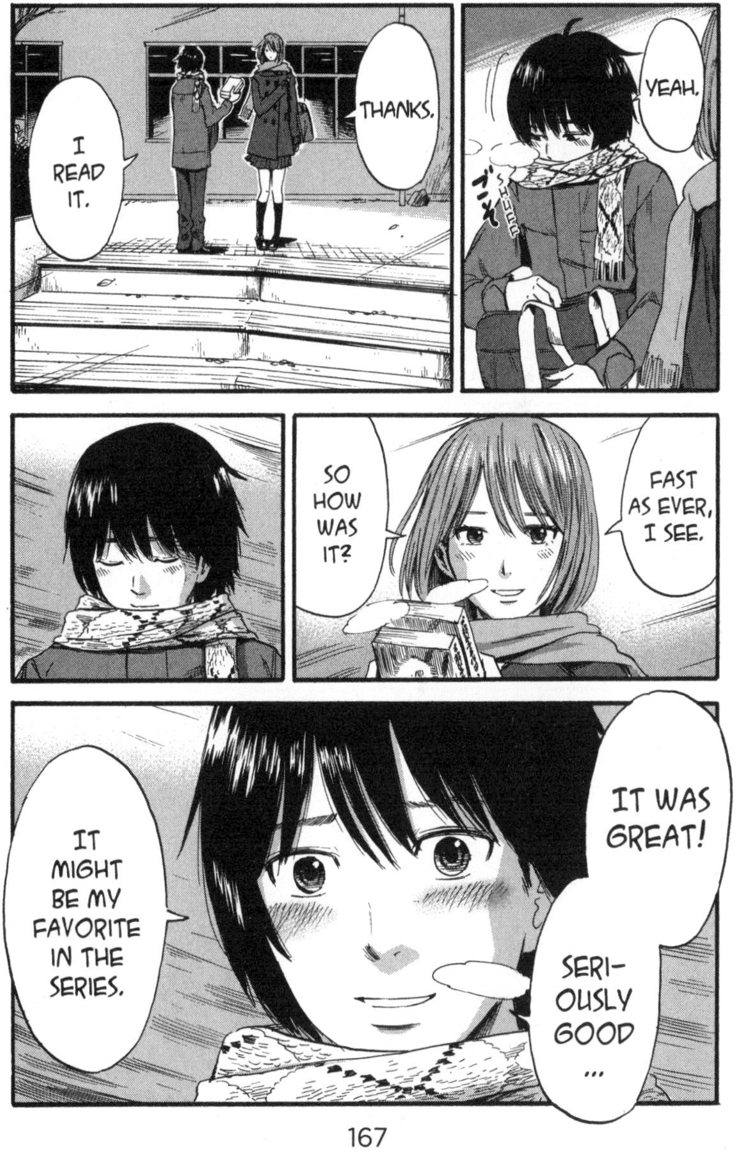
YEAH.
THANKS.
I READ IT.
FAST AS EVER, I SEE.
SO HOW WAS IT?
IT WAS GREAT!
SERI-OUSLY GOOD ...
IT MIGHT BE MY FAVORITE IN THE SERIES.

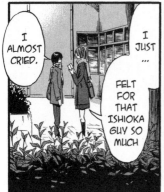

I KNOW, RIGHT?!
IT IS SOMETHING ELSE, ISN'T IT?
I JUST...
FELT FOR THAT ISHIOKA GUY SO MUCH
I ALMOST CRIED.
YEAH, I KNOW!
THAT SENSE OF BEING ABANDONED, OF BEING LEFT BEHIND!
BUT THEN HE SOLVES IT ON HIS OWN.
THAT PART'S JUST... REALLY TOP-NOTCH.
I KNOW, IT DOES MAKE YOU WANNA CRY!
AWW, I'M STARTING TO WANT TO READ IT AGAIN!

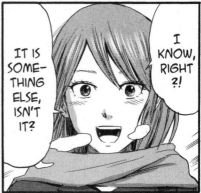

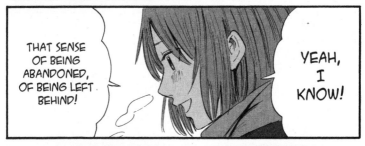

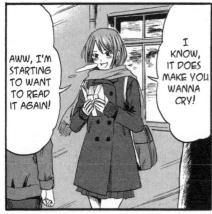

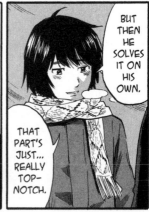

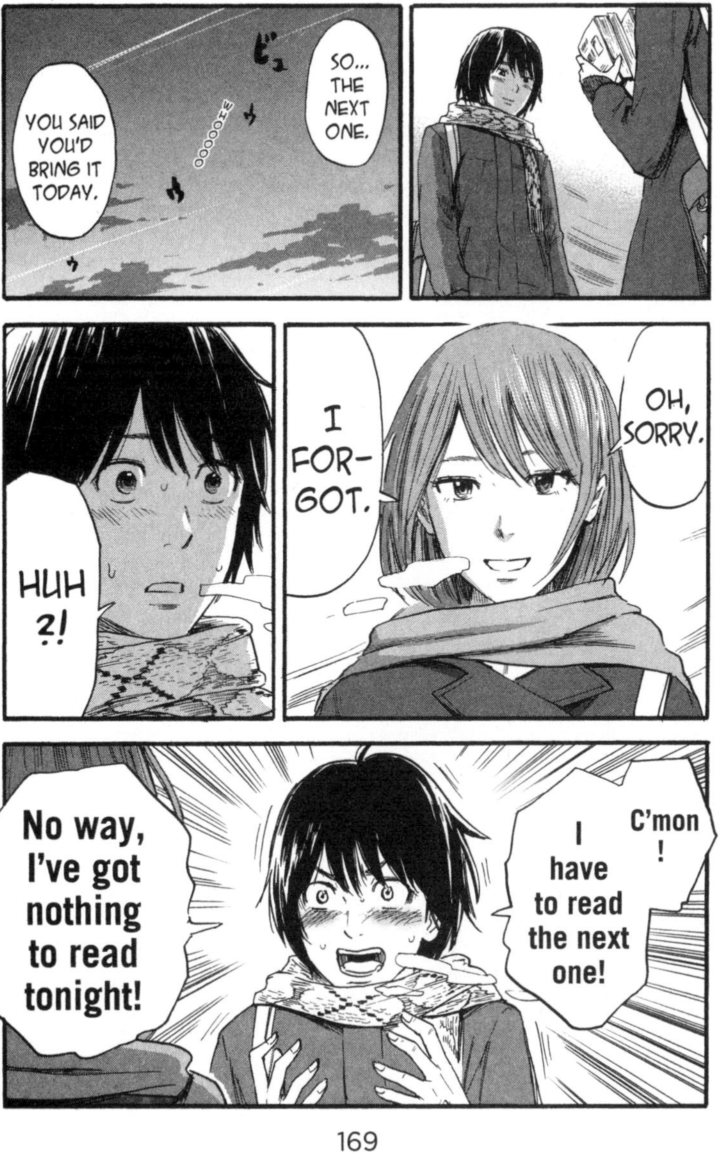
SO... THE NEXT ONE.
OOOOOOIE
YOU SAID YOU'D BRING IT TODAY.
OH, SORRY.
I FOR-GOT.
HUH ?!
C'mon!
I have to read the next one!
No way, I've got nothing to read tonight!

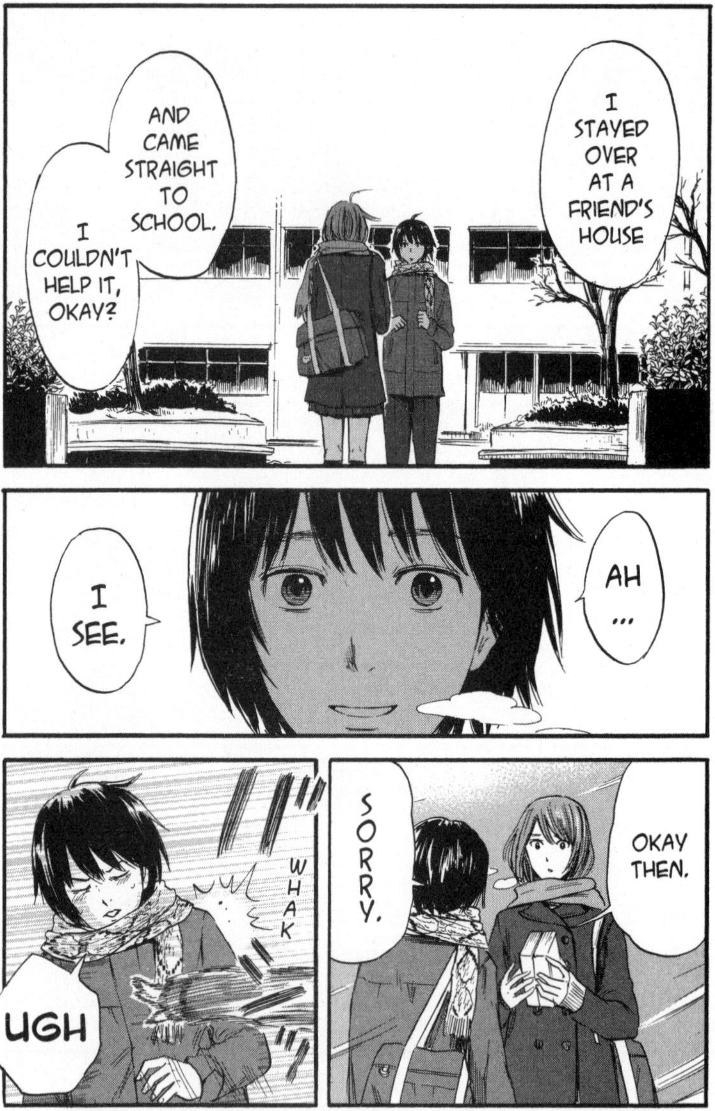
I STAYED OVER AT A FRIEND'S HOUSE
AND CAME STRAIGHT TO SCHOOL.
I COULDN'T HELP IT, OKAY?
AH ...
I SEE.
OKAY THEN.
SORRY.
WHAK
UGH

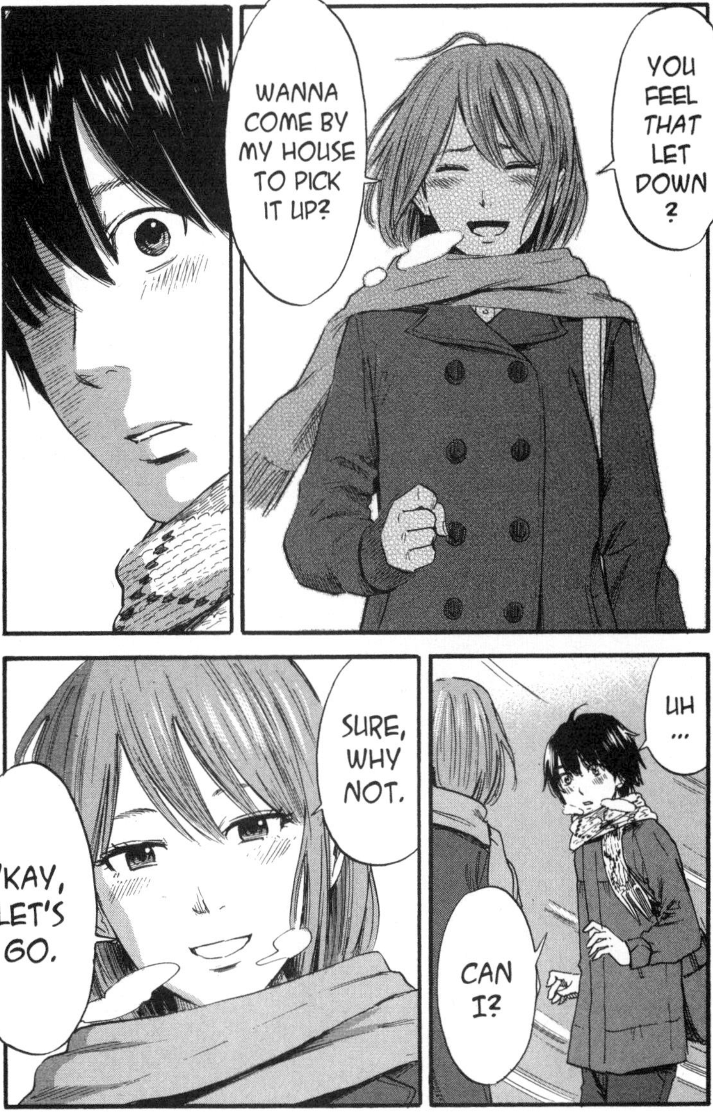
YOU FEEL THAT LET DOWN?
WANNA COME BY MY HOUSE TO PICK IT UP?
UH ...
CAN I?
SURE, WHY NOT.
'KAY, LET'S GO.

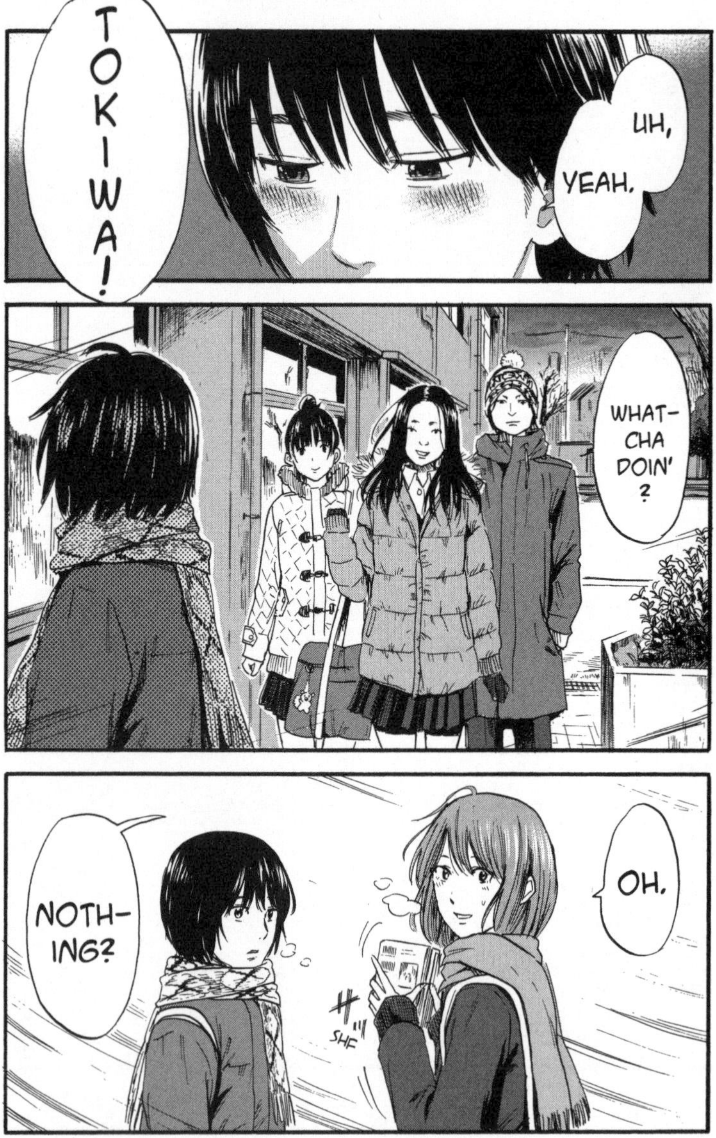
UH, YEAH.
TOKIWA!
WHAT-CHA DOIN'?
OH.
NOTH-ING?
SHF

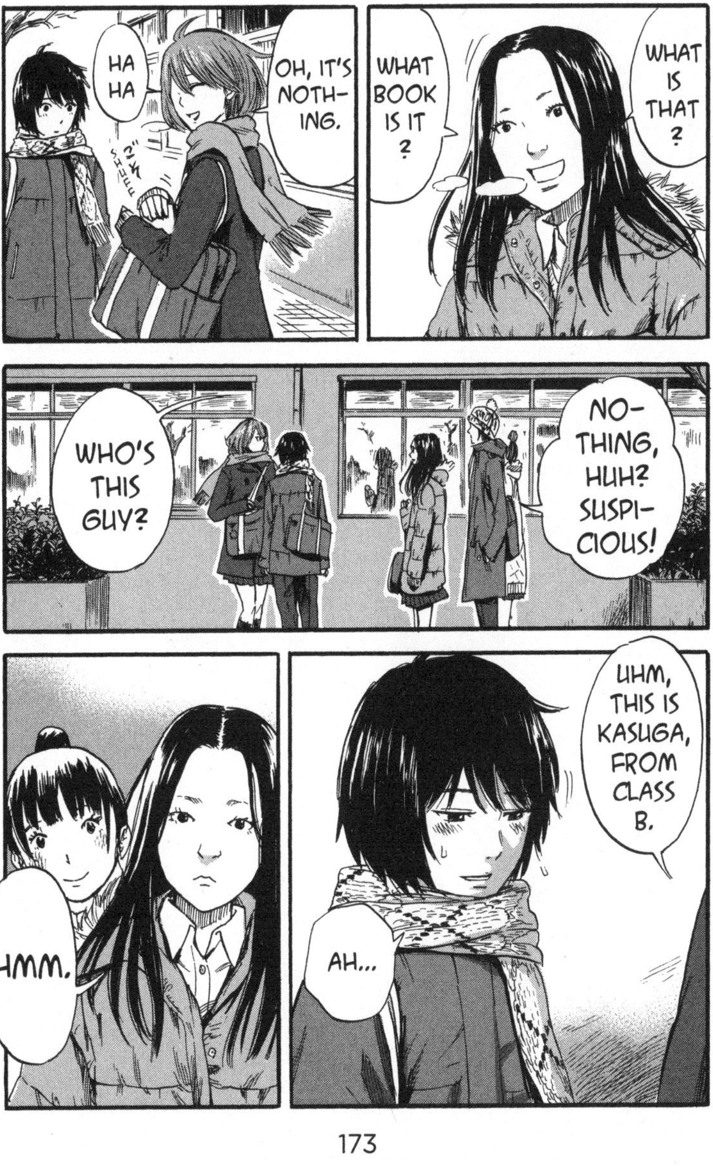
WHAT IS THAT?
WHAT BOOK IS IT?
OH, IT'S NOTHING.
HA HA
ごそ
SHUFFF
NO-THING, HUH? SUSPI-CIOUS!
WHO'S THIS GUY?
UHM, THIS IS KASUGA, FROM CLASS B.
AH...
HMM.

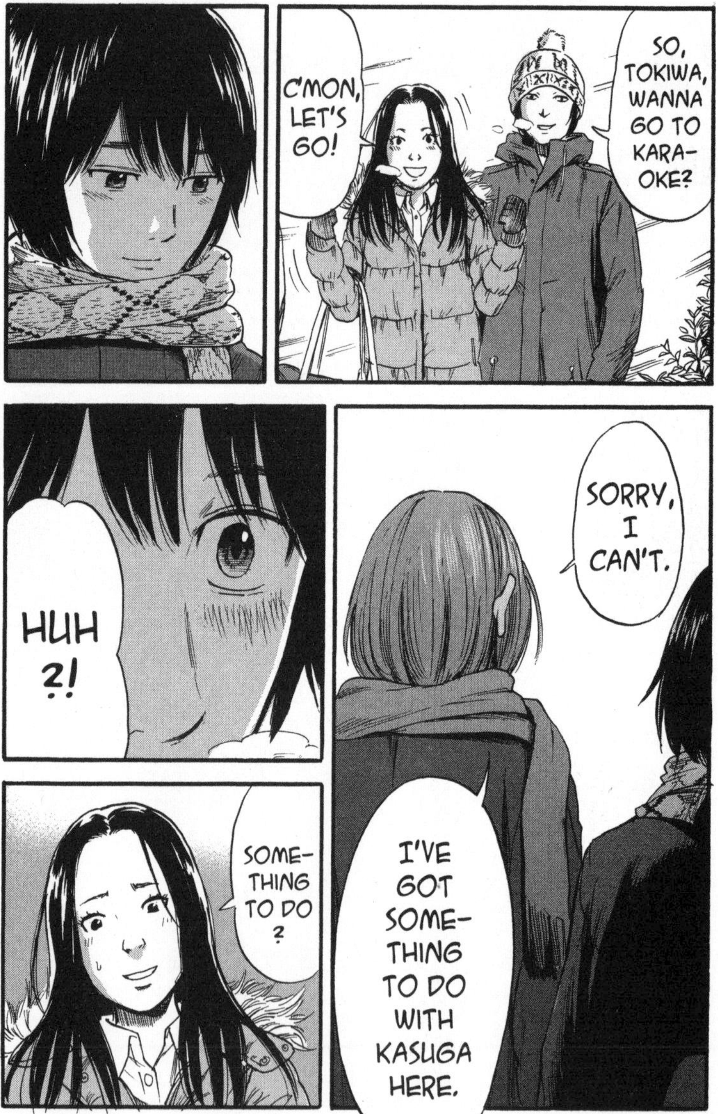
SO, TOKIWA, WANNA GO TO KARA-OKE?
C'MON, LET'S GO!
SORRY, I CAN'T.
I'VE GOT SOME-THING TO DO WITH KASUGA HERE.
HUH ?!
SOME-THING TO DO ?

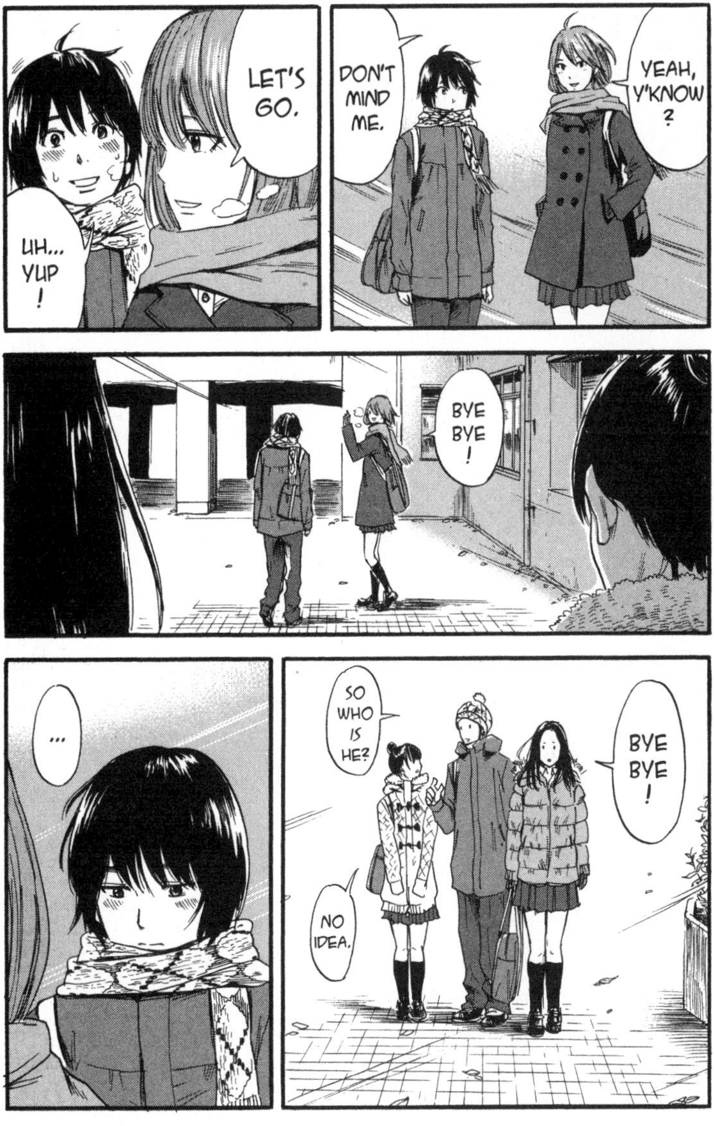
YEAH, Y'KNOW ?
DON'T MIND ME.
LET'S GO.
UH... YUP !
BYE BYE !
BYE BYE !
SO WHO IS HE?
NO IDEA.
...

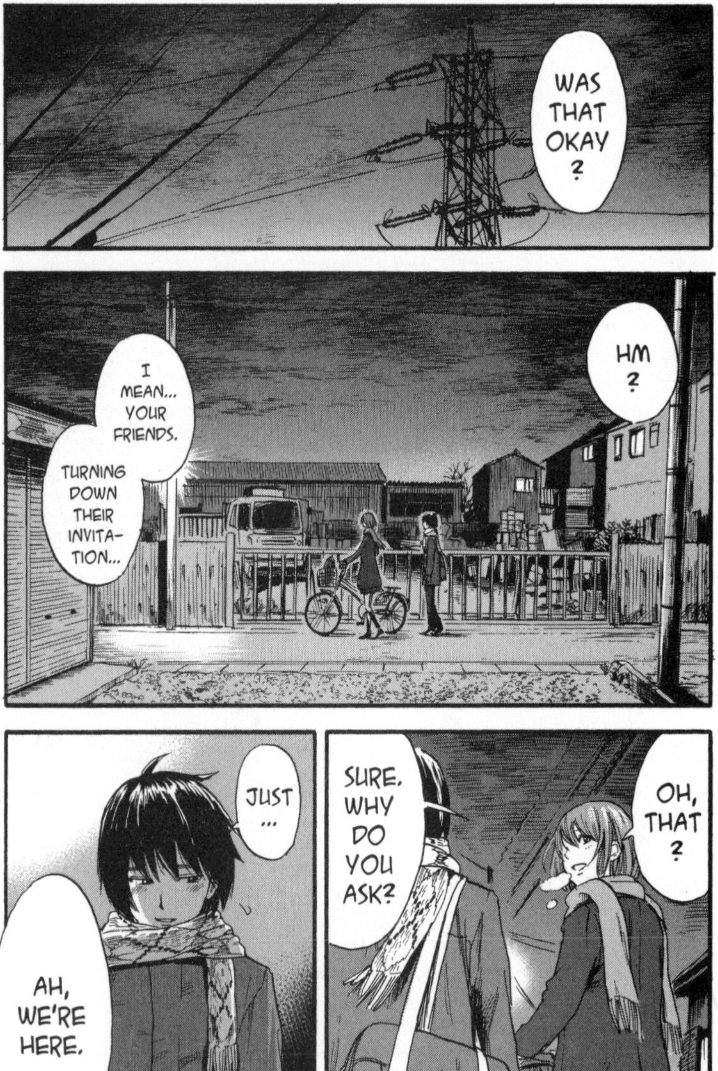
WAS THAT OKAY?
HM?
I MEAN... YOUR FRIENDS.
TURNING DOWN THEIR INVITATION...
OH, THAT?
SURE. WHY DO YOU ASK?
JUST...
AH, WE'RE HERE.

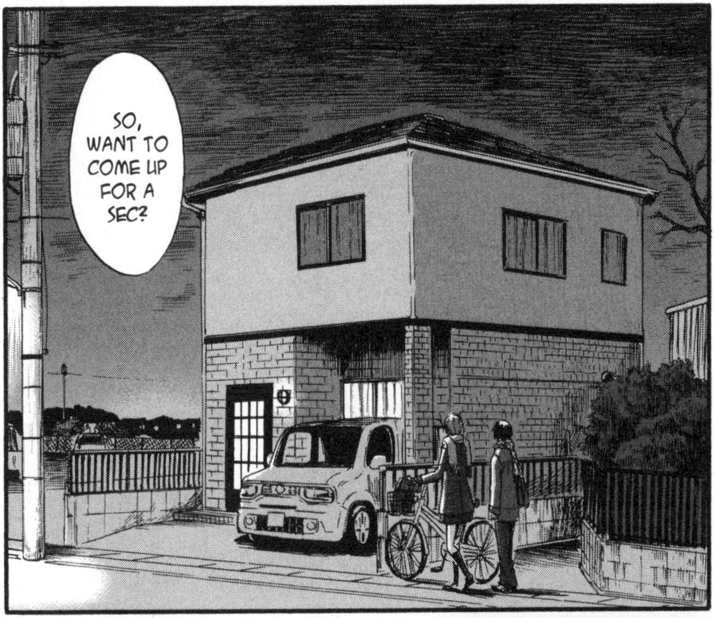
SO, WANT TO COME UP FOR A SEC?
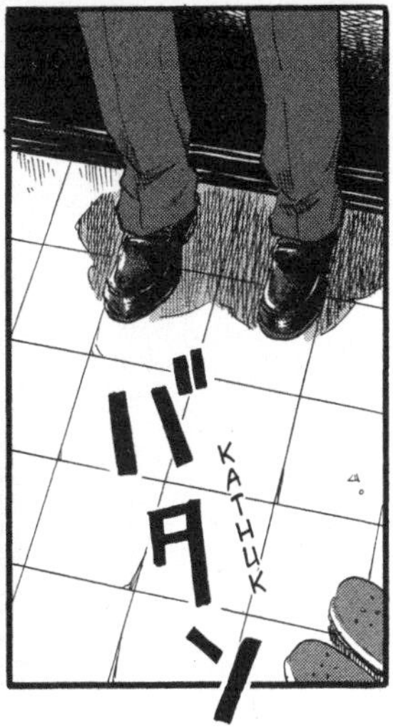
バタン
KATHUK
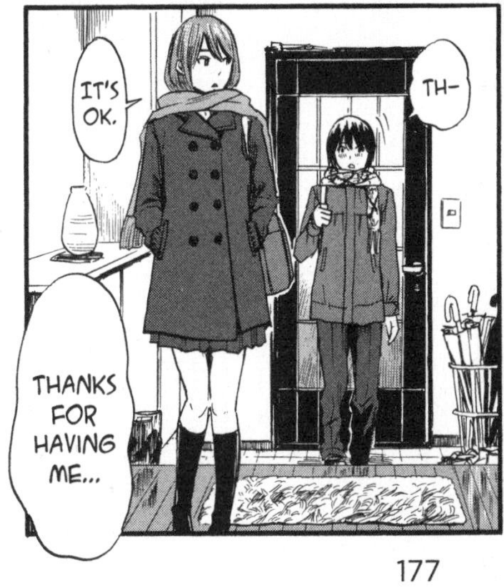
TH-
IT'S OK.
THANKS FOR HAVING ME...

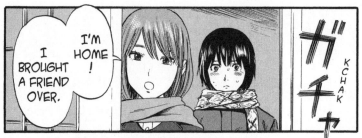

ガチャ
KCHAK
I'M HOME!
I BROUGHT A FRIEND OVER.
OH, MY.
WEL-COME.
UH... HI.
PARDON THE INTRU-SION.
MY ROOM'S UP-STAIRS.
C'MON UP.

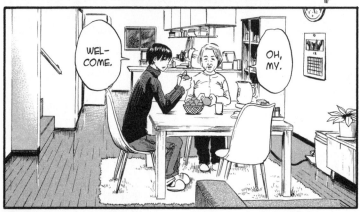

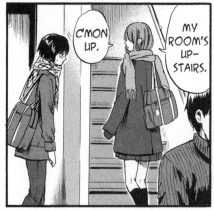

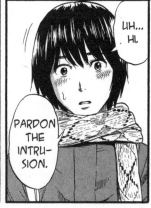

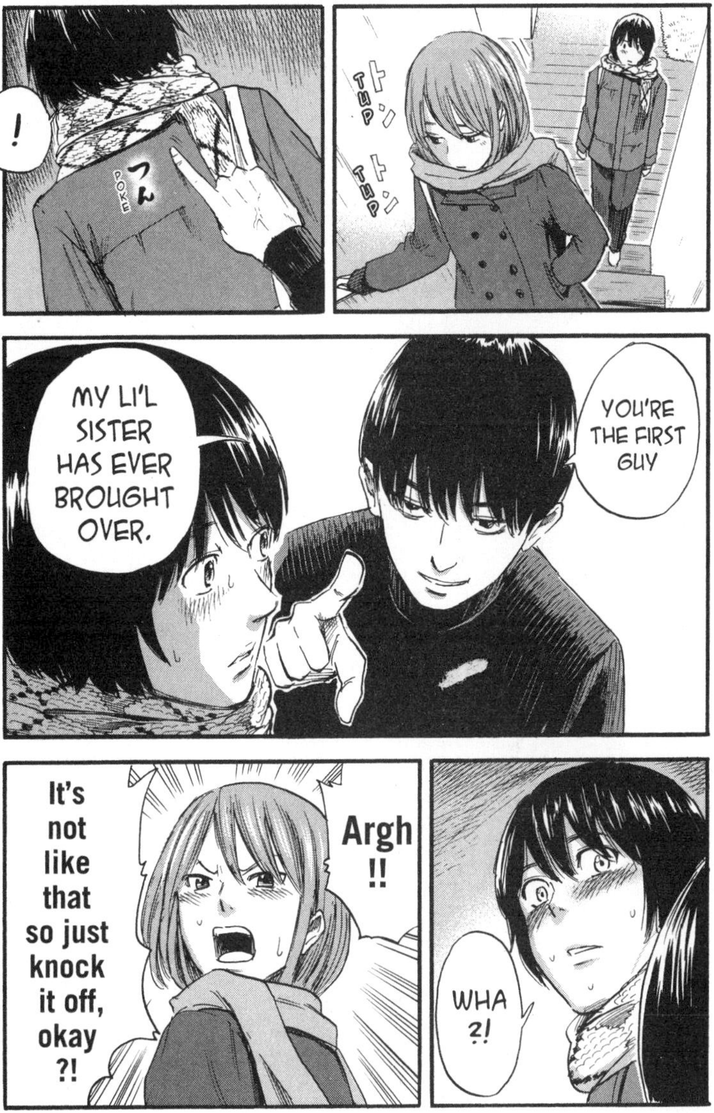
トン TUP
トン TUP
!
つん POKE
YOU'RE THE FIRST GUY
MY LI'L SISTER HAS EVER BROUGHT OVER.
WHA ?!
Argh !!
It's not like that so just knock it off, okay ?!

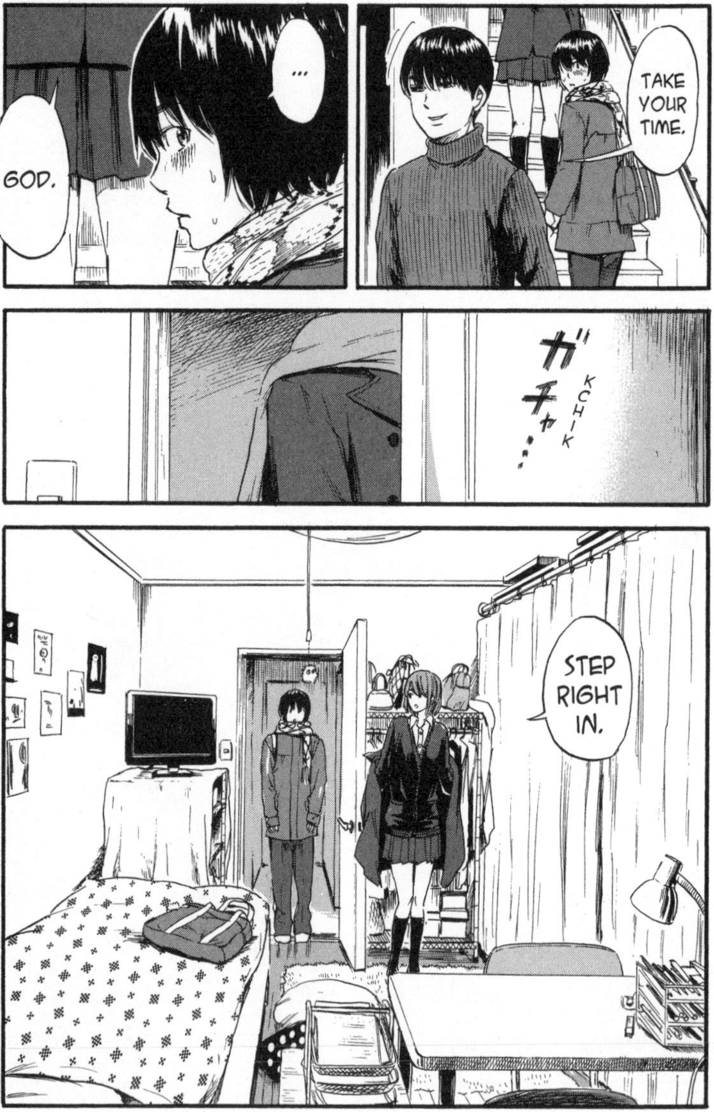
TAKE YOUR TIME.
...
GOD.
ガチャ…
KCHIK
STEP RIGHT IN.

HOLLYWOOD
GHOST WORLD
JUST SIT WHEREVER.
...
NOW ...
TOTT
とて
TOTT
とて
SWISH

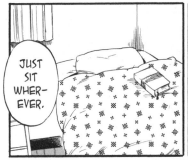

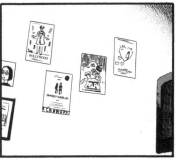

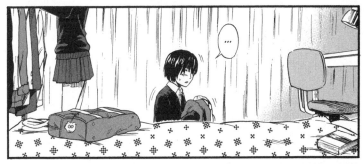

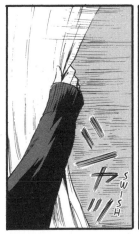

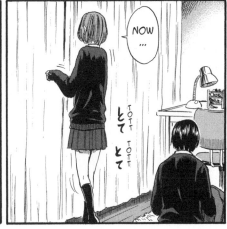

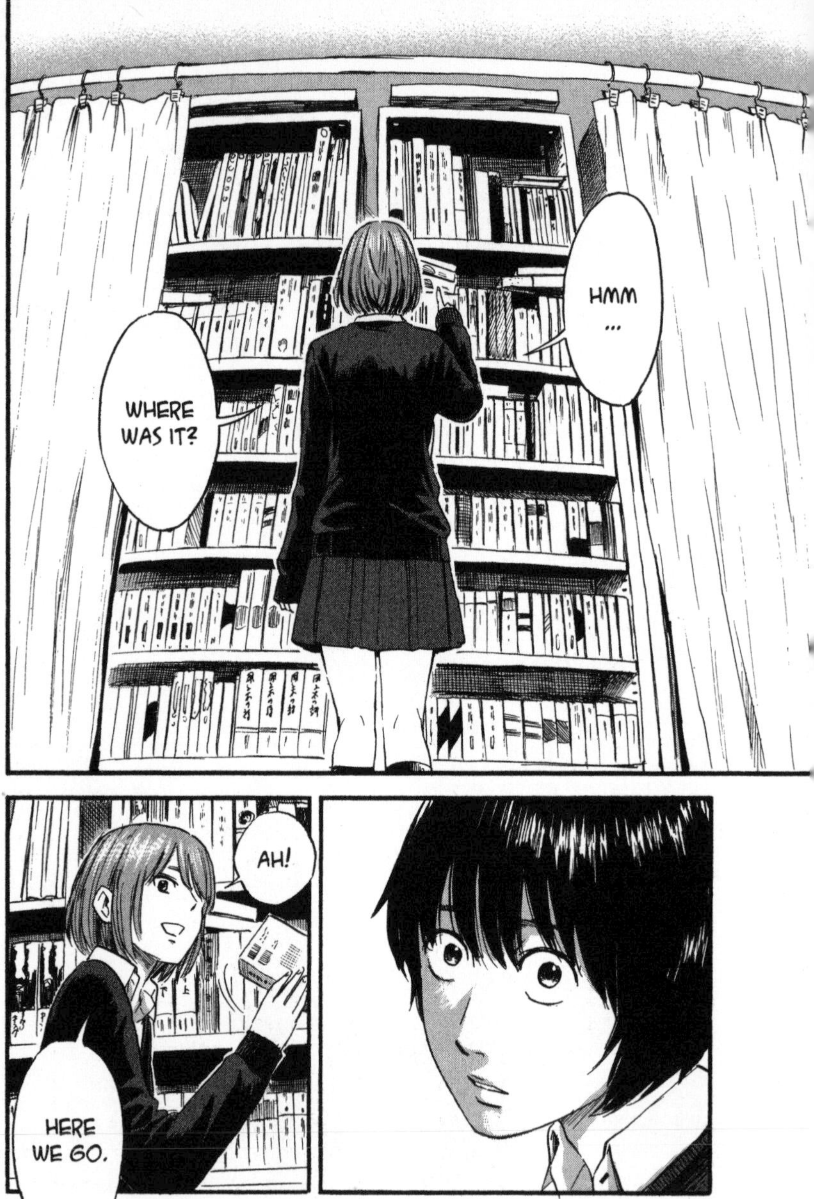
HMM ...
WHERE WAS IT?
AH!
HERE WE GO.

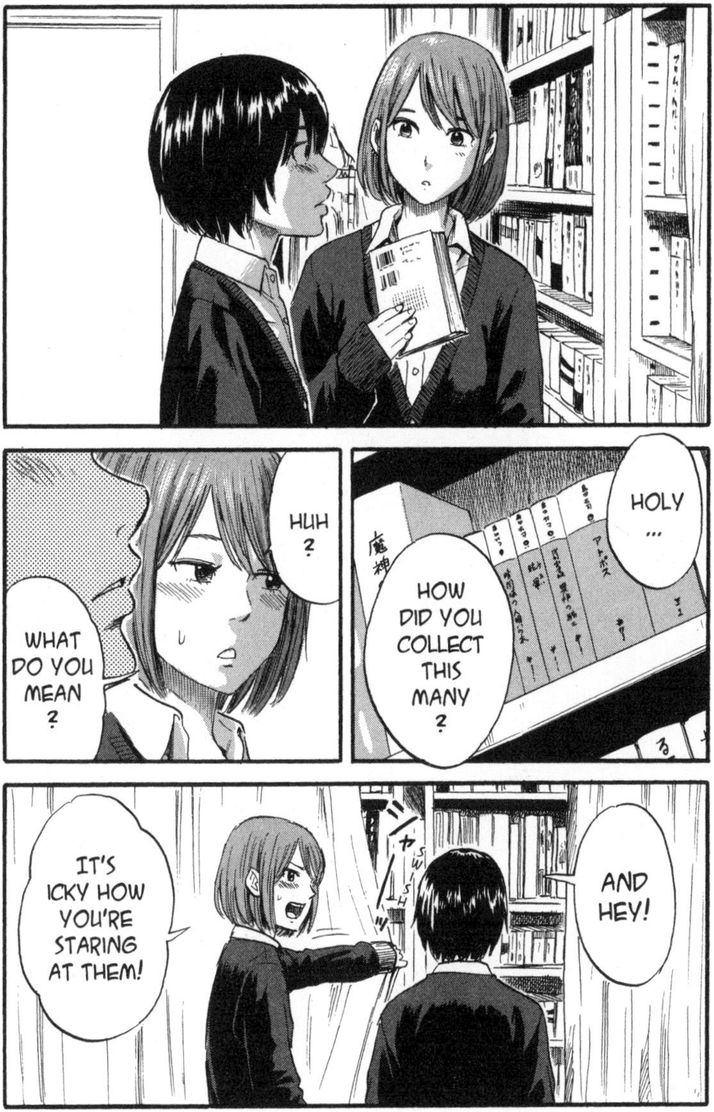
HOLY ...
HOW DID YOU COLLECT THIS MANY?
HUH?
WHAT DO YOU MEAN?
AND HEY!
SWISH
IT'S ICKY HOW YOU'RE STARING AT THEM!

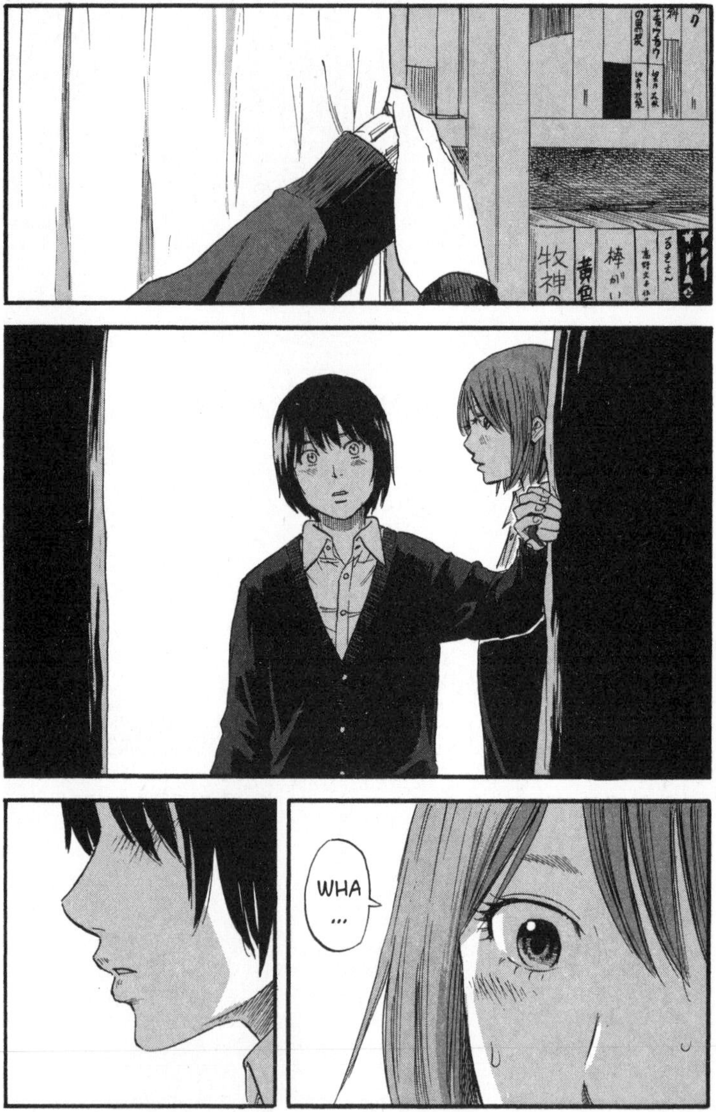
WHA ...

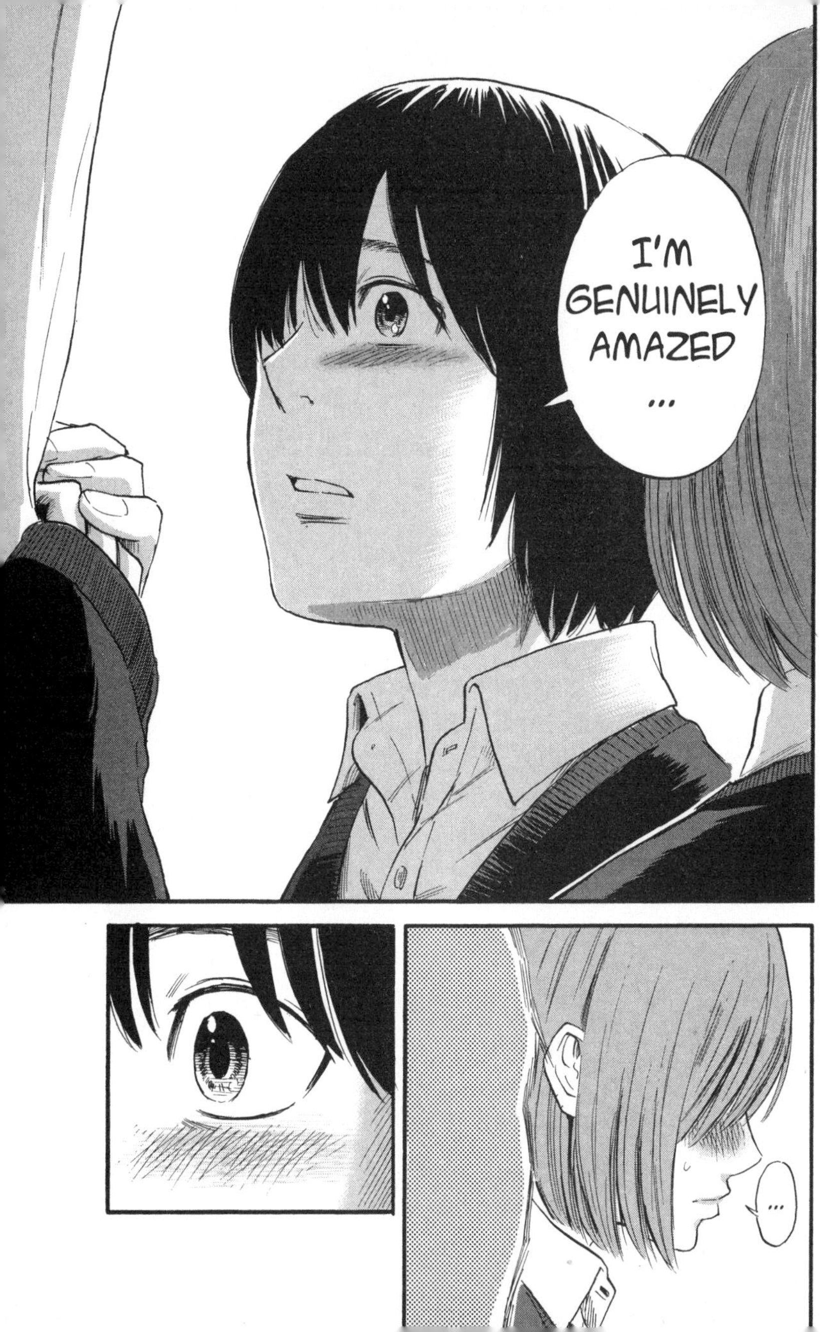
I'M GENUINELY AMAZED ...
...

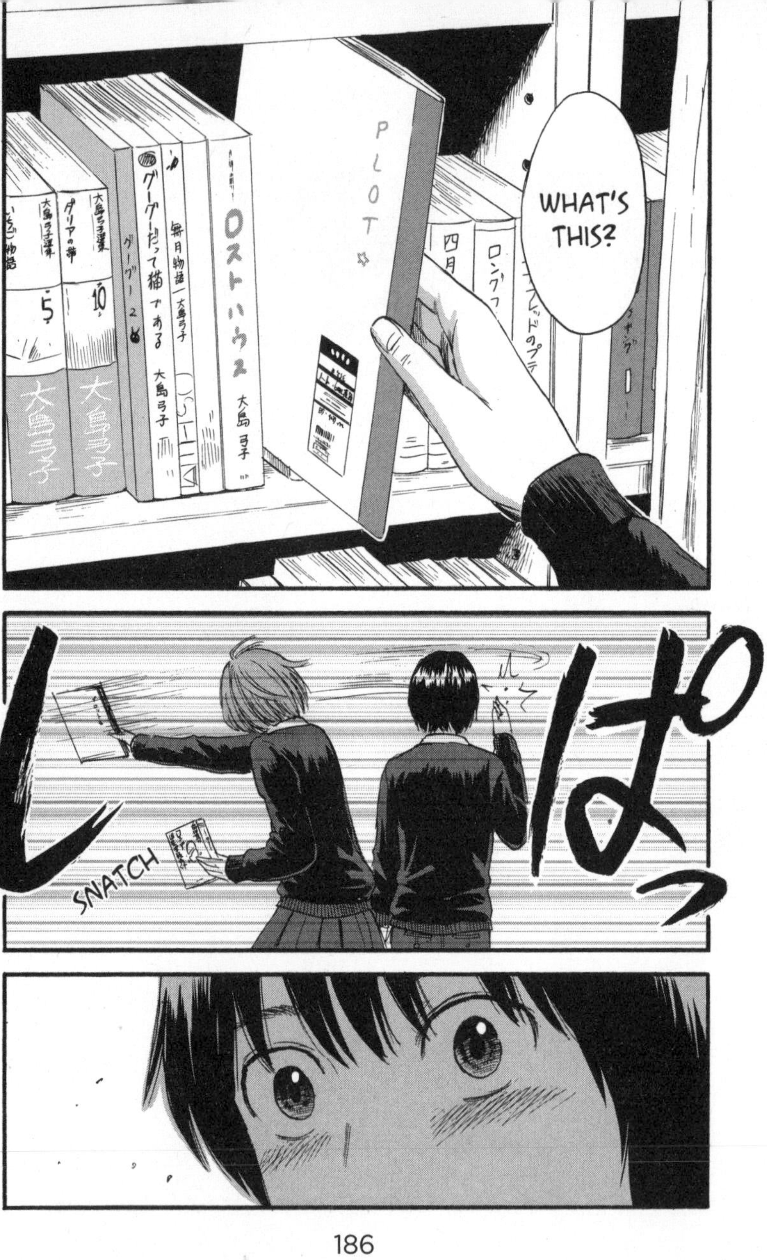
PLOT
WHAT'S THIS?
しぱっ
SNATCH

THIS ONE IS

OFF-LIMITS.

IS IT

SOMETHING YOU WROTE, TOKIWA?

BY ANY CHANCE...

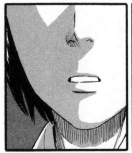

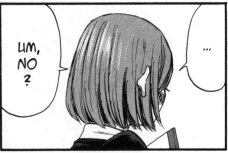

...
UM, NO?
SHOW ME! WHAT IS IT?
DON'T TELL ME IT'S A NOVEL!!
N—
I SAID NO, ALL RIGHT?!

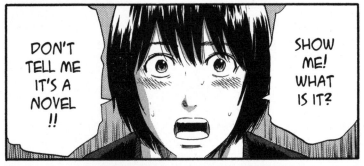

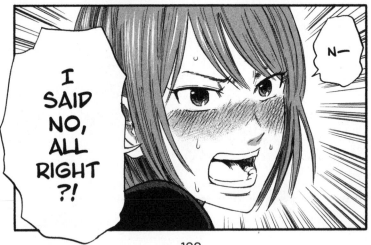

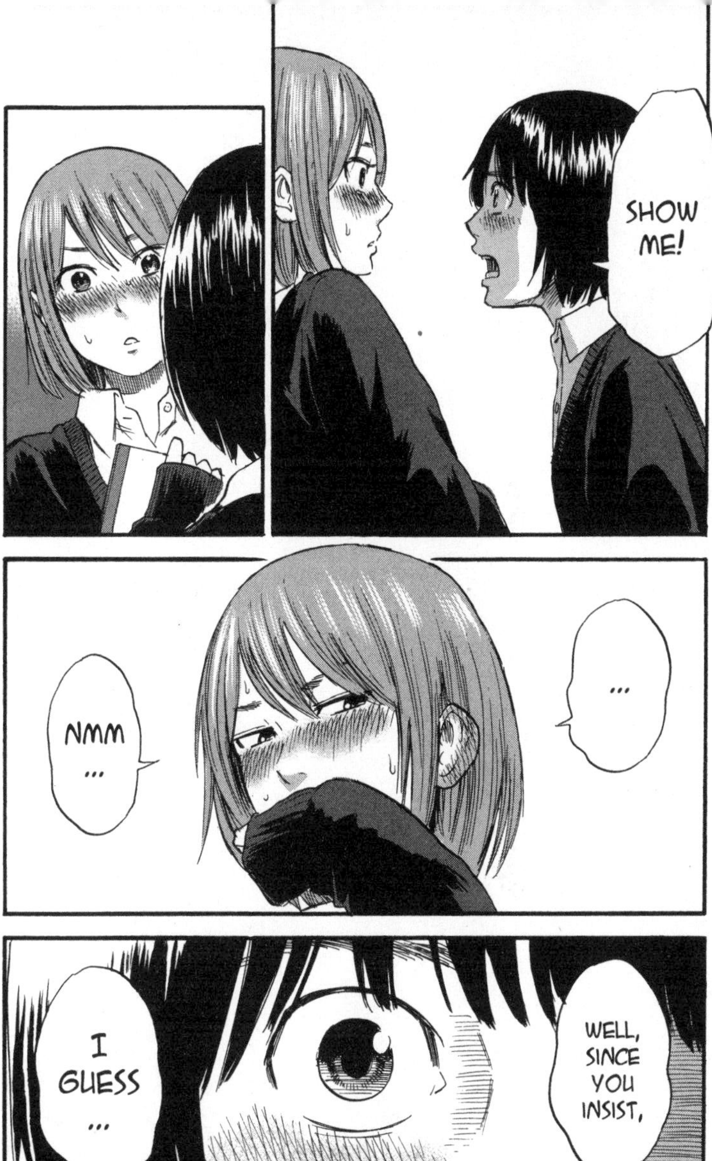
SHOW ME!
...
NMM ...
WELL, SINCE YOU INSIST,
I GUESS ...

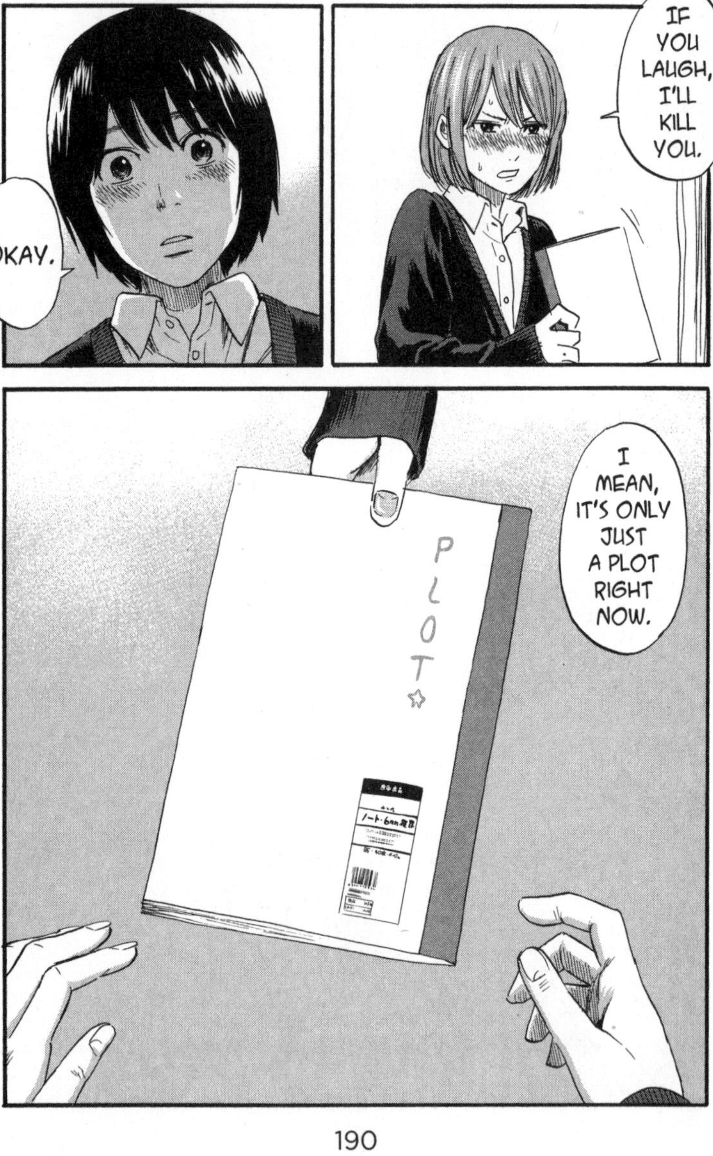
IF YOU LAUGH, I'LL KILL YOU.
OKAY.
I MEAN, IT'S ONLY JUST A PLOT RIGHT NOW.
PLOT

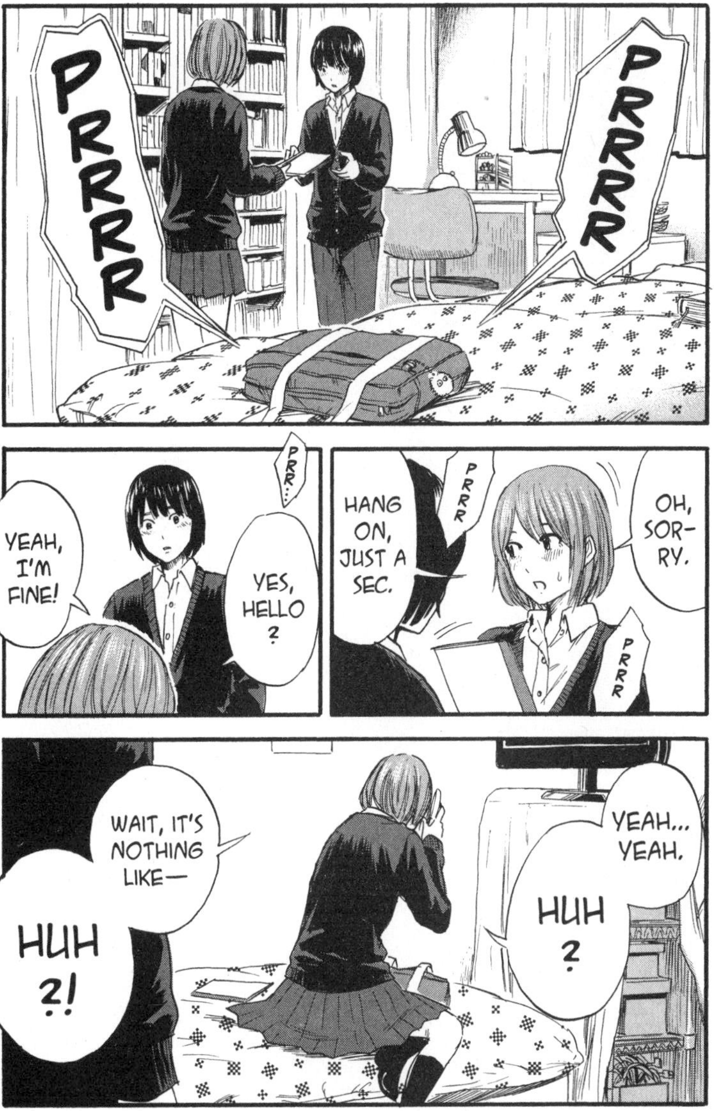
PRRRR
PRRRR
OH, SOR-RY.
PRRR
HANG ON, JUST A SEC.
PRRR
PRR...
YES, HELLO?
YEAH, I'M FINE!
YEAH... YEAH.
HUH?
WAIT, IT'S NOTHING LIKE—
HUH?!

どた
STOMP
どた
STOMP
どた
STOMP
カララ…
RATTLE
WHOOO
OH.
WHOOO
UH, KASUGA
MY BAD ...

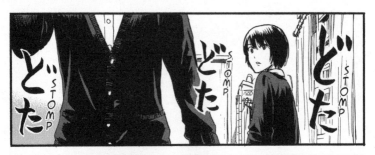

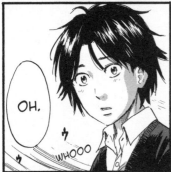

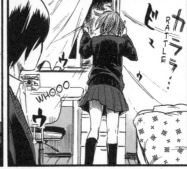

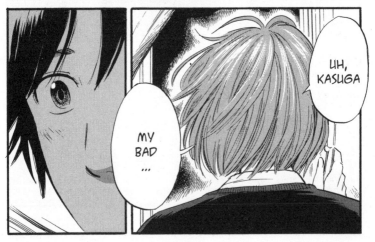

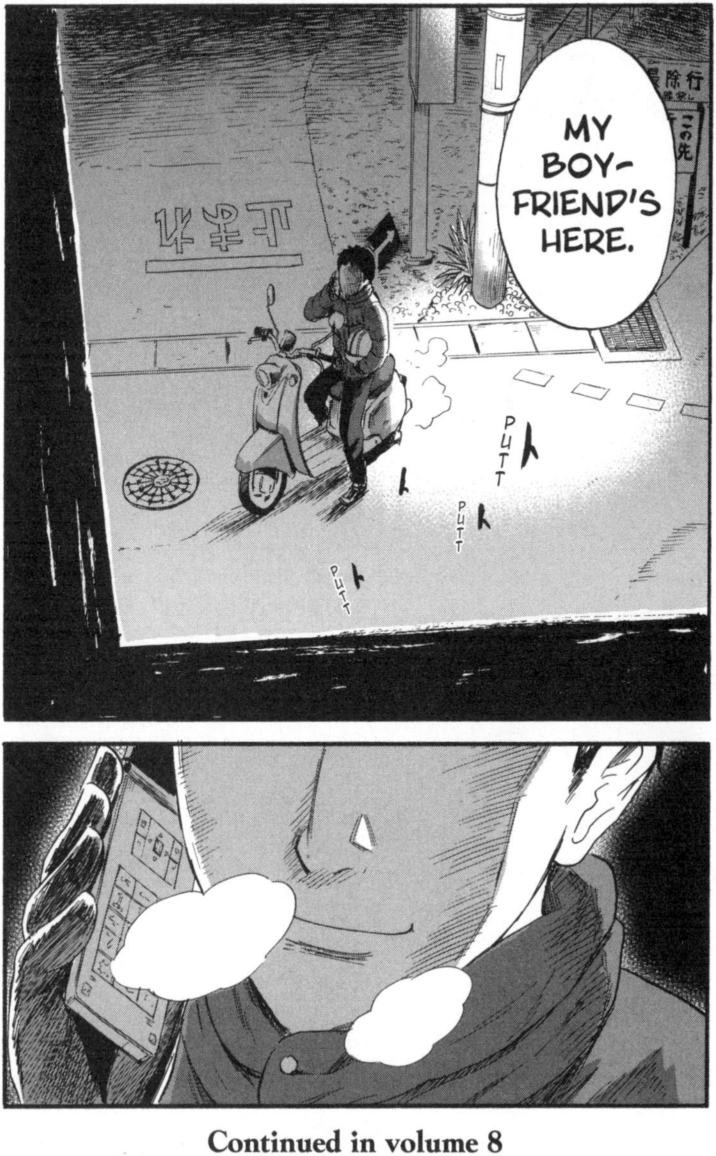
MY BOY-FRIEND'S HERE.
PUTT
PUTT
PUTT

Continued in volume 8

DESPAIR!!

When college freshman and future
psychotherapist Kazuma Futaba
responds to a curious call for a
room to let, he ends up living
in a mansion owned by Emiru,
a frail beauty his own age.

Although neighborhood kids
call the place haunted,
if anything the young mistress
nurses a darker affliction in
this thoughtful diptych.

PART 1 Of 2 NOW AVAILABLE
WHEREVER BOOKS ARE SOLD

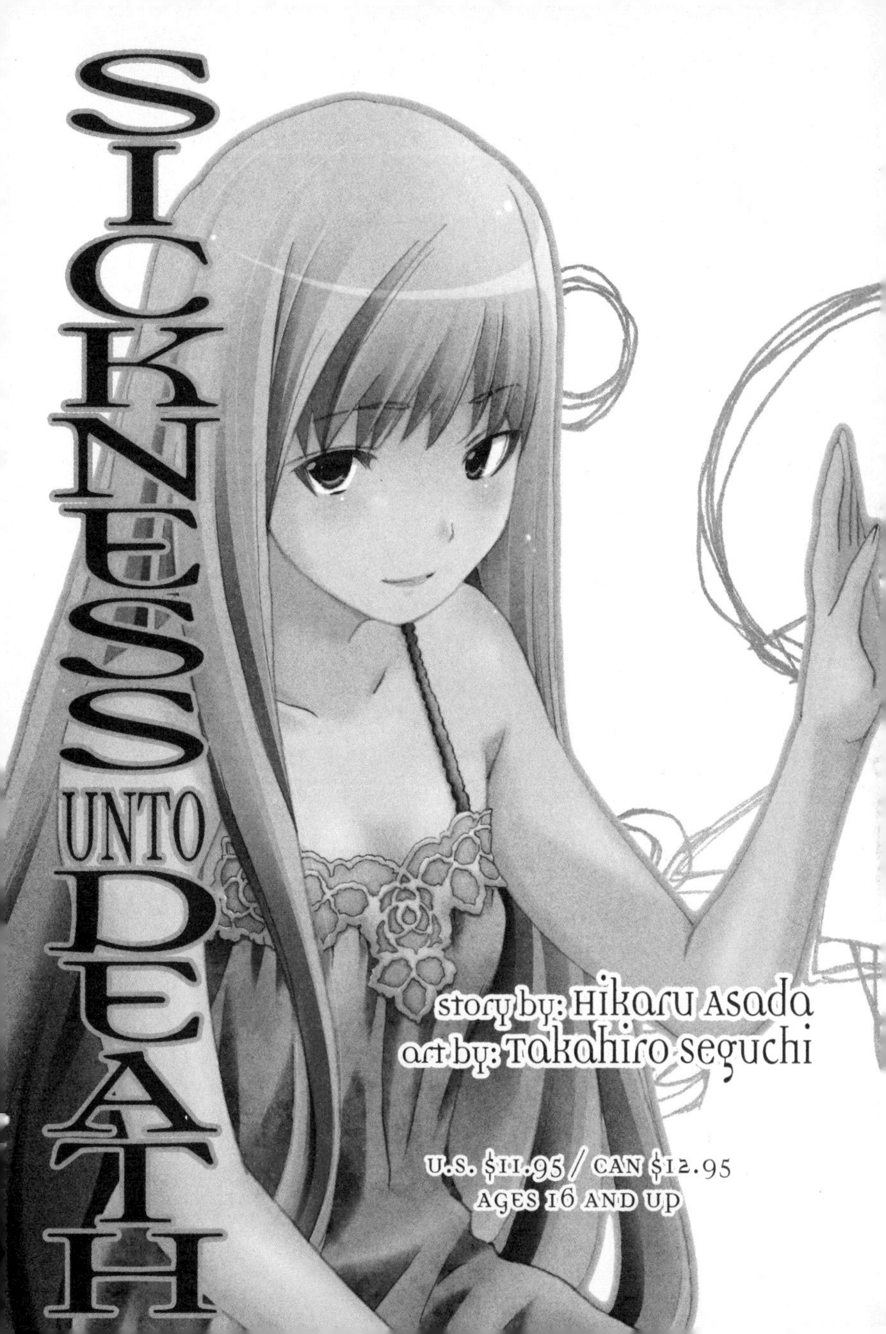
SICKNESS UNTO DEATH
story by: Hikaru Asada
art by: Takahiro Seguchi
U.S. $11.95 / CAN $12.95
AGES 16 AND UP

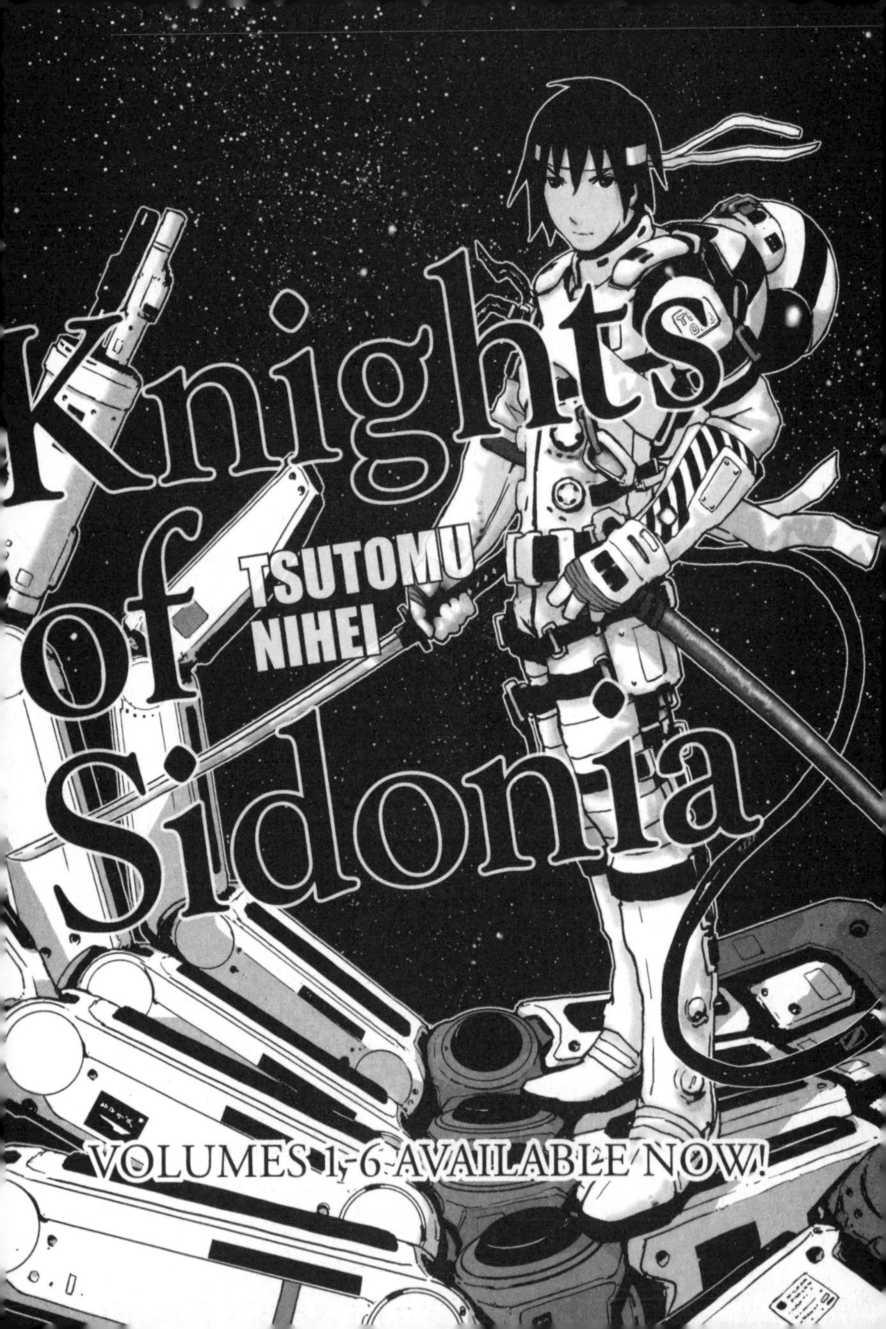
Knights of Sidonia
TSUTOMU NIHEI
VOLUMES 1-6 AVAILABLE NOW!

CORE EXPOSED

Outer space, the far future.

A lone seed ship, the *Sidonia*, plies the void, ten centuries since the obliteration of the solar system. The massive, nearly indestructible, yet barely sentient alien life forms that destroyed humanity's home world continue to pose an existential threat.

Nagate Tanikaze has only known life in the vessel's bowels deep below the sparkling strata where humans have achieved photosynthesis and new genders. Not long after he emerges from the Underground, however, the youth is bequeathed a treasured legacy by the spaceship's coolheaded female captain.

"One of **Knights of Sidonia**'s chief strengths is that it doesn't bog down the intrigue of its world with too much unnecessary, bloated dialogue... It's definitely a solid pick-up for Vertical; there's not really anything else in their catalog like it. Dig into the first volume and see if Nihei's gorgeously depicted wreck of a sci-fi future doesn't secure an immediately tight grip."
— *Otaku USA*

"**Knights of Sidonia** is off to a solid start with its first volume... All in all it's a promising and entertaining offering and one that's left me chomping at the bit for the next volume."
— *Comic Book Resources*

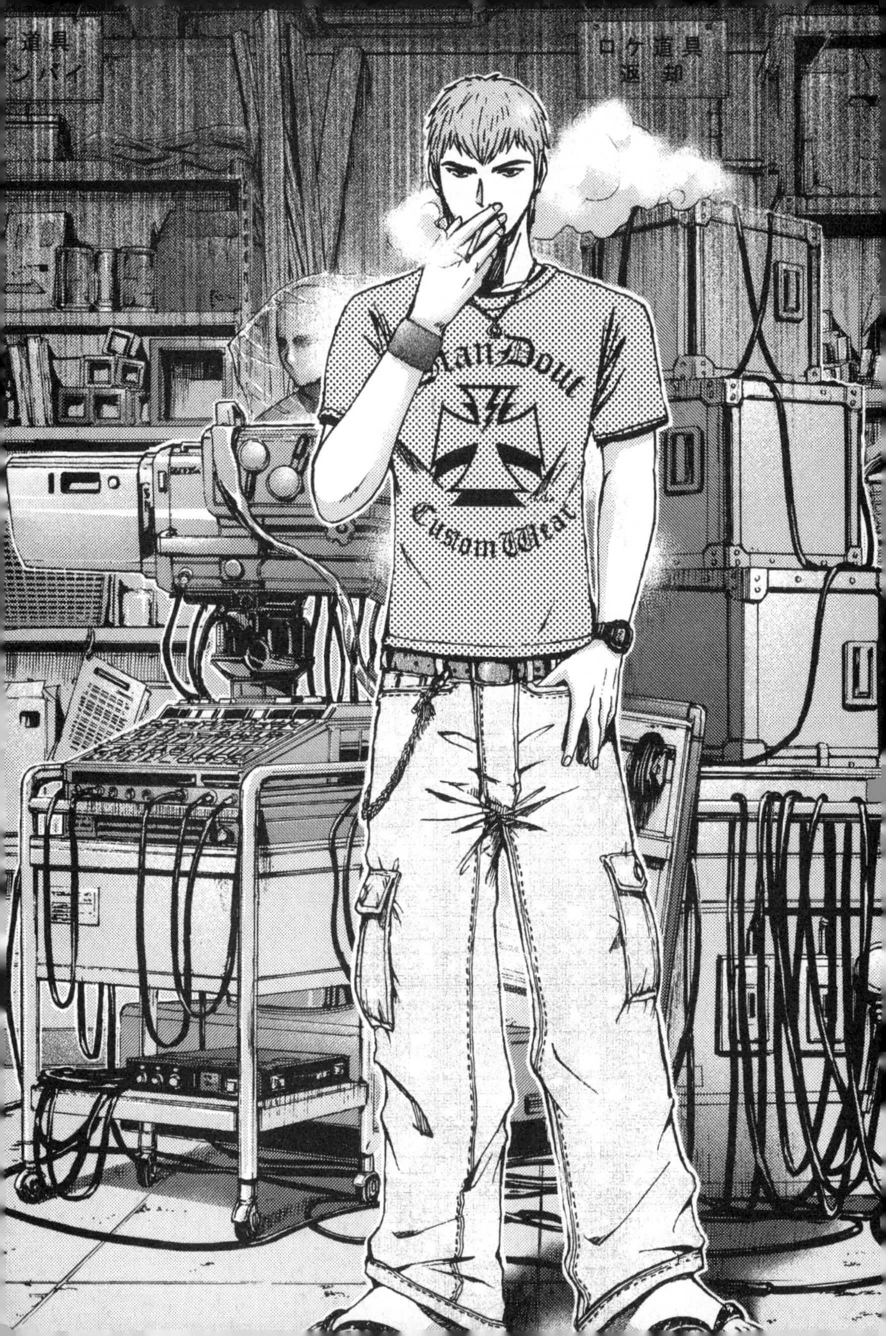
ロケ道具
返却

The Flowers of Evil, volume 7

Translation: Paul Starr
Production: Risa Cho
          Nicole Dochych

Copyright © 2013 Shuzo Oshimi. All rights reserved.
First published in Japan in 2012 by Kodansha, Ltd., Tokyo
Publication for this English edition arranged through Kodansha, Ltd., Tokyo
English language version produced by Vertical, Inc.

Translation provided by Vertical, Inc., 2013
Published by Vertical, Inc., New York

Originally published in Japanese as *Aku no Hana* by Kodansha, Ltd., 2012
Aku no Hana first serialized in *Bessatsu Shonen Magazine*, Kodansha, Ltd., 2009.

This is a work of fiction.

ISBN: 978-1-939130-00-6

Manufactured in Canada

First Edition

Vertical, Inc.
451 Park Avenue South
7th Floor
New York, NY 10016
www.vertical-inc.com